Settlement and Economy in Later Scandinavian Prehistory

edited by

Kristian Kristiansen

BAR International Series 211
1984

B.A.R.

5, Centremead, Osney Mead, Oxford OX2 0ES, England.

B.A.R. -S211,1984 :'Settlement and Economy in Later Scandinavian Prehistory'.

ISBN 9780860542728 paperback
ISBN 9781407336596 e-book
DOI https://doi.org/10.30861/9780860542728
A catalogue record for this book is available from the British Library
This book is available at www.barpublishing.com

CONTENTS

PREFACE

The idea for this book was conceived in 1978 and draft versions of the papers were presented at a 3-days seminar in Elsinore north of Copenhagen in the spring of 1980. Here a selection of papers from Denmark, Norway and Sweden spanning from the Mesolithic to the Medieval period were discussed. However, as it turned out that a substantial number of the original papers could not be published for various reasons, and as the book could not be published by the National Museum Press in Copenhagen as originally planned, it was decided to re-organize it around a number of especially Swedish and Norwegian papers dealing mainly with later prehistory.

I want to thank Jens Jönsson for taking care of all practical arrangements at the seminar and Carsten Larsen and Catharina Oksen for editorial assistance.

The Nordic Council of Ministers generously financed the seminar through their cultural secreteriat.

Copenhagen, January 1984.

Kristian Kristiansen.

LIST OF PARTICIPANTS IN THE ELSINORE SEMINAR FROM 2-5 MARCH 1980.

Niels H. Andersen	Forhistorisk Museum, Moesgaard.
Søren H. Andersen	Forhistorisk arkaeologisk institut, Moesgaard.
Torben Grøngärd Jeppesen	Fyns Stiftsmuseum, Odense.
Lotte Hedeager	Stoltenberggade, Copenhagen
Steen Hvass	Vejle Kulturhistoriske Museum
Jörgen Jacobsen	Fyns Stiftsmuseum, Odense.
Stig Jensen	Forhistorisk arkeologisk institut, Maesgaand.
Christian Keller	Universitetets Oldsakssammling, Oslo.
Kristian Kristiansen	Fredningsstyrelsen, Copenhagen.
Lars Larsson	Historiska Museet, Lunds Universitet.
Torsten Madsen	Forhistorisk Arkaeologisk Institut, Moesgård.
Egil Mikkelsen	Universitetets Oldsakssamling, Oslo.
Viggo Nielsen	Fredningsstyrelsen, Copenhagen.
Per Persson	Inst. för Nordisk Arkeologi, Göteborg Universitet
Erland Porsmose	Historisk Institut, Odense Universitetscenter.
Jan Skamby	Vikingeskibsmuseet, Roskilde.
Bergljot Solberg	Historisk Museum, Bergen.
Ulf Sporrong	Kulturgeografiska Institut, Stockholms Universitet.
P. Harder Sørensen	Bjellerupparken, Randers.
Henrik Thrane	Fyns Stiftsmuseum, Odense.
Stig Welinder	Universitetets Oldsaksamling, Oslo.
Mats Widgren	Kulturgeografiska Institut, Stockholms Universitet.

Berngt Windelheld	Kulturgeografiska Institut, Stockholms Universitet.
Einar Østmo	Universitetets Oldsakssamling, Oslo.

INTRODUCTION

Kristian Kristiansen

The articles in this book represent 3 major aspects of modern Scandinavian archaeological research: Human Geography, Ecology and Spatial Analysis.

The interaction between archaeology and human geography represents an important feature of recent Swedich archaeology and 5 of the major exponents of this research tradition have contributed to the present book. For the early Iron Age the application of methods of human geography to archaeology was originally carried out by S.-O. Lindquist in Ostergötland (Lindquist, 1968) and on Gotland (Lindquist, 1974), followed by Widgren, Windelhed and Carlsson (see articles in this volume). For the later Medieval and historical periods the dominant figure has been David Hannerberg, followed by e.g. Sporrong and Göransson (see articles in this volume). However, a strong ecological tradition is also running through these contributions, especially explicit in the article by Widgren. The strength of the approach presented in these articles is its ability to trace a settlement system in great details within a rather small area, whereas archaeologists traditionally are dealing with larger regions (for a discussion see Näsmann, 1979 and reviews in Fornvanen, 1987). These 5 contributions cover most of the settlement history from 500 B.C. to the Medieval period, but should for the late Iron Age/Wiking period be supplemented with the works of Ambrosiani (1964) and Hyenstrand (1973). Although mainly dealing with Central Sweden it is apparent that the major trends in settlement organization are valid for most of Scandinavia: from the Celtic fields of the Pre-Roman Iron Age, through the infield outfield system of individual farms in the Roman Iron Age/Germanic Iron Age to the new organization of the Medieval period (see discussion in Norwegian Arch. Review, 1974, vol. 7, no. 1).

The ecological tradition in Scandinavian archaeology may be said to originate in the interdisciplinary research commission headed by J.A. Worsaae during the 1850's which lead to the recognition of an early Stone Age hunting subsistence. Also today such interdisciplinary research projects are an important feature of Scandinavian archaeology (e.g. Bertha Stjernquist's contribution). Modern ecological research, however, is clearly linked to the development of pollen analysis as a cultural historical discipline by Johannes Iversen (1941) and Troels-Smith (1953). For many years such ecological studies were separated from the dominant archaeological research, mainly dealing with archaeological objects and less with settlement analysis. This situation, however, has greatly changed throughout the 1970's and Stig Welinder is probably the most prominent exponent for this integration of archaeological and ecological studies. In his contribution to this book he has summarized some of the major long term trends in settlement, economy and ecology, based on his previous research. An ecological approach is also apparent in the contribution from Bergljot Solberg, but it is rather linked to the exploitation of natural resources. It is interesting to note again that also in this region patterns of expansion and recession of settlement conforms with similar patterns in other areas of Scandinavia throughout the later Iron Age. In the regional context of Western Norway Solberg's work is further illuminated by the works of Myhre (1978) and Odner (1972).

It is a specific feature of Scandinavian archaeology that total registrations of all prehistoric monuments and sites have been carried out. In Denmark it was begun in 1873 and finished in 1930. In Sweden it has only recently been finished and Norway is still on its way (see articles in Fornvännen, 1978). Thus there exist in Scandinavia central registers of all known monuments and sites - in Sweden approx. 500,000, in Denmark only a little more than 115,000. These registers represent a great potential for landcsape - and settlement studies, due to the fact that in more marginal areas in Norway and Sweden the number of surviving monuments is very close to the original one. Several studies throughout the last 10-15 years have demonstrated the potential of this database when linked to modern methods of analysis (Ambrosiani, 1964; Hyenstrand, 1979 a & b and 1981; Selinge, 1979). These registrations have naturally also been vital for the research of human geography, which in local areas could be easily complimented by test excavation of selected sites. In combination with a very large number of archaeological objects from sites, burials, and hoards this evidence holds a great analytical and explanatory potential when treated by modern methods of spatial analysis. Already in the 1960's Mats Malmer applied some of the methodological principles of spatial analysis borrowed from especially the Swedish human geographer Hägerstrand (Malmer, 1957). In recent years new geographical methods of spatial analysis have been developed and examples of such applications on the rich Swedish evidence are demonstrated in the 2 contributions by Lundström and Larsson. Here the focus is rather on the relationship between spatial organization and social and political organization.

Throughout the last 20 years a group of Swedish and Norwegian archaeologists developed a research tradition based on an integration between human geography, ecology, and settlement analysis, thereby in many ways preceding the developments of New Archaeology. Unfortunately, this has not been sufficiently recognized among Anglo-American archaeologists. It is hoped that the present selection of articles will help to change this situation.

BIBLIOGRAFI

Ambrosiani, B. 1964. Fornlämningar och bebygelse. (English summary). Uppsala.

Hyenstrand, A. 1973. *Centralbygd - randbygd*. (Central Settlement - outlying Districts). Studies in North-European Archaeology 5. Stockholm.

Hyenstrand, A. 1979a. *Arkeologisk regionindeling av Sverige*. Riksantikvarieämbetet. Stockholm.

Hyenstrand, A. 1979b. *Ancient Monuments and Prehistoric Society*. Riksnatikvarieämbetet. Stockholm.

Hyenstrand, A. (ed.) 1981. *Dokumentation - forskning*. (English summaries). Riksantikvarieämbetet. Stockholm.

Iversen, J. 1941. *Land Occupation in Denmark's Stone Age*. A Pollen Analytical Study of the Influence of Farmer Culture on the vegetational Development. D.G.U. II. Raekke, nr. 66, Copenhagen.

Lindquist, S.O. 1968. *Det förhistoriska kulturlandskapet i Ostra Ostergötland* (mit deutscher Zusammenfassung). Studies in Northern European Archeaology 2, Stockholm.

Lindquist, S.O. 1974. The Development of the Agrarian Landscape on Gotland during the Early Iron Age. *Nordic Archaeological Review*, vol. 7, No. 1, Oslo.

Malmer, M. 1957. Pleionbegrebets betydelse för studiet av förhistoriska innovationsförlopp. *Finska fornminneforeningens tidsskrift 58*.

Myhre, B. 1978. Agrarian Development, Settlement History and Social Organization in Southwest Norway in the Iron Age. In *New Directions in Scandinavian Archaeology*. Edited by K. Kristiansen and C. Paludan-Müler. National Museum of Denmark, Copenhagen.

Näsman, U. 1979. En arkeologs syn på kuturgeografisk grävnings, metod, med exempel särskilt från Mellansverige. In *Fra jernalder til middelalder*. Skrifter fra Historisk Institut, Odense Universitet, nr. 27. Edited by Henrik Thrane.

Odner, K. 1972. Ethno-historic and ecological settings for economic and social models of an Iron Age society: Valldalen, Norway. In *Models in Archaeology*. Edited by David D. Clarke Methuen. London.

Selinge, K.G. 1979. *Agrarain Settlement and Hunting Grounds*. Theses and Papers in North-European Archaeology 8, Stockholm.

Troels-Smith, J. 1953. Ertebøllekultur - bondokultur. Resultater af de sidste 10 års undersøgelser i Aamosen. (Ertebølle culture - Farmer culture. Results of the past ten years of Excavations in Aamosen Bog, West Zealand), *Aarbøger for Nordisk Oldkyndighed*. Köenhavn.

A SYSTEMIC APPROACH TO UNDERSTANDING LONG-TERM CHANGE IN A CULTURE LANDSCAPE

Stig Welinder

1. A model landscape
2. The archaeological record of the model landscape
3. The systemic view
4. An operational system
5. Long-term change within the system
6. Economic models
7. Energy-use estimations
8. Explaining long-term change

This essay is a summary and perhaps implicitly a critical review of a 10 year attempt to understand growth and change within the prehistoric and early historical culture landscape in temperate Europe. In the process examples of various prehistoric societies from the period 7000 - 1000 B.P. in the Scandinavian Peninsula have been analysed. The main publications in this effort are:

(1) Welinder 1975. In this book three variables regarded as basic for the understanding of the culture landscape were selected: Agricultural technology, demography, and ecology (in the following denoted the three-variables-model). In Figure 5, and the preceding Figures 3-4, these variables are worked out in more detail explicitly using a systemic approach. The three-variables-model was used to transform the pollen analytically demonstrated expansion - stagnation dynamics within the culture landscape (Berglund 1969) into terms of human production - consumption. The attempt made it obvious that purposefully designed case studies of expansion and stagnation stages, respectively, in the development of the culture landscape were needed. Thus, two case studies were planned, before the model of Welinder 1975, pp. 91-94, was to be worked out into something of more interest.

(2) Welinder 1977a. In this book a model of expansion within a given society was suggested (op.cit., pp. 182-184). Especially the agricultural technology variable was discussed and outlined as a subsistance economy and social structure system. The book has been severely critizised both as concerns the analysis of the specific case study (e.g. Larsson 1978, Widholm 1980) and the terminology and concepts chosen for the model building (e.g. Spång 1978, Hyenstrand 1979). I myself, found the primitive demographic and ecological

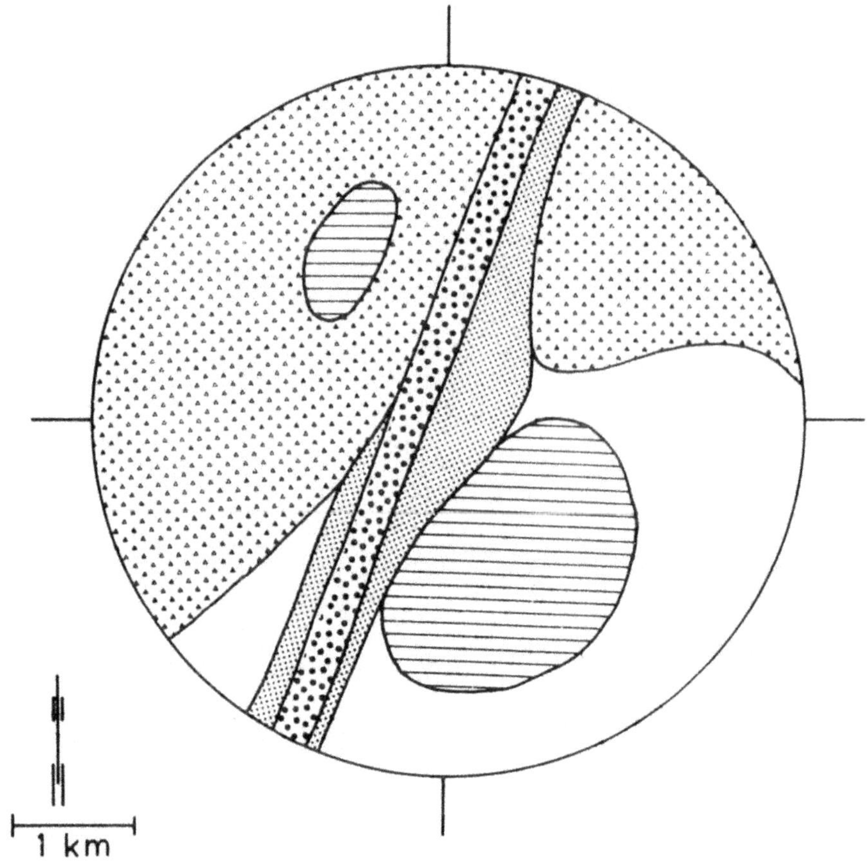

Fig. 1a. The Quaternary geology of the model landscape (triangles = naked rock, till; rings = glacifluvial eskar, dots = sandy sediments; horizontal lines = marshy areas; no signiture = clay sediments).

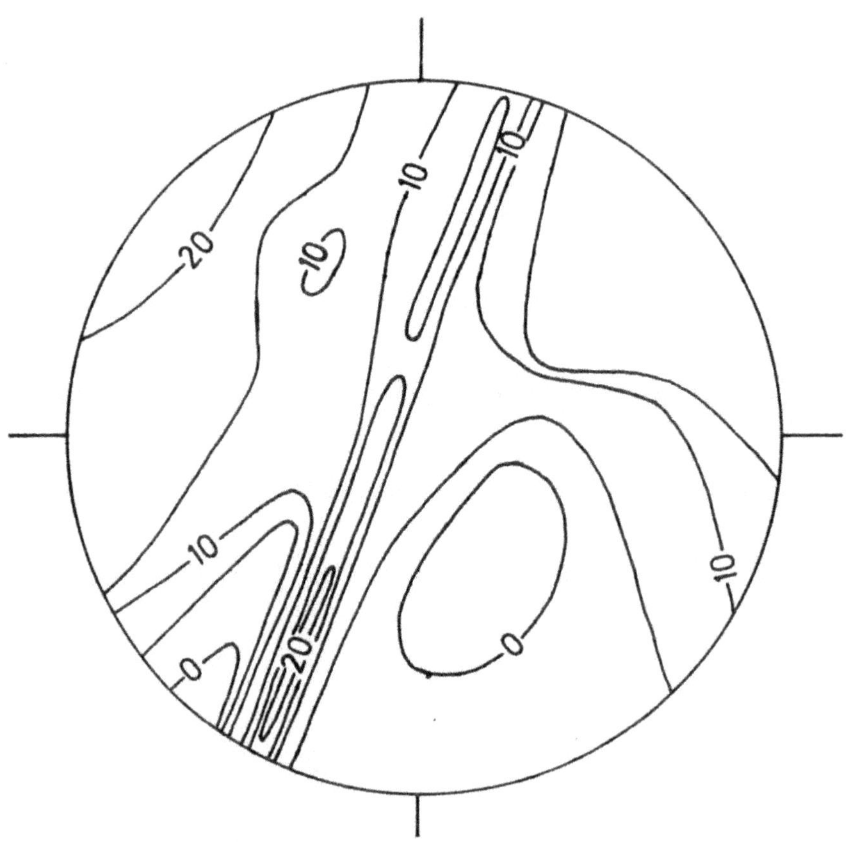

Fig. 1b. The topography of the model landscape (heights in m above the bottom of the landscape).

analysis of the case study most annoying.

(3) Welinder 1979. In this book a serious attempt was made to reconstruct the demography of prehistoric societies at the Scandinavian Peninsula, both as concerns demographic structure of a defined society at a defined point of time and as concerns demographic long-term change. The attempt was not successful. The archaeological source material simply did not allow detailed reconstructions of demographic change independent of economic and ecological change. Thus, it turned out to be moderately encouraging to start an analysis of a specific stagnation stage and modelling general features of the expansion - stagnation dynamics in terms of demography. Only close to trivial long-term demographic growth could be demonstrated, not short-term fluctuations in relation to for example technological innovations.

(4) Welinder, 1983a. In this book the long-term growth of the culture landscape was outlined in terms of ecosystems change and energy-use. This had to be done for discrete stages. The continuous, dynamic description of the culture landscape development announced in Welinder 1975, 1977 has not been possible for me to present by the selected approach.

In the present essay the main ideas of the above publications are summarized, and at the end of it a model of culture landscape growth is presented (Figure 9). The model is neither exciting nor instructive when trying to explain change within human societies. Perhaps it is the best that can be obtained from the approach selected.

In the following a model landscape is used for illuminating the ideas. This will emphasize generality, although when refering to actual field and laboratory data these will be derived from Central Sweden.

1. A Model Landscape

The model landscape has features typical of much of the Scandinavian primary rock area, although the Central Swedish landscape has most features in common with both the model landscape and its archaeological record to be presented in the next paragraph. It is divided into a high-lying part covered by till with a marsh in a depression and a low-lying area covered by sediments (Figure 1). The till is typically a wave-washed till, sandy and with boulders at the surface. The sediments are typically silty and clayey deposits from the Early Holocene covered by gyttja and peat at the bottom of the landscape.

The glacifluvial eskar running across the model landscape is a characteristic element of the Central Swedish culture landscape. The kind of terrain associated with eskars are richer than any other kind of terrain in Central Sweden as concerns archaeological sites. Thus, the presence of an eskar might justify the concentrated occurrence of sites inserted in the model landscape. The reason is the presence of sand-sediment terraces free from stones and boulders along the foot of an eskar. In addition the complex geology around an eskar generates a varied biotop with many ecological niches, some of which in connection to the fine-grained sediments offer the maximum biological production in the Scandinavian primary rock type of landscape.

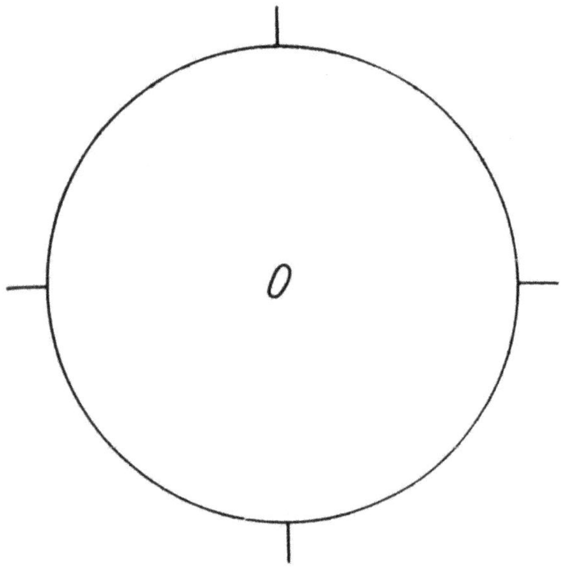

Fig. 2a. The archaeological record of the Mesolithic, c. 5000 B.C. (settlement site).

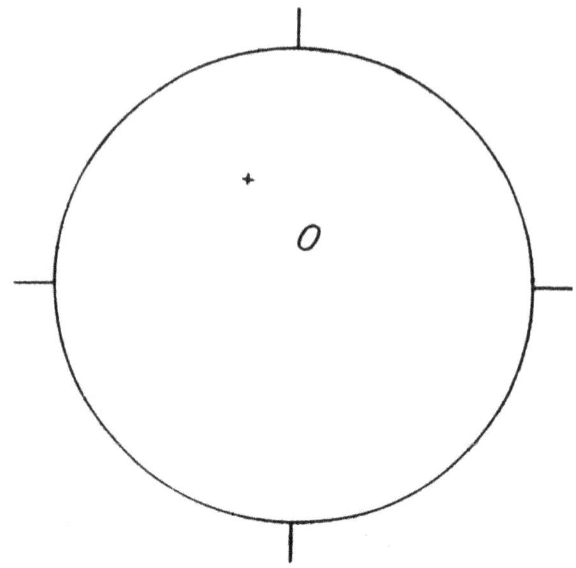

Fig. 2b. The archaeological record of the Early Neolithic, c. 3500 B.C. (settlement site and sacrificial deposit of pottery).

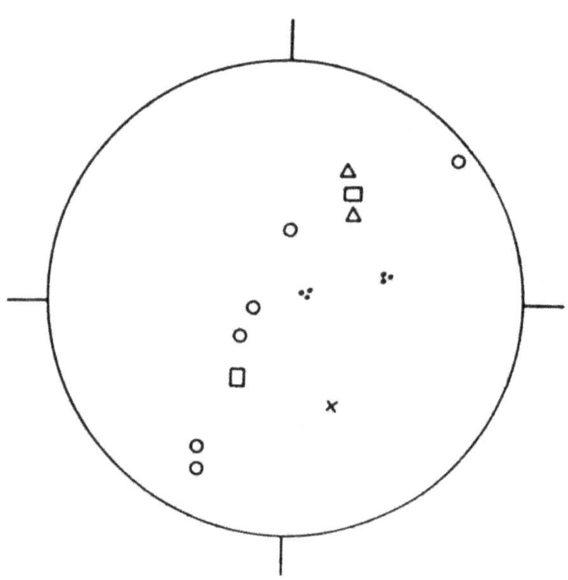

Fig. 2c. The archaeological record of the Late Bronze Age, c. 700 B.C. (rectangles = settlement sites; circles = cairns; triangles = heaps of fire-cracked splinter-stones; tripods = cupmark sites; cross = sacrificial deposit of bronze objects).

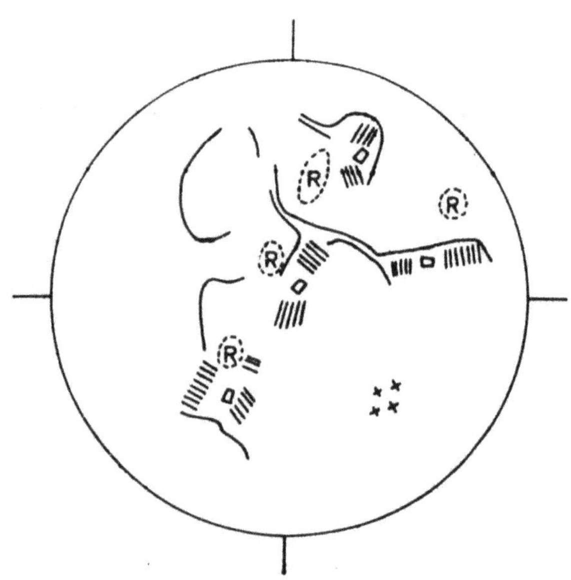

Fig. 2d. The archaeological record of the Early Iron Age, c. A.D. 400 (rectangles = house foundations; striped areas = various indications of arable land, lines = henges; R-marks and lines of dashes = burial grounds with mounds and stone-settings; crosses = ritual deposits of pottery, farming implements etc.).

Figure 1a presents the Quaternary geology of the model landscape. Due to the Holocene land upheaval the prehistoric landscape partly differed from this map. This has to be included in a systemic study of the landscape. Likewise, site catchment analyses has to be based on reconstructed past environments.

2. The Archaeological Record Of The Model Landscape

The recording of archaeological sites in an area is dependent on what kind of analyses one has in mind. The maps of the archaeological record of the model landscape (Figure 2) display the types of features that to me have been useful in the case studies of subsistence economy in the Central Swedish culture landscape. The following description of the record merely is a list of publications with the full details of the field monuments from the various mapped periods:

(1) The Mesolithic, c. 5000 B.C. Settlement sites (Welinder 1977b, 1980)

(2) The Early Neolithic, c. 3500 B.C. Settlement sites and ritual deposits (Hulthén et al. 1981, Welinder 1982)

(3) The Late Bronze Age, c. 700 B.C. Settlement sites, burial cairns, and ritual sites and deposits (Kjellén et al. 1977, Jaanusson 1981, Löthman 1981)

(4) The Early Iron Age, c. A.D. 400. Settlement sites, burial grounds, ritual deposits, henge systems and deserted arable fields (Lindquist 1968, Baudou 1973, Widgren 1978, 1983)

It is notable that detailed maps of the archaeological record from the periods inbetween the above periods cannot be presented today. The recorded and excavated sites are too few in number and too little informative for the purposes of this essay. This is valid for the main part of the South and Middle Scandinavian primary rock area.

One idea is that since the introduction of farming c. 3500 B.C. the periods with an abundant and informative source material coinside with the expansion periods, while the intervening stagnation periods are less well apprehensible as concerns the structure of the cultural landscape. To an archaeologist interested in for example social relations or trade relations the case might be quite another. Likewise, the maps presented in Figure 2 for expansion periods might look quite different when compiled by an archaeologist interested in relations of that kind.

During the stagnation periods the farming landscape is presumed to have contracted to the very best areas from an agricultural point of view. These areas have been plowed continuously since the beginning of the Neolithic. Thus, the archaeological record is either destroyed or hard to get hold of. Settlement sites from the expansion periods can be presumed to be situated in areas that have been plowed only sporadically or not at all since the occupation period, thus being preserved until recent time. The prerequisite for this idea on the varied quality of the archaeological record is economic change from one expansion period to the next. The idea works best for marginal areas.

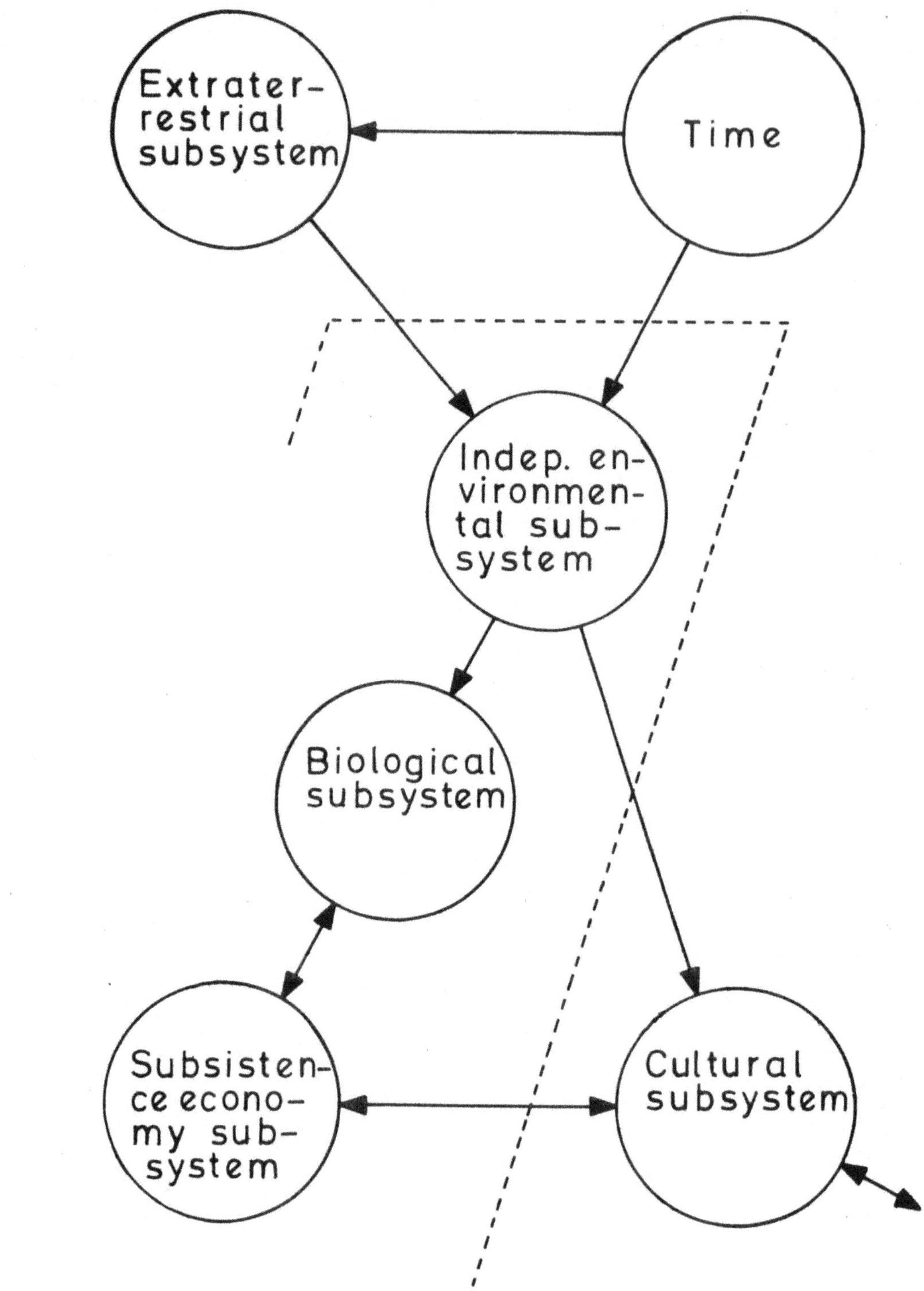

Fig. 3. General model of a human ecosystem. The dashed lines encircle the subsystem regarded to be of basic interest in a long-term perspective on culture landscape development.

3. The Systemic View

Figure 3 summarizes the subsystems of a cultural system and its biological and social environment. It is a matter of taste whether to name the system a cultural system or a human eco-system. At least for the part of the system within the dashed line the latter term is preferable. Only that part will be elaborated in the following. The idea is that the interaction between a society and its biological environment is the essential part of the system when trying to understand the function and development of a culture landscape. In the following the term "total human ecosystem" will be used for the system of Figure 3.

Figure 4 are elaborated details of Figure 3 on the way towards the operational system of Figure 5, which is to be used in the actual analysis of the prehistoric field and laboratory data.

The total system of Figure 3 contains a part, which is independent of human activity, that is the independent environmental subsystem (Figure 4). The components of this subsystem are climate (macro climate), geology (bedrock and Pleistocene deposits), and topography. These components together form the environmental background of the rest of the human ecosystem. This background changes along the time-axis due to i.a. climatic change and the land upheaval dynamics. At the bottom these changes are dependent on large scale forces, either extra terrestrial (e.g. solar radiation) or terrestrial (e.g. orogenesis, glaciation).

It is tempting to explain changes in the culture landscape by changes in the independent environmental subsystem. Especially climatic change has been frequently exploited in explanations in the past. When this is not necessarily false, at least it is an oversimplification not taking the full biological subsystem in consideration.

The biological subsystem (Figure 4) produces living biomass from solar energy and simple compounds. This production, from which the human society benefits by hunting-gathering or farming, is involved in complex production-consumption food webs. The general green plants - animals - decomposers - humus chain is the main pathway for energy and nutrients. The internal function and human manipulation of the biological subsystem is an essential point in the total human ecosystem to understand in an attempt to understand long-term change within a culture landscape.

It is notable that the biological subsystem is unilaterally dependent on the independent environmental subsystem, although the climate might be locally modified by vegetation change (micro climate).

The human subsystem (human society) of Figure 4 is modelled in the first place to pinpoint those parts of the subsystem that interact with the above subsystems. These are gathered in the economic activities component, while internal relations between individuals and groups of individuals are gathered in the social activities and religion components. The demography component is the quantitative aspect of the human subsystem, the number of consumption units.

Like the independent environmental subsystem the demography component of the human subsystem has been regarded an independent variable in explaining change within the culture landscape. This was frequently tried during the late 1960's with i.a. the Boserup model as a source of

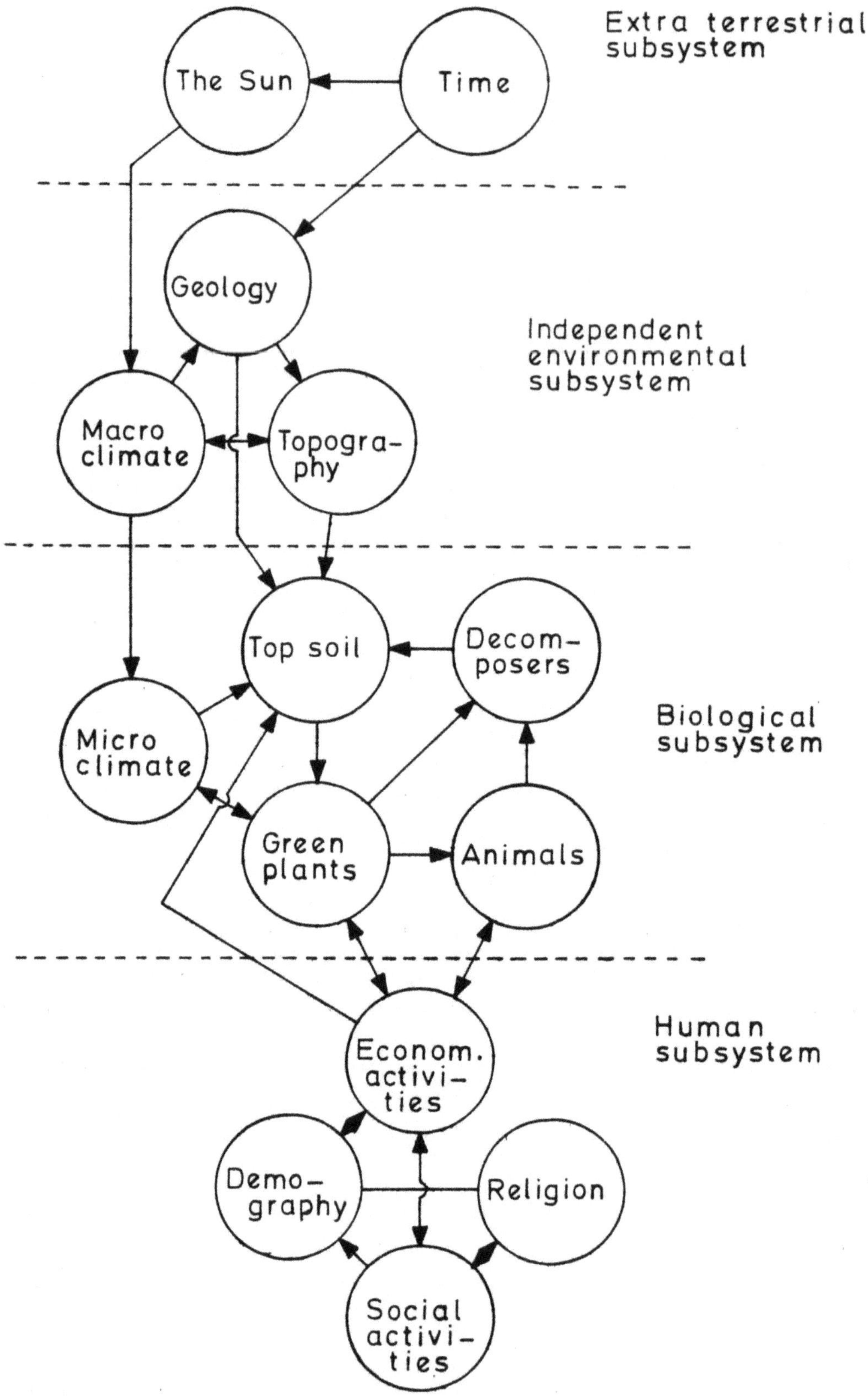

Fig. 4. Modified version of Figure 3.

inspiration (Boserup 1965, e.g. Spooner 1972). Since then the population pressure concept has declined from an agent in explanations to a cliché.

The interaction between the human subsystem and its physical-biological environment is presented in Figure 4. From this overview it is evident that there are four groups of explanations of change in the culture landscape:

(1) Change dependent on the independent environmental subsystem

(2) Demographic change

(3) Internal change within the human subsystem

(4) Change in the relations between the human and biological subsystems

The first two groups of explanations are one-factor-explanations that have lost most of their interest during the last decades. In this essay the fourth group will be looked upon. Its use in practical research work has produced some brilliant results (e.g. Rappaport 1967, Clark 1972). Nevertheless, as a basis of interesting explanations of change this type of explanations has lost most of its glamour. The critizism works along lines like reductionism and determinism. Thus, the third group is in focus in the debate today. It is basic in analyses i.a. from a Marxistic point of view.

Explanations belonging to the above third group will need a detailed elaboration of the human subsystem, especially the interaction between the cultural and subsistence economy subsystems in Figure 3. A potential social subsystem will not be further discussed here. It occupies an insignificant place within the above fourth group of explanations to be discussed in this essay. From the systems analysis point of view this means that within the human subsystem (Figure 4) of the toal human ecosystem the economy component work as an independent variable interacting only with the demographic component. The latter is also used as a measurement of the size of the human subsystem.

4. An Operational System

The human ecosystem of Figures 3-4 present the theoretical framework to be used in explaining long-term change within the culture landscape. The system in Figure 5 is to be used in analyses of specific societies and their ecology at defined points of time. It is intended to be used in understanding the function of a culture landscape. It also allows the explanation of change from certain other points of view to be stressed below.

Central to the operational system of Figure 5 is the ecological succession of vegetation stages: Herbs - shrubs - high-ground forest. By introducing forest clearance into this succession, it is turned into a cycle, e.g. a short-term cycle of natural succession in a forest ecosystem due to forest-fires and storm-fellings.

The above succession cycle is stopped by human activity in three ways:

(1) Forest clearance to create arable land

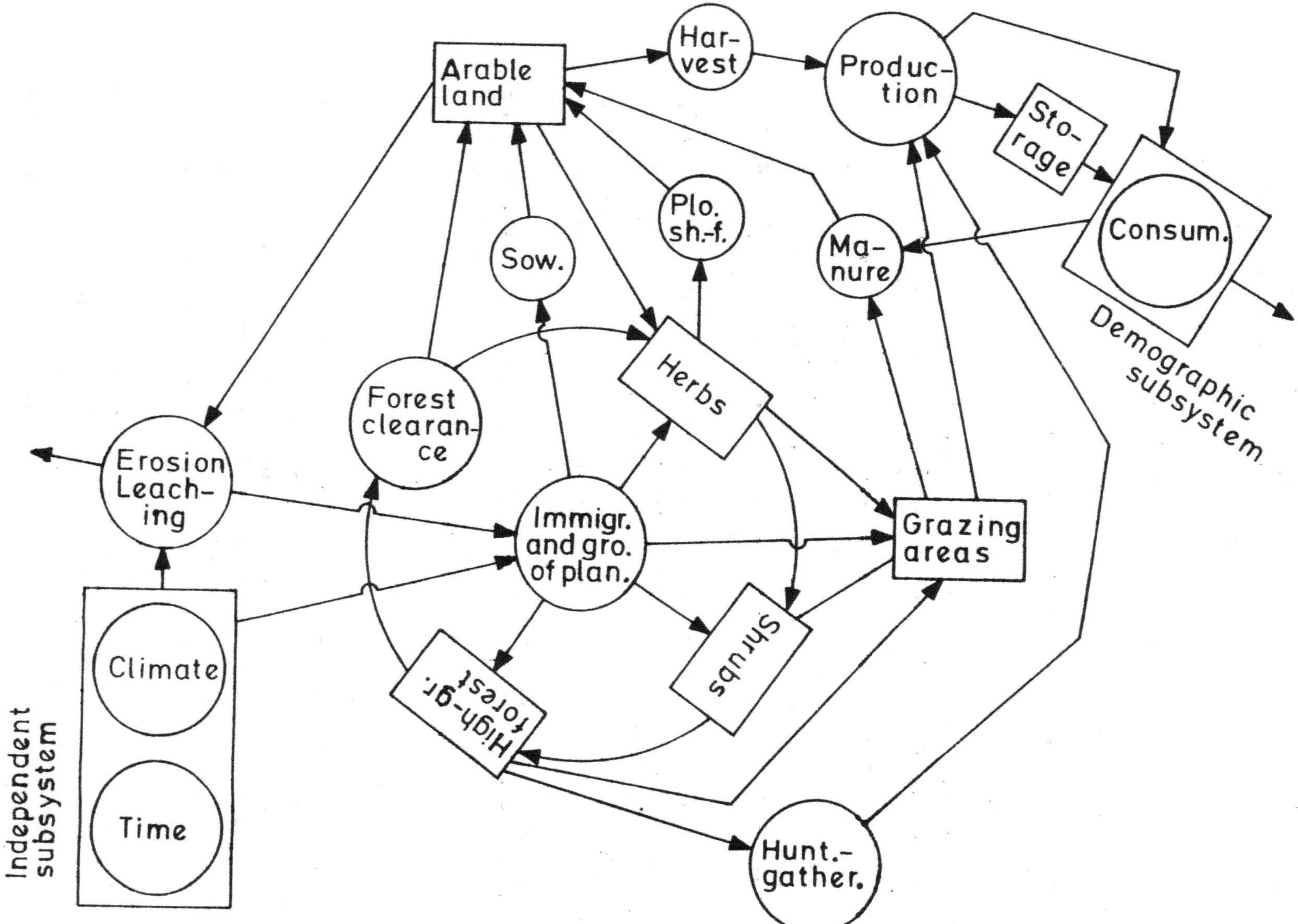

Fig. 5. The operational system to be used in the analysis of culture landscapes (abbr.: Immigration and growth of plants, Ploughing of short-fallow land; Sowing).

(2) Plowing of short-fallow land

(3) Grazing by domestic animals

All three activities prevent regeneration of the forest ecosystem, thus by force keeping it in an early state from an ecological point of view. The result is an increased net production per unit of surface area. This makes possible a bigger consumption within the human society than merely exploiting all stages of the natural succession cycle by hunting-gathering.

In this operational system the three-variables-model for understanding a human ecosystem is refound. The agricultural technology variable is explicitly incorporated in the system as the method of clearing and maintaining arable land (Fig. 5). The demography variable is incorporated as the consumption component within the system. The need of a minimum consumption to maintain the labour force needed in the system at a defined point of time is stressed. The ecology variable is implicitly incorporated as the general choice of components and relations in constructing this system (Fig. 5) and not another one.

According to the above "ecology" is defined as the relations between components of the biological subsystem and components of the human subsystem. This is an operational definition to be used in the study of culture landscapes. It is selfevident that "ecology" refers also to relations between components within the biological subsystems.

Internal to the system is long-term change dependent on time and climatic change (independent environmental subsystem). The main agencies are erosional and leaching processes (edaphic change). Due to the length of time involved and increasing humidity since the Late Subboreal these processes have been a main factor of the retrogressive interglacial development described by Iversen 1964, as part of his cyclic glacial - interglacial model. The result is acidification (podsolation) towards the end of an interglacial. The above described climatic-edaphic long-term changes present a more complex alternative of explaining change within the culture landscape than merely climatic change. It is, however, not less deterministic.

Forest clearance and maintenance of arable land and grazing areas by a human society increase both erosion and leaching. Thus, the retrogressive development is accelerated. This might result in a continuous need for more efficient farming techniques, or over-exploitation of the resources might be the result. Combined with demographic growth along the time-axis this offers a still more complex alternative of explaining long-term change within a culture landscape.

The operational system of Figure 5 is essentially an energy-flow system. It contains three natural vegetation types and two artificial ones (components) that function as energy stores in the system. Energy is also stored as food supplies and manure within the human subsystem. The rest of the system is built of energy path-ways (relations) and regulators (components) affecting the transport from one store to another. Energy is added to the system from the independent environmental subsystem (solar energy, nutrients from the subsoil). Energy is lost from the system by erosional and leaching processes and by consumption within the human susbsystem.

There are two ways to describe change along the time-axis within the system:

(1) The quantities of energy transported along one or several energy path-ways might increase or decrease.

(2) Components or relations might be removed or inserted.

In both cases an explanation is needed to tell why change takes place. It is not selfevident that the system contains a sufficient set of components and relations to produce an interesting explanation. It is not selfevident that the necessary minimal set of components and relations is present.

5. Long-term Change Within The System

In this paragraph examples of long-term change within the various subsystems of the total human ecosystem (Figure 3) will be presented. The examples are derived from case stuides of the Central Swedish culture landscape (Welinder 1974, 1975). They do not claim to give the full information neither available nor necessary for a reasonable understanding of the culture landscape development. They merely are examples of the potential information of the behaviour of the ecosystem along the time-axis.

Climatic change might be derived indirectly from a vegetational change, that is infering change in the independent environment subsystem from change in the biological subsystem. A more direct way, involving less risk of circuit conclusions, is to infere climatic change from water-level changes, either from sediment growth curves or from the peat growth of raised bogs. In Central Sweden an increasing humidity from c. 1000 B.C. is notable (Figure 6a).

The land-upheaval curve is the resulting sum of global climatic change and local isostatic rise. In Central Sweden, after c. 5000 B.C., no or only insignificant transgressions are noted (Figure 6b). This implies a continuous increase in low-lying nutritious sediment-covered areas in the coastal zone, especially well-suited for grazing and winter-fodder production. To the rest of the total ecosystem the land-upheaval is an independent variable belonging to the independent environmental subsystem (Figure 5).

The biological subsystem is during the latter half of the Holocene characterized by a long-term change from climax plant-communities on brown forest soil to more open plant-communities on podsols. In Central Sweden this development, as concerns forest species, is characterized by the decline of the broadleaf forest and the immigration of spruce (Figure 6c). This is a major change in the central ecological succession cycle of the operational system (Figure 5), due to climatic change and, in the first place, leaching processes regulated by the "immigration and growth of plants" component. It is notable that farming activity (including grazing) is a major agent in this process. Increasing input of energy to compensate for impoverishing of farming land, thus, is an important self-reinforcing effect of farming activity (positive feed-back).

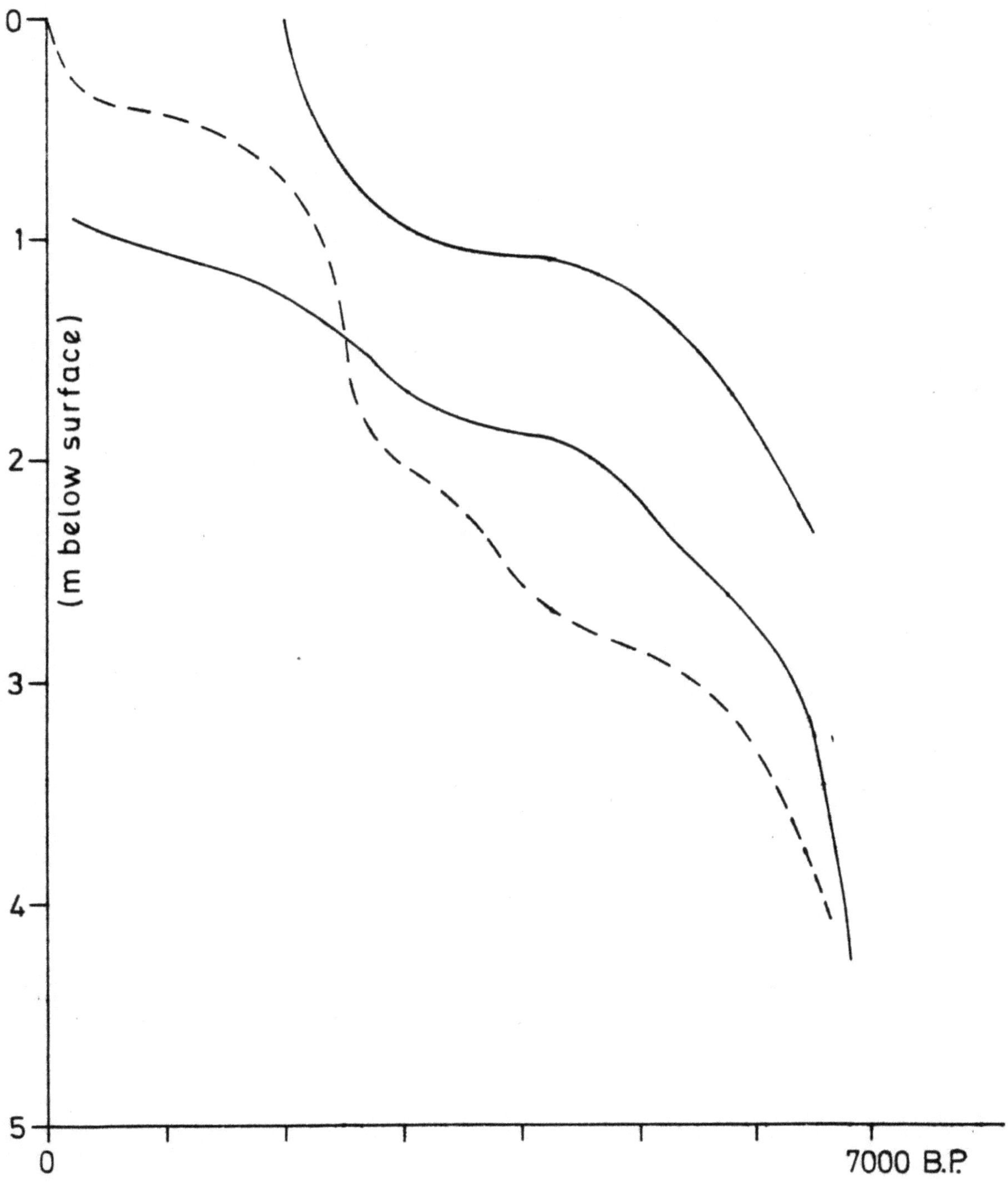

Fig. 6a. Sediment growth of lakes (full lines) and peat growth of a raised bog (from Welinder 1974).

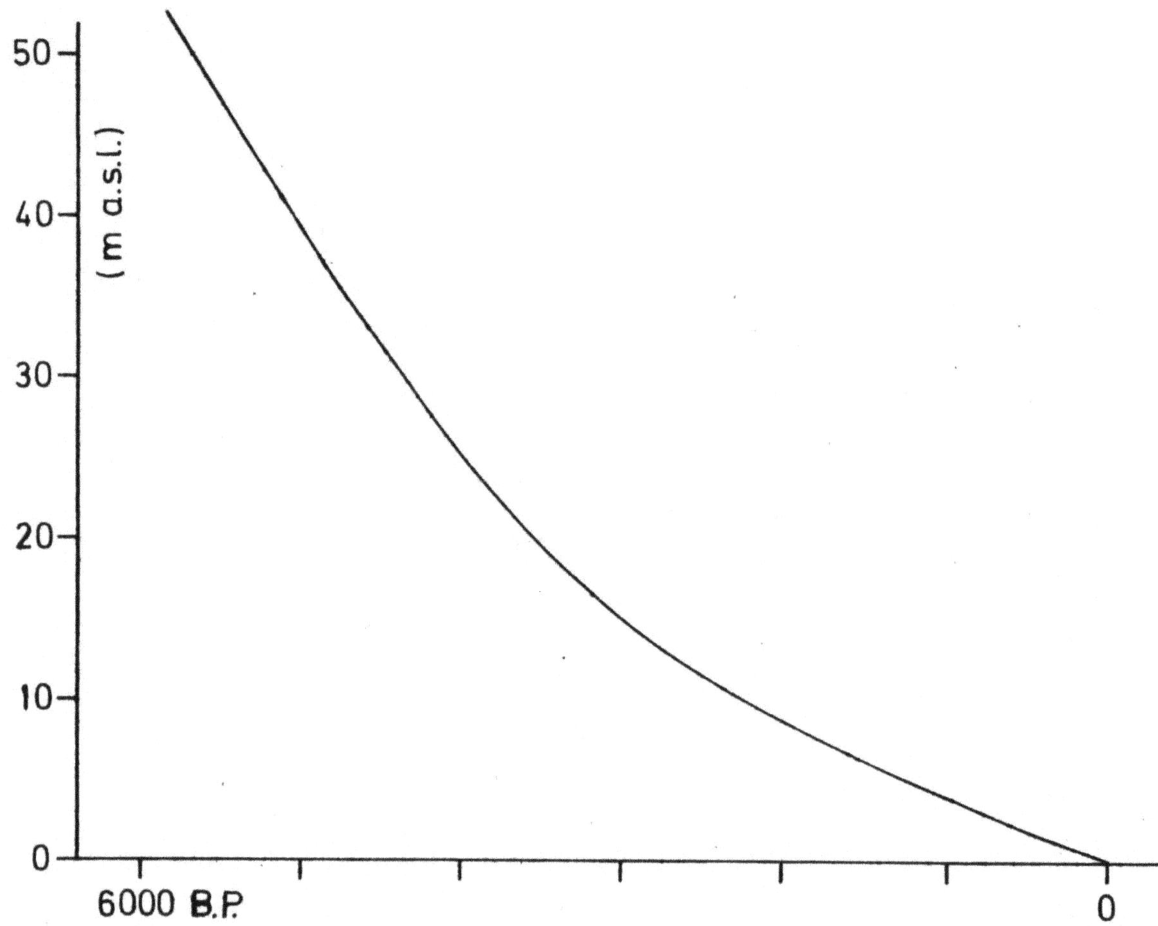

Fig. 6b. The land-upheaval curve (from Ase 1970 and others).

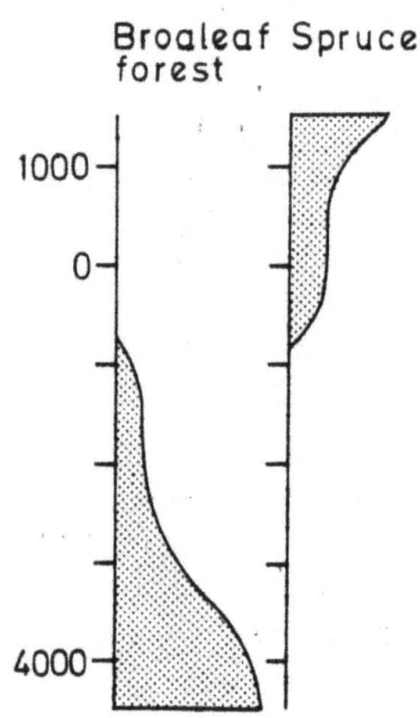

Fig. 6c. The decline of the broadleaf forest and the immigration of spruce (from Welinder 1975).

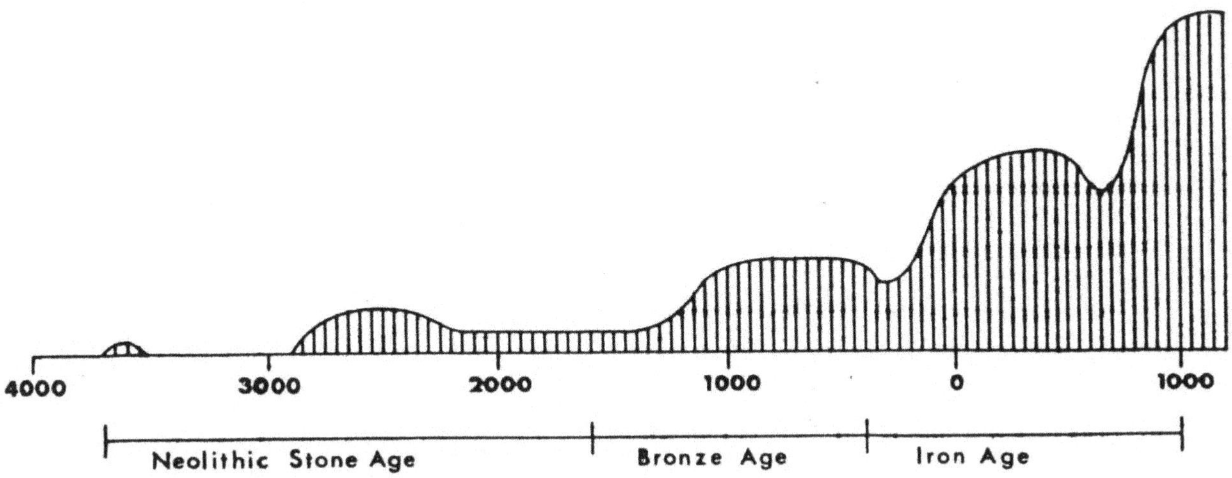

Fig. 6d. Influence diagram (from Welinder 1975).

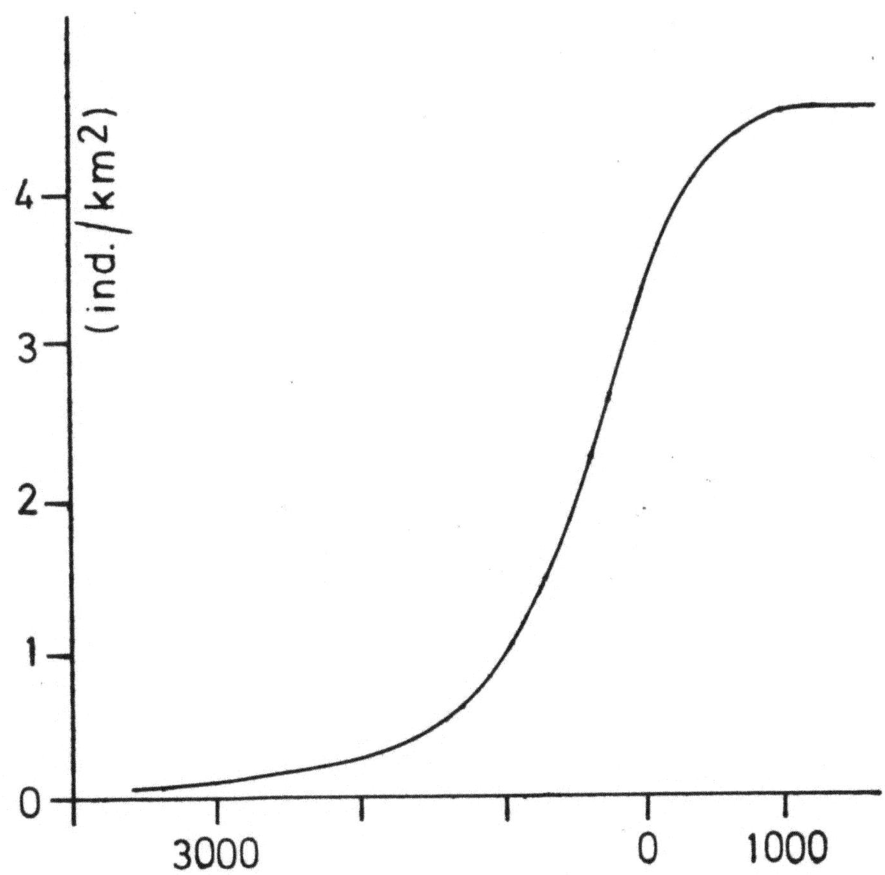

Fig. 6e. Population density curve (from Welinder 1975).

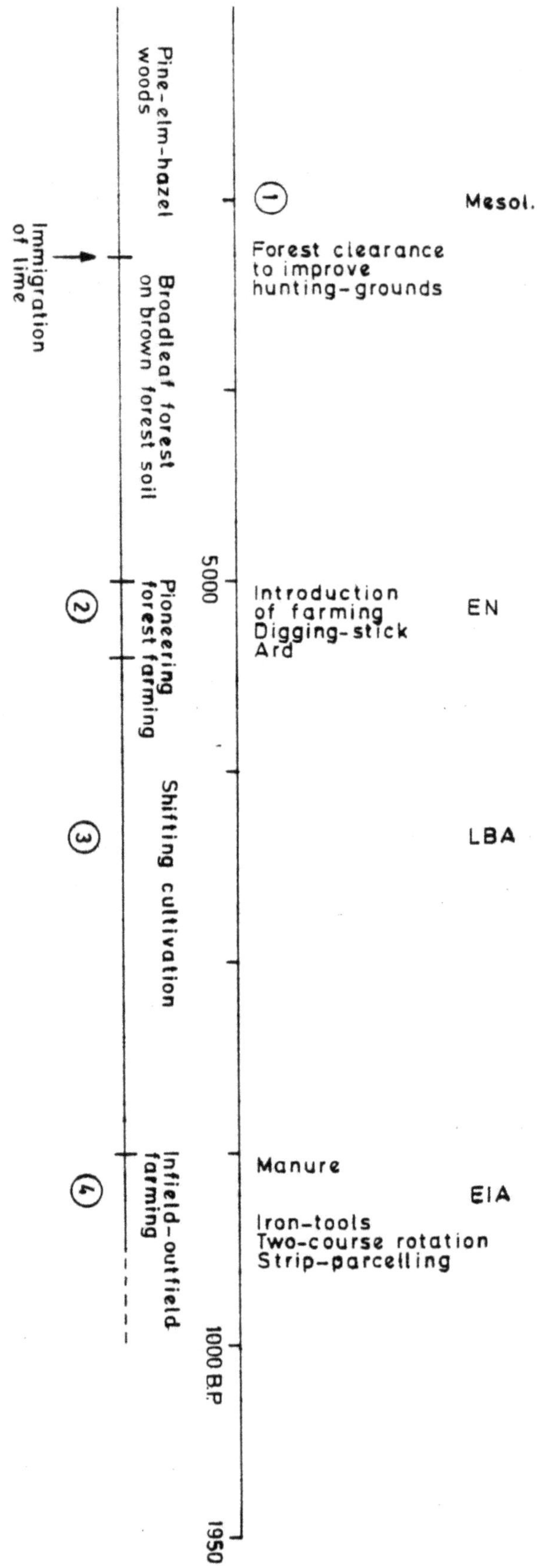

Fig. 6f. Summary of economic development of the model landscape.

An influence diagram is a complex output from the total human ecosystem. It reflects change both in the biological and human subsystems. The scale of the diagram measures the size of the arable land and grazing area of the system (Figure 5). The underlying emperical base is the amount of pollen grains produced by certain plans. All of these plants are manipulated by the human society (either sown or involuntarily favoured).

In Central Sweden the influence diagram (Figure 6d) displays both a general exponential growth and a number of expansion and stagnation stages. As discussed above the points of time selected for the recording of field monuments in the model landscape coinside with the expansion stages.

The size and growth of the human subsystem, that is the minimum size of the consumption component of the operational subsystem, is measured by demographic variables. From prehistoric source material it is, perhaps, possible to reconstruct demographic change. To reconstruct absolute population sizes or densities is almost impossible. Analogies or extrapolations comming close to circuit conclusions are hard to avoid.

The Central Swedish population density curve in Figure 6e is based on the number of sites in a defined area. The absolute numbers are extrapolations from historical data. The exponential population growth since the introduction of farming to the area c. 3500 B.C. is remarkable. The growth came seemingly to a stop around A.D. 700. Actually, around this date expansion outside the earlier settled areas started, while expansion before this date took place in the first place within the old culture landscape. Phrased in another way, emmigration began around that date (Welinder 1974).

Figure 6f summarizes the main types of vegetation on high ground within the culture landscape, the main technical innovations as concerns farming technology, and the main cultivation systems in use in central areas in Central Sweden. Thus, the figure summarizes essential features of structure and change within the agricultural technology variable of the three-variables-model (Figure 5). It is based upon interpretations of the archaeological record, pollen data, and ecological theory. The element of analogy is problematic. To which extent are the economic models to be presented in the next paragraph reconstructed from field and laboratory data, and to which extent are they selected among possible analogies to suite the paleoecological record? This is a crucial question to answer before introducing explanations of change within the human ecosystem. If the economic models are not reconstructed from data and ideas independent of the data and ideas used in the reconstruction of the ecological (that is relations between the human and biological subsystems) and the biological subsystems (that is the ecological succession cycle of the operational system) explanations will be based on circuit conclusions and, thus, will be of little interest. The same is valid for the demographic variable.

6. Economic Models

Four economic models will be suggested for the model landscape (Figure 1). The models are based on the field and laboratory data presented in the previous paragraph, or better phrased, interpretations of these data and appropriate analogies. The models will be shortly described as concerns the following aspects (Figure 7):

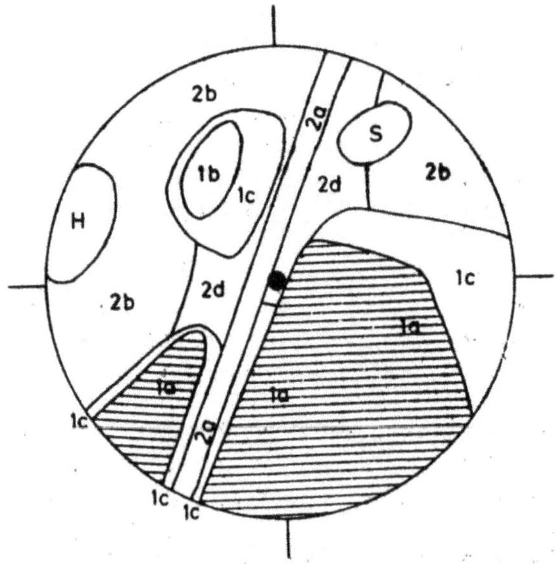

Fig. 7a. The resource exploitation in the model landscape during the Mesolithic, c. 5000 B.C. (lines = open water expanses; 1 = low-ground vegetation, a = reeds, b = Carex marshes, c = brushwood, mostly alder; 2 = forest, a = pine, b = pine, birch, c = pine, birch, spruce, d = elm, hazel, pine, e = broadleaf forest; 3 = manmade vegetation, a = grassland with stands of broadleaf species, b = open grassland, c = juniper-grassland; A = arable land, F = fodder production; G = grazing, browsing; H = the herbs stage in forest generation, P = pannage, S = the shrubs stage in forest generation; dotted line circumscribes the landscape used for farming).

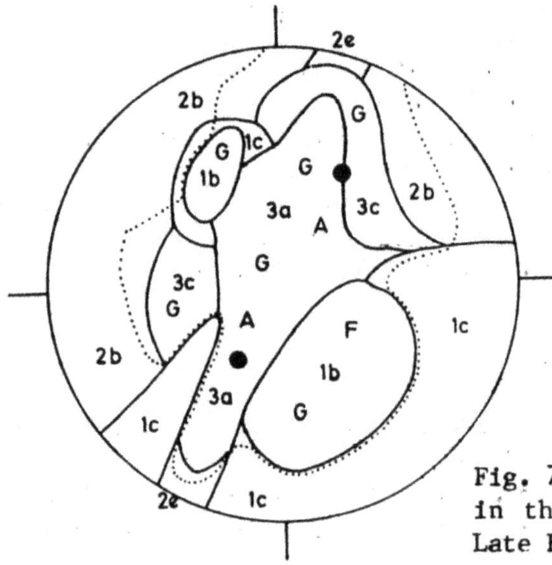

Fig. 7c. The resource exploitation in the model landscape during the Late Bronze Age, c. 700 B.C.

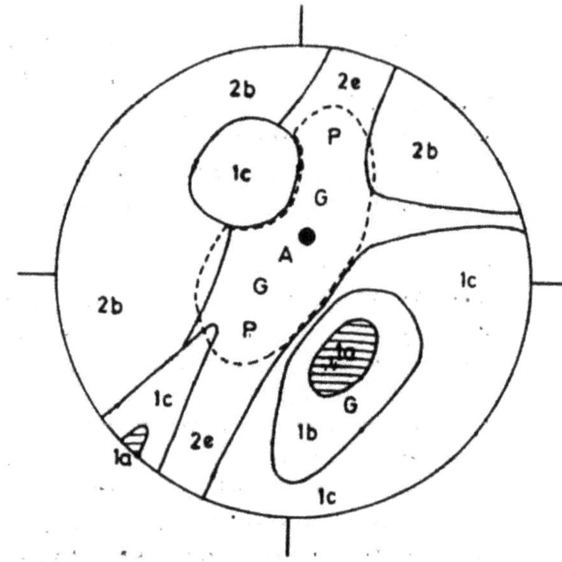

Fig. 7b. The resource exploitation in the model landscape during the Early Neolithic, c. 3500 B.C.

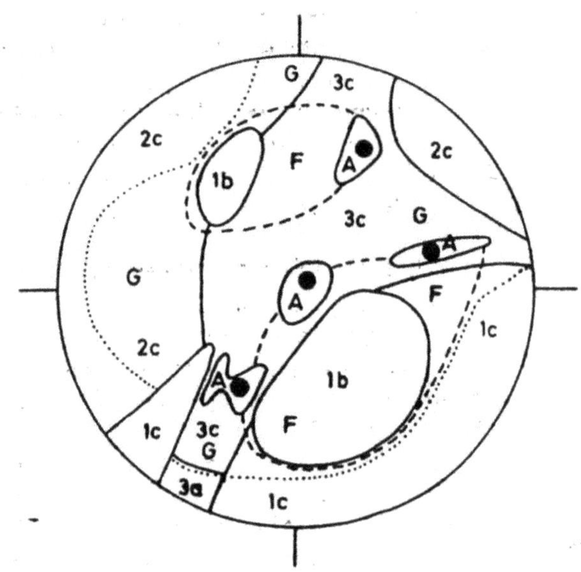

Fig. 7d. The resource exploitation in the model landscape during the Early Iron Age, c. A.D. 400.

(1) Vegetation types

(2) Food-production technology (mainly agricultural technology)

(3) Human manipulation of the vegetation

(4) Technological change

(5) Demographic growth (population density change)

The core of the descriptions are references to publications, where the cultural landscape is discussed in detail. The publications are selected among my own case studies as well as studies by other researchers working along similar lines or at least along lines useful for the purpose of this essay.

(1) The Mesolithic, c. 5000 B.C. (Figure 7a). A base camp for hunting-gathering at an inlet of the sea. The site is situated in a landscape of optimal production due to erosion of clay sediments by the regressive sea. Patches of the high-ground forest have been cleared by fire to improve hunting grounds. The varied biotop along the eskar at the innermost bays of the sea forms the basis for a year around exploitation. Task sites for big game hunting might be situated at lakes in the inland (Welinder 1980, 1983a).

(2) The Early Neolithic, c. 3500 B.C. (Figure 7b). A farming site is situated in a broadleaf forest area above a shallow lake surrounded by marshy areas. A few square kilometers of broadleaf forest around the site are in a dynamic state of clearance and regeneration with plots of arable land and herbs and shrubs vegetation. The latter is used for browsing by sheep and goats. Swines are herded in the broadleaf forest still to be cleared. Winter-fodder is gathered from the Carex marsh and from girdled elms and other trees surrounding the site.

A task site for exploitating marine resources might be situated further down the eskar. Another task site might be situated in the other direction along the eskar at an extensive Carex marsh used as grazing area or for the gathering of winter-fodder (Hulthén et al. 1981, Welinder 1982).

(3) The Late Bronze Age, c. 700 B.C. (Figure 7c). Two contemporary sites are situated along the eskar above extensive Carex marshes used for grazing and winter-fodder gathering. The eskar is covered by grassland with stands of girdled and pruned broadleaf trees. Plots of arable land is situated in this area. In areas permanently grazed by cattle juniper shrubs are found (Kjellén et al. 1977, Welinder 1983b).

(4) The Early Iron Age, c. A.D. 400 (Figure 7d). Four contemporary farms are situated regularly spaced within the model landscape. They are surrounded by henged, permanently plowed arable land and fodder-producing areas including the low-lying Carex marshes. Only occasional broadleaf trees are found. An extensive grazing area around these infield areas is covered by grassland and juniper shrubs. It is edged by a mixed forest with i.a. spruce (Widgren 1983, Welinder 1983a).

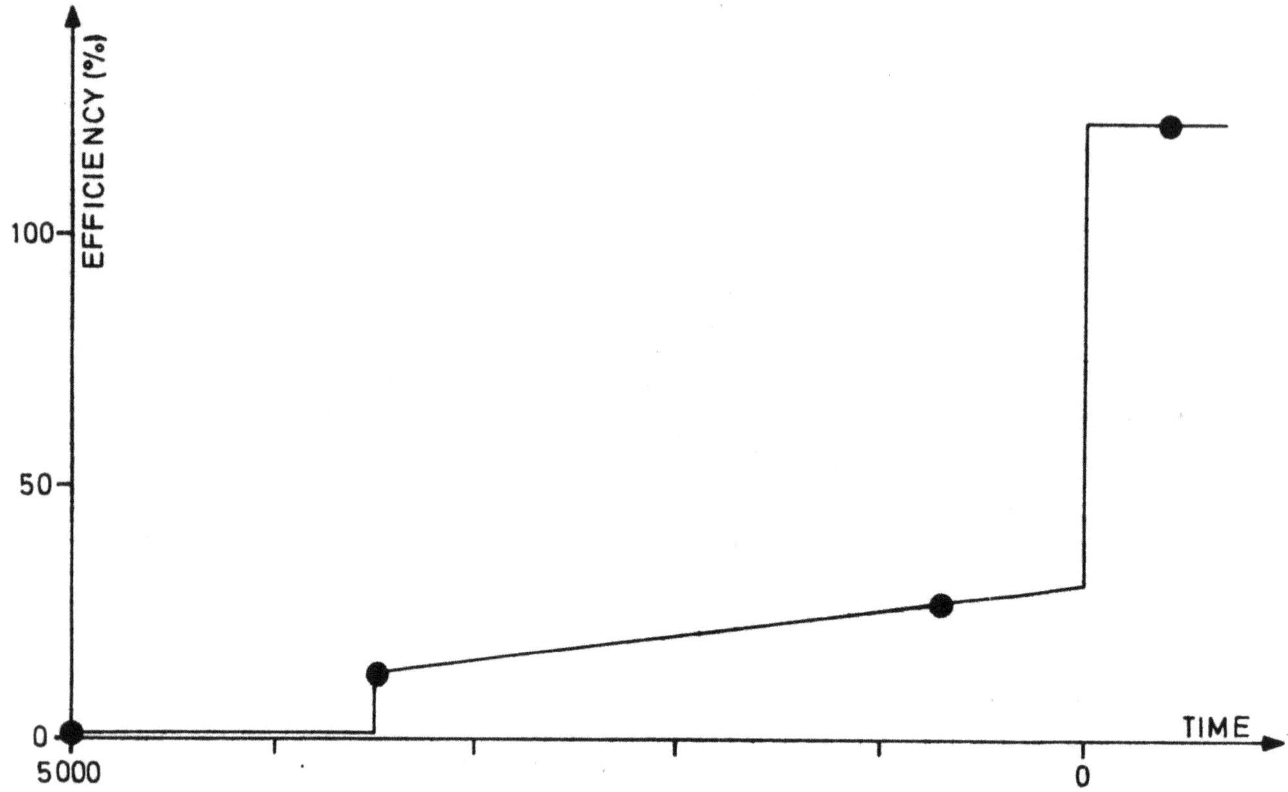

Fig. 8. The estimated efficiency of human societies in Central Sweden (cf. Table 1).

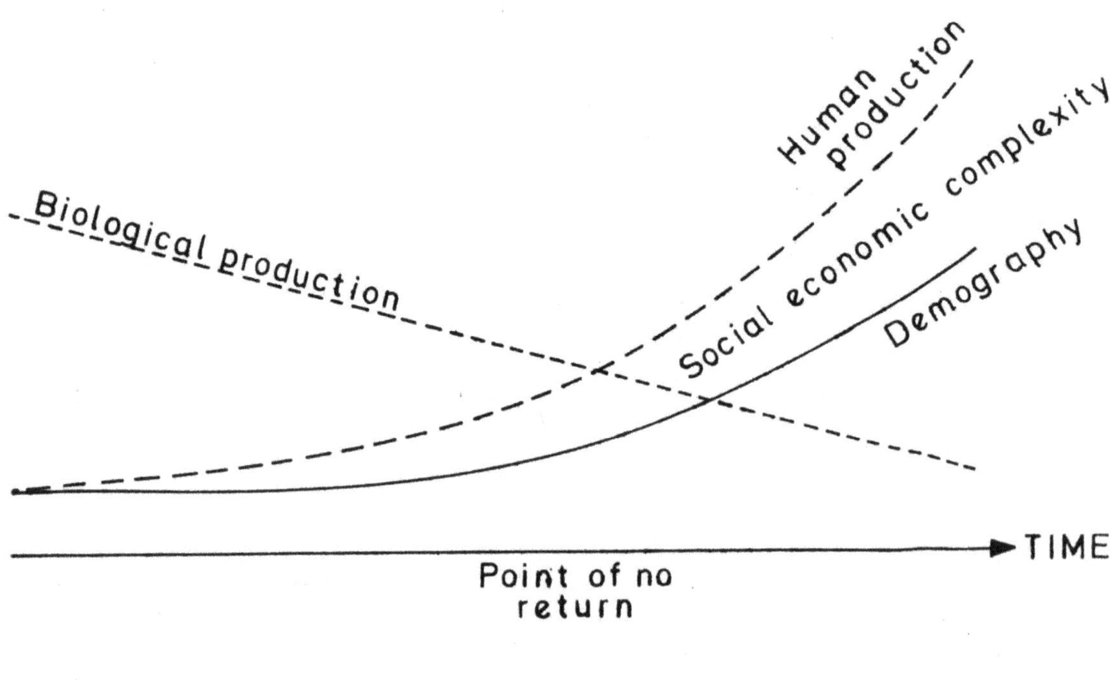

Fig. 9. Summarizing model of the growth and change of the human ecosystem in the model landscape in the long-term perspective.

7. Energy-use Estimations

The operational system is an energy-flow system. The amount of energy stored and annually circulating within the system ought to be possible to estimate. Attempts have been made for various types of Scandinavian culture landscapes (e.g. Malmer 1969, Enckell et. al. 1979, Widgren 1983, Welinder 1983a). A summary mainly based on Welinder 1983a is presented in Table 1.

In the energy-use and efficiency estimations the site catchment area have been used as the basis. Thus, the estimations are valid not for the total landscape exploited but for the most efficiently exploited part of it. For the time after the introduction of farming, hunting-gathering activities are not considered. Likewise, energy stored in living biomass or in humus released after forest clearances are not taken into account. An attempt of this is presented in Welinder (1983c).

The efficiency is measured as the percentage of the total biological production of the site catchment area used by the human society for its own benefit. As the vegetation has been manipulated by human activities to increase the net production, the net production of the landscape before the introduction of farming is used as the basis in the estimations. Probably this is not appropriate, as a hypothetical natural net production have decreased since that time due to the retrogressive development.

The efficiency of the human society seems to have increased stepwise during the Holocene (Figure 8). Two main steps are the introduction of farming per se and the introduction of the infield/outfield system. Analytical studies of change have in the past concentrated on the first one of these two events.

8. Explaining Long-term Change

In terms of the operational system (Figure 5) the development of the culture landscape in Central Sweden (the models of Figure 7 are in their general aspects valid for most of temperate Furope) is described as biological, technological, and demographic change against an independent background of environmental change (climate, topography). Technological and demographic change most probably infere change in organization. Thus, social-economic change is perhaps a more relevant term.

Using the selected systematic approach the structure and function of the culture landscape might be understood from a number of essential aspects at defined points of time, e.g. resource exploitation pattern, ecological relations, energy-flow, production - consumption balance etc. Also how changes take place along the time-axis might be understood, a.i. which components and relations that change either qualitatively or quantitatively. With a reasonable set of ideas and analogies and with an informative set of field and laboratory data at disposal the understanding might be quite detailed and profound.

The description of the culture landscape and the change along the time-axis within the landscape will take the form of a complex interaction (feedback loops) between a number of selected, essential variables.

The retrogressive development of the Holocene involves a decreasing biological production (leaching of nutrients, podsolation). Demographic growth inferes an increasing human production (without stating which depends on which). At some point along the time-axis (Figure 9) this makes necessary manipulation of the environment to increase the production by adding high-quality energy to the system. This was a point of no return. From that point onwards an increasing social-economic complexity was needed to keep the production both at a level higher than the natural one and sufficiently high for the demands of the human society. From here on the general trend in the development will appear deterministic.

The above is a statement, not an explanation. It is based on interpretations of field and laboratory data combined with a set of ideas on culture landscape development derived from ecological theory. Is it possible to come closer to an explanation of change ?

BIBLIOGRAPHY

Ase, L.E. 1970. Kvartärbiologiska vittnesbörd om strandförskjutningen vid Stockholm under de senaste c. 4000 åren. Geol. fören. förh. 92:1. Stockholm.

Baudou, E. 1973. Arkeologiska undersökningar på Halleby 1. Halleby-undersökningen II. Acta univ. stockh. Studies in North-Europ. arch. 3. Stockholm.

Berglund, B.E. 1969. Vegetation and human influence in South Scandinavia during prehistoric time. Oikos, suppl. 12. Copenhagen.

Boserup, E. 1965. The conditions of agricultural growth. Lund.

Clark, J.G.D. 1972. Star Carr: A case study in bioarchaeology. Module 10. Reading, Mass.

Enckell, P.H., Königsson, E.S. & Königsson, L.-K. 1979. Ecological instability of an Iron Age human community. Oikos 33:2. Copenhagen.

Hulthén, B. & Welinder, S. 1981. A stone age economy. Theses and papers in North-Europ. arch. 11. Stockholm.

Hyenstrand, A. 1979. Ancient monuments and prehistoric societies. Central Board of National Antiquities. Stockholm.

Iversen, J. 1964. Retrogressive vegetational succession in the Post-glacial. British ecolog. soc. jubilee symp. Journ. of ecol. 52. Oxford.

Jaanusson, H. 1981. Hallunda. The Museum of National Antiquities, Stockholm. Studies 1. Stockholm.

Kjellén, E. & Hyenstrand. Å. 1977. Hällristningar och bronsålderssamhälle i sydvästra Uppland. Upplands fornm.fören. Tidskr. 49. Uppsala.

Larsson, M. 1978. Resenion. Fornv. 73. Stockholm.

Lindquist, S.-O. 1968. Det förhistoriska kulturlandskapet i östra Ostergötland. Acta univ. stockh. Studies in North-Europ. arch. 2. Stockholm.

Löthman, L. 1981. Bronsåldersstråk i Västmanland. Västmanl. fornm.-fören. Arsskr. 1981. Västerås.

Malmer, N. 1969. Organic matter and cycling of minerals in virgin and present ecosystems. Oikos, suppl. 12. Copenhagen.

Rappaport, R. 1967. Ritual regulations of environmental relations among a New Guinea people. Ethnology 6. Pittsburgh.

Spooner, B. (ed.) 1972. Population growth: Anthropological implications. Cambridge, Mass. London.

Spång, L.-G. 1978. Teorier om förhistorisk ekonomi. Kontaktstencil 14. Lund.

Welinder, S. 1974. Kulturlandskapet i Mälarområdet I-IV. Univ. of Lund. Dept. of Quater. Geol. Reports 5-6. Lund.

Welinder, S. 1975. Prehistoric agriculture in Eastern Middle Sweden. Acta arch. lund. 8° min. 4. Lund.

Welinder, S. 1977a. Ekonomiska processer i förhistorisk expansion. Acta arch. lund. 8° min. 7. Lund.

Welinder, S. 1977b. The Mesolithic Stone Age of Eastern Middle Sweden. Ant. arkiv 65. Stockholm.

Welinder, S. 1979. Prehistoric demography. Acta arch. lund. 8° min. 8. Lund.

Welinder, S. 1980. The disappearance of a hunting-gathering economy. Veröff. des Mus. fürur und Frügesch. Potsdam 14/15. Potsdam.

Welinder, S. 1982. The hunting-gathering component of the Central Swedish Neolithic Funnel Beaker (TRB) economy. Fornv. 1982:3. Stockholm.

Welinder, S. 1983a. The ecology of long-term change. Acta arch. lund. 8° min. 9. Lund.

Welinder, S. 1983b. The Ecology of the Bronze Age landscape in Central Sweden. In Struktur och Förändringi: Bronsålderns Samhälle. Ed. B. Sternquist. University of Lund, Institute of Arch. Report Series No. 17. Lund.

Welinder, S. (1983c). Ecosystems change at the Neolithic transition. Norw. Arch. Rev. 16:2. Oslo.

Widgren, M. 1978. Kulturlandskap och bebyggelse under äldre järnålder. Ostergötland 1978. Linköping.

Widgren, M. 1983. Settlement and farming systems in the early Iron Age. Acta. univ. stockh. Stockh. studies in Human Geog. 3. Stockholm.

Widholm, D. 1980. Problems concerning Bronze Age settlements in Southern Sweden. Medd. fr. Lunds univ. hist. mus. 1979-1980. Lund.

Table 1: Energy-use and efficiency estimations for Central Swedish prehistoric human ecosystems (from Welinder 1983a and others).

	(1)	(2)	(3)	(4)	(5)	(6)
Mesolithic	25	31 400	0.001	3	0.01	0.2
Early Neolithic	50	1 260	0.04	3	0.4	13
Late Bronze Age	20	600	0.03	3.5	0.8	27
Early Iron Age	10	70	0.14	4.1	3.7	123

(1) = individuals per site
(2) = site catchment area (ha)
(3) = population density within the site catchment area (individuals/ha)
(4) = biological net production (x 10^3 kg/ha)
(5) = the part of the net production used by humans and domestic animals (x 10^3 kg/ha)
(6) = efficiency (the part of the net production used by humans and domestic animals as a percentage of the biological net production of the Mesolithic landscape).

THE GÅRDLÖSA RESEARCH PROJECT

The Ecological Analyses in the Archaeological Framework

Berta Stjernquist

Introduction

In the period following the second World War, settlement archaeological research has underdone great changes. This is true both of material and of theory and method. Modern social planning has encouraged and made possible very comprehensive excavation projects, which have resulted in large quantities of material. At the same time, the discipline of archaeology has undergone changes of an interdisciplinary nature. The interdisciplinary changes involve a complicated process which cannot be simply explained but which means among other things that research has become more problem-oriented and that ecological relationships are in a central position. The research situation has awakened interest in and made possible the analysis of questions which touch the totality of a society, in which man as a social being stands in relation to both the natural environment and to other individuals and societies (Stjernquist 1978a, p. 251 ff.).

Gårdlösa. Background knowledge

The village of Gårdlösa is located in Smedstorp parish in southeastern Scania (Fig. 1). Within the village area there is an unusually well-defined ridge, whose southern part is encircled by the water system of the Tommarp river. The river continues meandering towards the east, and issues finally into the Baltic.

The ridge is an offshoot of the large Linderöd ridge. It is prominent and has somewhat steep sides. During the Iron Age there was a settlement on the southern part. The parish church, Smedstorp Church, and the present village of Gårdlösa, lie below.

It was long known that there was an Iron Age grave-field up on the ridge. This was marked by stone-settings in the form of ships, stone circles and occasional upright stones. In the 1920's a gravel-pit was opened on the ridge, and this revealed an inhumation grave from the Late Roman Iron Age (Stjernquist 1951, p. 37 ff. and 1955, p. 168). Although the gravel-pit was infrequently exploited, it later came to disturb further graves as well as occupation layers and remains of pit-houses. These random finds indicated the presence of an extensive Iron Age settlement. Moreover, it was clear that the settlement included both graves and remains of house foundations. Everything pointed to the context being sufficiently rich and differentiated so as to shed light on various aspects of prehistoric society. Furthermore, the finds showed that the settlement was in existence during the major part of the Iron Age. As mentioned previously

FIG. 1: Map showing the location of Gårdlöa.

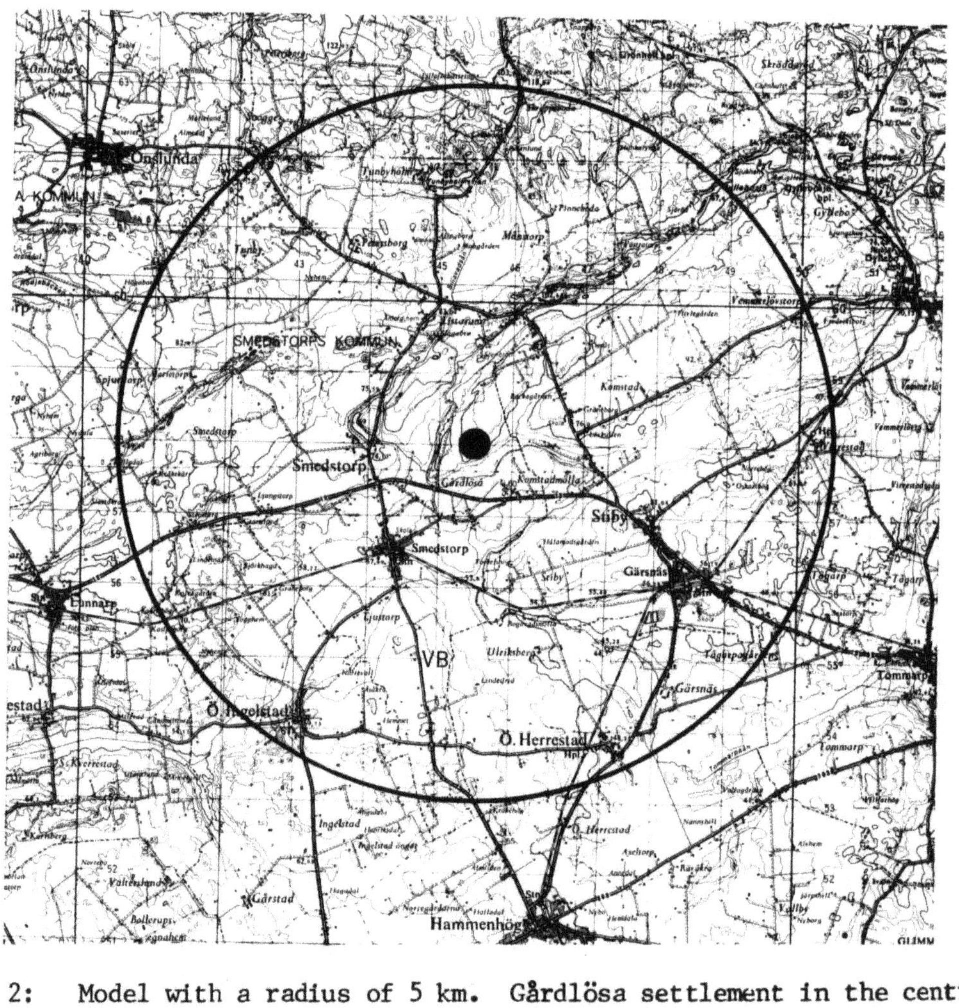

FIG. 2: Model with a radius of 5 km. Gårdlösa settlement in the centre.

the area was well delimited geographically. All these factors indicated that the settlement should be a suitable object for an analysis of an Iron Age community (Stjernquist 1978b, p. 167 ff.).

Problems

Although it was impossible to assess the extent of the finds at the start, the goal of the Gårdlösa investigation was from the beginning to analyse the settlement as a whole, where the interrelation of the different factors and of man's adaptation to his environment was to be studied. During the first stages of the fieldwork, the theory and the problems to be treated were worked on and developed. In order to be able to make an investigation of a settlement as an entity, the chronological aspects have to be taken into account; i.e., it must be possible to study social changes over a certain period of time. Such changes may occur in the structure of the settlement, the resources, and the population. The main object of the investigation, however, is the study of human activity on all levels. (Stjernquist 1981b).

It is logical to follow Higgs and Vita-Finzi and define a site as a place where there is a deposit or sets of deposits which contain evidence of human activity (Higgs and Vita-Finzi 1972, p. 28). This is basic but not sufficient for delimiting an area to be investigated.

Delimitation of the research area

During the planning of the Gårdlösa Project it became clear that the material situation was favourable for an investigation of the Iron Age settlement as a whole, including a study of the various functions involved. But it was not equally clear how the material should be delimited. However, it should be possible to draw limits for such an investigation, starting from the groupings of the archaeological units, or with the help of the topographical conditions. The way in which house foundations are grouped can thus indicate social contemporaneity, such as for example at Vallhagar (Stenberger and Klindt-Jensen 1955) or Eketorp (Stenberger 1974). The topographical delimitation can consist of the occurrence of settlement on an island, a peninsula, a ridge, or of a limited settlement on an open plain. There are many variations. A larger area can have several settlement concentrations which stand in relation to one another (cf. Kossack, Harck, Reichstein 1975; Jankuhn 1976).

For the Gårdlösa Project, the ridge was delimited as a primary area for intensive investigation, in which all features should be investigated as much as possible (the site). But activities in a society are not limited to the site. There are many functions which are linked to the subsistence situation which, for the individual outside the settlement area, make him dependent on a large area. Different variations in the question of this resource have been discussed in the literature (cf. Higgs and Vita Finzi 1972, p. 27 ff., Vita Finzi 1978). In this connection the term "the site territory" was used for the area habitually exploited from the site. In discussions of the resource area in modern scientific literature, this is usually portrayed as a circle with the settlement as the centre. Attention is given to the assumed mobility in the calculation of the size of the area. A common model is one that assumes a resource area with a radius of 5 km (an hour's walk) for stationary settlements, while mobile societies are accorded a resource area with a 10 km radius (2 hours' walk).

The discussion of the resource area, inspired by ethnographic analogies, has been important among other things because it has quickened interest in the study of the varying activity patterns practiced by man. However, uncertainty about the size of the resource area can be characterized as great. Variations in the question of mobility, and therefore the size of the resource area dependent on local conditions, can be seen in ethnographic material (Bakels 1978, p. 5 f.).

It is wholly theoretical to picture a resource area in this schematic fashion, even if the model is useful for indicating which adjacent area should have been easily accessible to the inhabitants of the settlement (Fig. 2). Such a model cannot be used without question for all settlement analyses. The size of a resource area is undoubtedly dependent on a number of factors. The topography and other natural conditions play a large part (Linke 1976). The importance of the subsistence structure has been emphasized. It is also dependent on other settlements and their resource areas. If they are calculated in this way, the resource areas of settlements will no doubt be seen to have intersected each other.

In the Gårdlösa Project, the topographical conditions with the valley of the Tommarp river have been emphasized (cf. Fig. 3). Therefore, in part the closest surroundings, in part this valley have been accorded special importance, both as a resource area and as an area for contact. The settlement area itself has been intensively investigated, while the surrounding resource area has received a more cursory analysis in which relevant problems were taken into consideration.

The concentration on the Tommarp valley, natural for the Gårdlösa Project, has grown through the work with reconnaissance and excavation which has previously been done in the area. A grave-field from the Late Bronze Age and the Early Iron Age at Simris was totally excavated during the years 1949-1951 (Stjernquist 1955 and 1961). At this time, as well as later, extensive reconnaissance and minor excavations were carried out in the parish on either side of the Tommarp river. These works build the foundation for the reconstruction of the settlement pattern in the Iron Age, and thus are of importance for, and are a part of, the Gårdlösa Project (Stjernquist 1978b, p. 171). How large a part of this area can truly be called an area for external contacts depends on how the concept resource area is defined.

It should be noted that, in spite of the uncertainty which can prevail about the resource area, a motivated delimitation must be attempted so that a systematic analysis can be carried out. This means that the settlement area for the Gårdlösa Project, as noted above, was intensively investigated, while the extent and importance of the resource and contact areas will be tested with two alternatives in mind.

1. That the model for stable settlements most used in the literature is accurate and that the area which is enclosed in a circle with a 5 km radius is the primary resource area.

2. That the valley with the parishes on both sides of the Tommarp river has had special importance as a resource and contact area.

The excavation

Since the goal of the project was to analyse Iron Age society as a social system, it was necessary to conduct the excavation so that the greatest possible amount of information could be gained about the structures and about the connections between them. This meant in principle the total excavation of all the features. Culture layers, i.e. remains of demolished structures, were to be excavated by digging areas to give information about find frequency and dating. Source errors in the material must be critically examined, since it cannot be assumed that all features which once existed have been located. This is relevant in the reconstruction of the different parts of the settlement.

Systematic fieldwork started in 1963 and was terminated in 1976. In 1976 fieldwork was carried on for only a month, but otherwise the duration of the excavation season was about 3-4 months every year. The area which was investigated lay about 1500 m as the crow flies from the boundary of the parish of Stiby in the northern part to the south tip of the ridge at the Tommarp river. The width of the ridge part varies, but is about 500 m. For practical reasons, the excavation was conducted from north to south along the ridge and therefore was concluded at the tip of the ridge at the Tommarp river. The investigated area, like the ridge, runs mainly in a northeast/southwest direction. Parallel with the excavation, reconnaissance was carefully carried out area by area. The methods included test pits, probing, and removal of the surface layer, as well as study of the vegetation cover and surface layer under different weather conditions. Aerial photography was tried but did not prove to be useful. Supplementary excavations were carried out below the ridge in the present-day village of Gårdlösa, at Smedstorp church and at the Kungsgården lying nearby, during the final phases of the excavation. Other supplementary investigations were carried out at a greater distance from the settlement (Stjernquist 1978b, p. 178 ff.).

The investigations have shown that the ridge was occupied during the greater part of the Iron Age. There are, in addition, some traces of occupation from the later part of the Bronze Age. But this occupation has been less extensive. The Iron Age settlement, in contrast, has been intensive, lengthy and continuous. It has existed from the last centuries B.C. to an advanced stage of the Viking Period, the 11th century.

The excavated material consists of different sorts of graves, remains of house foundations, occupation layers, pits, wells, ovens and some refilled springs (Fig. 3). The excavations have naturally resulted in many objects of different sorts. Variations in burial practices can be followed in this material, and remains of house constructions can be studied. In addition, the grouping of structures and their location in relation to each other can be studied.

The house foundations lay in three different groups. The oldest complex was discovered in the northern part of the excavated area. Here, remains of house foundations, which had lain on the surface and which therefore were seriously damaged, were investigated. Occupation layers, post-holes with stone packing, and hearths were excavated. Even if it was not possible to delimit the house remains in relation to each other, one could clearly see that remains of house constructions with bearing posts built on the surface were involved. In this area a well and an oven were excavated. The finds in these structures were partly simple everyday

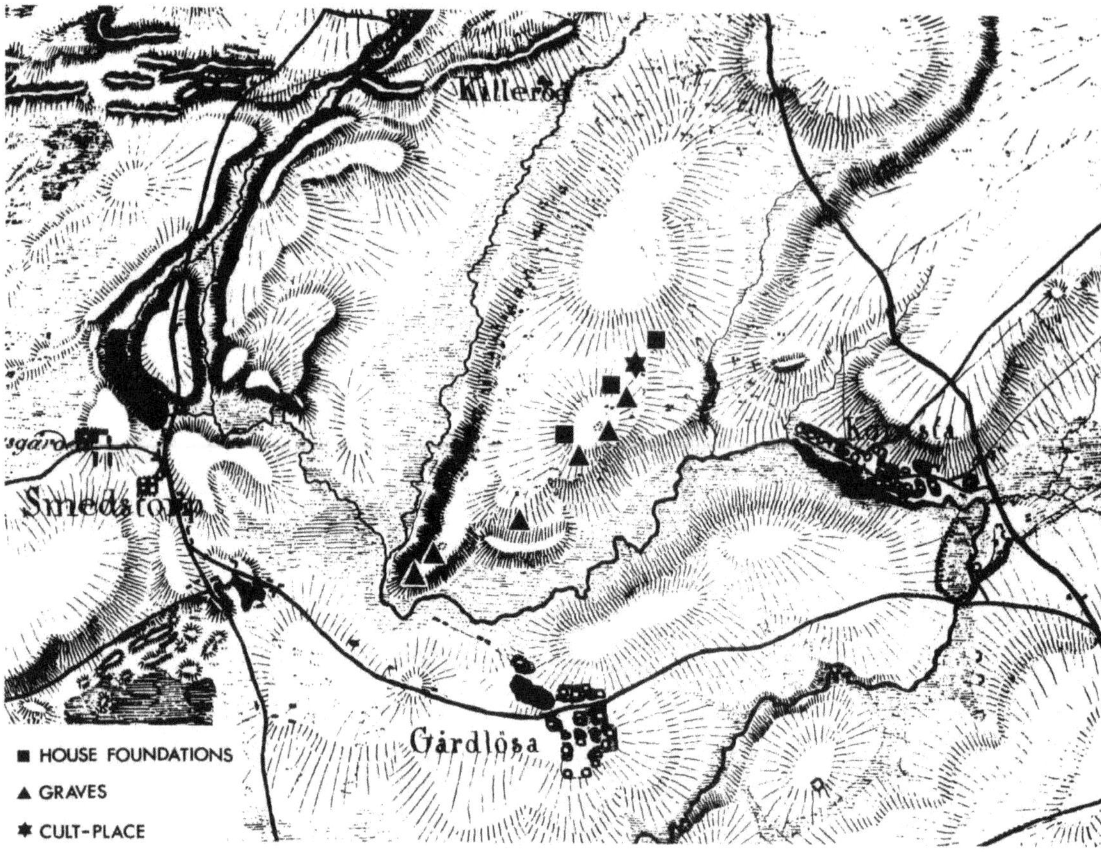

FIG. 3: Scanian survey map from 1816 with concentrations of investigated structures indicated. Note the Tommarp river system and its relation to the southern edge of the ridge.

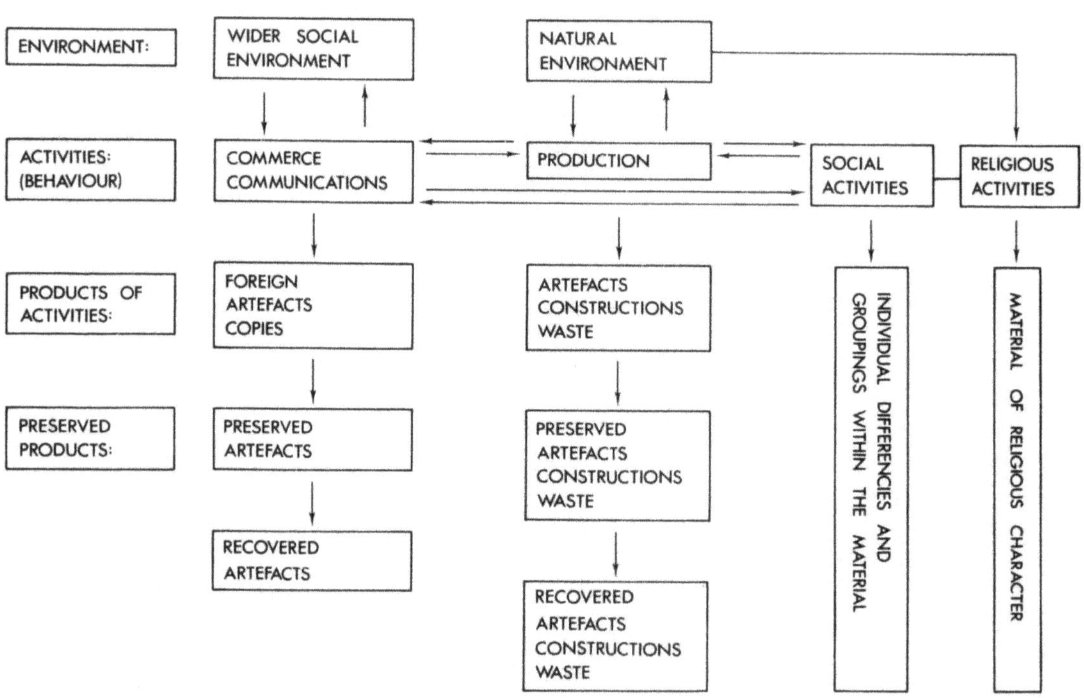

FIG. 4: Model of the components of a prehistoric community.

ceramics, burned clay and iron fragments, but there were also elements of fine polished ceramics with ornamentation and with profiled rim, which can be dated to the Roman Iron Age. Even the fourth century is clearly represented.

The next settlement complex was located ca 300 m southwest of the one described above. This was the largest and richest found on the ridge. It was dominated by a large number of partially subterranean small houses, pit-houses; but occupation layers and smaller features such as pits, hearths, ovens and post-holes were also found here. The pit-houses were spread out over a large area. They have a chronological range from the end of the fourth to the tenth century. A few remains of stone-settings indicate that perhaps larger houses, built on the surface, existed in this area. Because the entire area had been subject to cultivation, the uppermost layer was seriously disturbed. The large occupation layers which were found under the area can scarcely be explained from only the pit-houses encountered. No doubt the possibility that further constructions existed must be considered.

The pit-houses belonged to the standard type, with a post-hole at each gable end, but the structures varied in detail in regard to depth as well as size and the placement of the posts. The variations in the dating indicate a relatively short period of use. Thus, on the basis of this material, calculations about settlement changes during the period to which the constructions in this area belong can be made (Stjernquist 1970, p. 144 ff.).

Yet another complex was located ca 300 m southwest of the one just described. Here too occupation layers, hearths and a pit-house were found. However, the material was considerably less and was more damaged by cultivation than was the case for the large middle complex which was described above. This complex was wholly dominated by the occurrence of so-called Slavic ceramics. Large quantities of such ceramics were recovered as surface finds, and pottery also occurred in the structures. This indicates dating to the 11th century. The settlement can possibly have begun at the end of the 10th century, depending on how the ceramics are dated in detail.

The grave-field lay along the eastern edge of the ridge, where the graves lay in groups, often on the parts of the gently rolling ridge plateau which lay higher. There was no consistent horizontal straigraphy. Instead, the grouping was such that larger or smaller units with an inner chronological relationship could be distinguished. For example, a series of densely packed, large, low round stone constructions with graves from the period around the birth of Christ and from the beginning of the Roman Iron Age were excavated on the south tip of the ridge (Fig. 4), while a group of graves from the Viking Period was found just north of this grave complex. The occurrence of contemporary graves with the same construction in more than one place was considered to indicate burial places for different family units, a question which is being analysed in the working-up of the find material presently underway.

As a whole the period for the grave constructions agrees with that which the house remains represent. The question of the inner relationship will be more closely examined in connection with the intensive study of the finds. However, one can accept the hypothesis that the inner relationship is great.

Because the grave-field encompasses such a large part of the Iron Age

FIG. 5: Grave constructions on the southern edge of the ridge.

and is comparatively well preserved, it is possible, for the first time in south Swedish material, to see variations in burial practices at one and the same place during essentially the whole Iron Age. Therefore, the investigations of the grave-field do not only yield material for the interpretation of the inner connections in the settlement area, but also many new angles of approach for the interpretation of other grave-fields and for the question of the settlement's relation to the external social milieu (the contact net) (Stjernquist 1971 a, p. 99 ff.).

Many ship-settings, stone circles and other types of structures with upright stones are found among the characteristic grave constructions at the grave-field. The circular stone constructions have played a major role in the burial customs on the ridge. Inhumation graves from the Late Roman Iron Age with no visible marking above the surface, of the type known from a number of grave-fields in southern Sweden, are found among the burial structures (Stjernquist 1955, p. 166 ff.).

The ground water in the ridge is at a high level, and in a few places it emerges as a spring on the eastern edge of the ridge. Such a large spring lay in the settlement area. It is nowadays completely filled-in, but the place is still swampy in spite of having been drained with a line of tightly-packed large stones.

During the Iron Age the spring had originally stood open, but to judge from the stratigraphy it had been successively filled in. Remains of a large structure built of limestone slabs were excavated on the slope above the spring. Remains of hearths indicate that fires were repeatedly burned on the stone construction during a long time span. This activity can even be followed in the soot layers in the spring. This can be demonstrated from the Roman Iron Age until the Migration Period. The area has been interpreted as a cult location. With this is also included a pair of small refilled springs nearby (Stjernquist 1964, p. 180 ff.).

The three house foundation complexes are chronologically related to each other. Together, they cover the whole Iron Age from the first century B.C. to the eleventh century A.D. A variety of circumstances indicate that settlement relocations took place on two occasions. The house foundation complex was moved the first time in the transition period between the Roman Iron Age and the Migration Period, and the second time in the Viking Age, at the point in time when Slavic pottery made its appearance in the settlement. It is of particular interest that certain changes in settlement structure and in burial occur simultaneously with these relocations. Thus, the pit-houses appeared at the first relocation.

Dating

One of the conditions for completing the investigation is that the material should be set in a time perspective, i.e. that it should be possible to see a chronological relationship existing between the various entities. The methods used for this purpose are C 14 analyses and comparative analysis of the archaeological material with the help of typology. By employing both methods, increased certainty of the results will be assured. Both methods have sources of error. Combining them increases the possibilities of spotting uncertainties in the results. It was also possible to supplement the archaeological datings with C 14 analyses, and through C 14 analyses to obtain a chronological skeleton for the wood-anatomical identifications, so important for the milieu analyses. These are treated below.

A total of 79 C 14 analyses were carried out partly by Ingrid U. Olsson (Uppsala) and partly by Sören Håkansson (Lund). Dividing the analyses between the two laboratories was originally done for practical reasons. However, through double datings, this has subsequently been used for a study of error sources in the dating methods. Most of the analyses have been performed on charcoal, and only a few on bone or resin.

Theoretical background

One can of course construct an analysis of a settlement archaeological material in different ways. During the introductory phase of the investigation, problems and theories for an over-arching model were treated (Stjernquist 1971 c). The model is designed to be used for this investigation, but is general in character to enable use in an analysis of settlement complexes (Fig. 5). In a concrete manner it takes up all activities in a social system. Economic, social, and religious activities, relationships between them, and relations to the natural environment and to the social milieu are included here. Modern settlement archaeology aims at achieving a holistic picture of a society. A systematic analysis, starting from a model of this sort, does not only give positive results but is also of help in spotting gaps in the material. If the material is incomplete, it becomes clear in the analysis how far one can hope to go under the conditions given.

If one chooses to investigate a prehistoric society as a social system; that is, chooses a problem-orientation about conditions of life and man's way of living and forming his existence in society, an interdisciplinary method of analysis becomes necessary to investigate the ecological connections around and in the settlement. The natural surroundings and their resources are preconditions for the activities which affect subsistence. The interdisciplinary analyses play a central part even in the discussion of the area outside the settlement which could have contributed to the subsistence activities, the site territory (cf. above). Important factors creating resources are climate, hydrological conditions, soils, flora, fauna, technology, communication, and organisation. As noted, the categories of the model include all the productive, social, ecological and communicative connections.

To render the model operable, however, the major categories have to be broken down into minor ones, and at the same time they will be formulated more concretely. The study can concentrate on four dimensions, namely population, differentiation, integration and energy (Stjernquist 1978b, p. 178 ff., cf. Plog 1974) (Figs. 6 - 7). Within each one of these dimensions are a number of variables which can be made concrete and investigated in an archaeological material. For the study of all these dimensions, the study of technology is absolutely essential. Technology may be seen as a fifth dimension in relation to all the others. Population becomes the background for activities. Differentiation is an aspect which belongs to the productive activities. The social activities, such as institutions or social organisation, belong to integration. Energy is an aspect which belongs to the natural environment. Technology is another aspect of productive activities.

Interdisciplinary analyses

In order to carry out the analysis according to this model, an integration of the information which the archaeological material yields with that from the interdisciplinary analyses is needed (Berglund 1977). A number of researchers from scientific and humanistic disciplines have taken part in and contributed to the analyses of Iron Age society. The basic information which has emerged from these analyses has been presented and are now published in a first part of the Gårdlösa Research Project (Stjernquist 1981a). In connection with this, some of the main points of this analytical work and its importance for the research project are indicated.

The interdisciplinary analyses in the Gårdlösa Research Project have many angles of approach.

A geological investigation has been carried out by Jan Mikaelsson and Per Sandgren (Mikaelsson and Sandgren 1981). This work has produced a map showing bedrock and soils as a basis for the analysis of vegetation through time. It also yields information about the occurrence of various materials, for example where limestone can be found. Limestone was used in the structures at the settlement, and it should have been quarried in one of the localities near the settlement, as shown.

A vegetation reconstruction analysis has been completed through co-operation between Björn Berglund (Quaternary Geology), Thomas Bartholin (dendrochronology and wood anatomy) and Nils Malmer (plant ecology) (Bartholin, Berglund, Malmer 1981). It is not possible to obtain material for pollen analysis near the settlement. Instead, the standard profile which exists for Bjärsjöholm lake, ca 25 km from Gårdlösa, was used. However, this has been supplemented by material from the locality. In this work, two independent methods have been used.

The first of these methods is wood anatomy; that is, the identification of charcoal from hearths on the site. Through this an idea could be gained as to which trees and bushes were used and therefore existed near the site. Thomas Bartholin has been responsible for this part of the analysis.

The other method used here was developed by Nils Malmer and consists of drawing conclusions about the potential vegetation from present-day vegetation. This involves a theoretical construction to describe how the vegetational landscape today would have developed if it had been left alone without interference from man. In this way the area can be divided up into comprehensible ecological units and this can be used in the vegetation analysis. The paper which Hakon Hjelmqvist has written concerning the cultural plants is also included in the vegetation analysis. The analysis of cultural plants also yields information for many questions which concern subsistence life (Hjelmqvist 1979 and 1981).

The Iron Age landscape and its background in preceeding periods has been reconstructed from these different angles. A picture of the vegetation commensurate with soils and other surface conditions, for instance humidity, has emerged. A mosaic landscape with small open areas existed on the lighter soils on the ridge during the Iron Age. The forest was dominated by oak; but birch, ash and Sorbus species existed as well. It can be seen that the vegetation became more open after ca A.D. 500; a grazing landscape. One can assume that conditions for agriculture grew worse during the Vendel Period due to the hydrological and nutritional conditions in effect.

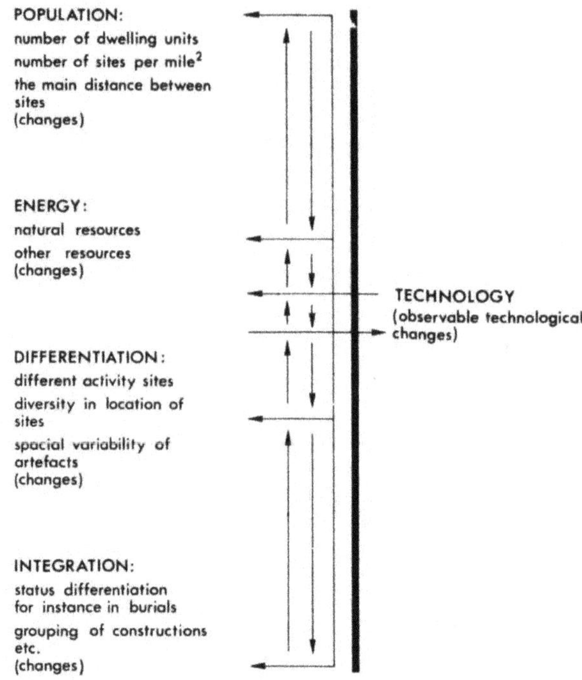

FIG. 6: Dimensions and some variables important for the study of change in a prehistoric community.

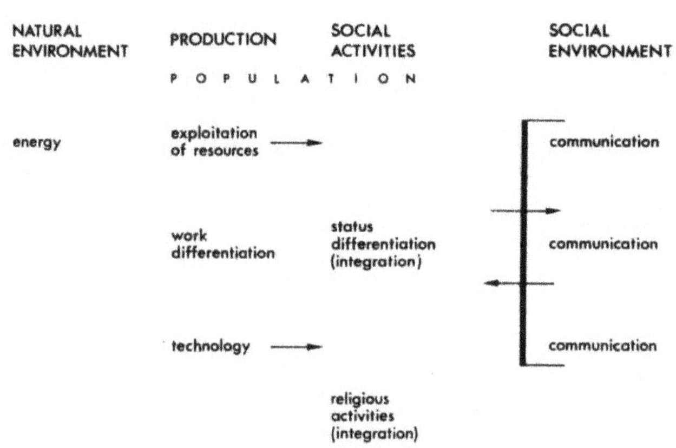

FIG. 7: Part of the model broken down into concrete, operable variables.

It is assumed that the climate from A.D. 700 became warmer and drier, and this could have contributed to lowered productivity and to the fact that the settlement moved from the ridge.

Through the vegetation reconstruction analysis it has been possible to gain a fairly good impression of the environmental conditions for subsistence.

The osteological material is a rich source of information about the settlement and of course also about the activities involved. Nils-Gustaf Gejvall has completed a thorough analysis of this material. It includes burnt and unburnt human and animal bone (Gejvall 1981).

In order to carry out the analysis of the society it is necessary to gain as much information as possible about the size and composition of the population. The basic source for such calculations is found in the osteological material, but the conclusions are not very evident. It should be pointed out that there are many sources of error in such a source material, which must be taken into account as much as possible and which Gejvall discusses. It is necessary to combine different methods which can be of use for such calculations if one wishes to investigate population conditions.

The animal bones give information about the activities and subsistence conditions at the settlement. Cattle were the most common domestic animal, but sheep and pigs were of importance and horses occurred as well. There are also a few bones from some wild species of particular interest such as seal and beaver. The informative paper which Gejvall has produced touches the investigation as a whole in many different ways regarding resources and activities.

A culture geographical analysis has been carried out by Staffan Helmfrid (1981). He has examined and worked-up the cartographic material. Since this material is relatively late and poor in information, and since fossil traces of cultivation are not and are not likely to be preserved in the sandy soil up on the ridge, the result of the analysis consists of possible hypotheses about culture geographical relationships. The preconditions for cultivation and forms for resource exploitation are discussed in this connection. This gives different interpretive possibilities.

The problems surrounding the removal and cessation of the settlement up on the ridge are central to the investigation. The cause of such changes can of course be wholly local, but on the other hand there may be causal connections and adaptive problems of more general nature in such a process. The interdisciplinary analyses play a central part in the microanalysis which is necessary to illuminate this. There is some support for the idea that the natural resources in the area very easily and relatively quickly could be over-exploited, especially if there was a period of dessication during the later part of the Iron Age.

The problems of the cessation of the settlement up on the ridge at the end of the Viking period also belong to the question of movements. Here the investigations touch problems of settlement changes during the transition from prehistoric times to the Medieval Period.

As was noted above, some test excavations in the village of Gårdlösa and at the church and Kungsgården were carried out in the last phases of the excavations. The aim here was to try to obtain evidence for the Medieval settlement below the ridge. However, it was not possible, with such limited attempts, to confirm the Medieval settlement, although considering the church building it must be assumed that it existed nearby. Nor has it been possible to reach so far back in time in the written source material so as to approach the prehistoric archaeological material.

As a part of the interdisciplinary analyses, Sten Skansjö has studied and analysed the written source material (Skansjö 1981). In this material the village of Gårdlösa is not mentioned before the end of the 15th century. Skansjö's paper, however, provided essential information to the analyses, among other things through the information which can be used for analogies in the study of the Iron Age material.

In addition to the interdisciplinary papers named, special investigations of ceramics and other material categories have provided information for the whole picture. Hans-Åke Nordström has carried out the analyses of the ceramics (Nordström 1981); the glass fragments have been analysed at the Glass Research Institute in Växjö; and slag products and iron have been analysed by Ebbe Langer at Danmarks Tekniske Højskole (Stjernquist 1971 b, p. 150 ff.).

That part of the investigation of the Iron Age settlement which is now at hand in the form of archaeological research results and interdisciplinary reports is the starting point for the integrated analysis of the settlement as a social system. The five dimensions which were advanced above in connection with the theoretical working-up of the problems are essential in this connection. At the present stage, a first part of the investigation is being published, with papers mentioned above which treat the investigation's problem-orientation, the archaeological framework, and the interdisciplinary analyses (Stjernquist 1981a).

BIBLIOGRAPHY

Bakels, C.C. 1978. Four Linearbandkeramik Settlements and their Environment: a Paleoecological Study of Sittard, Stein, Elsloo and Hienheim. Analecta Praehistorica Leidensia XI (Leiden).

Bartholin, T.S., Berglund, B.E. & Malmer, N. 1981. Vegetation and Environment in the Gårdlösa Area during the Iron Age, in Stjernquist, Gårdlösa 1981.

Berglund, B.E. 1977. Biological/Paleoecological Analyses for Modern Archaeological Research. Proceedings of the Nordic Conference on Thermoluminescence Dating and Other Archaeometric Methods, Uppsala University, Sweden, 25-26 November 1976. Risø National Laboratory, (Denmark 1977).

Cejvall, N.-G. 1981. Skeletal Remains from Gårdlösa, Smedstorp Parish, Scania, Sweden, in Stjernquist, Gårdlösa 1981.

Helmfrid, S. 1981. The Village of Gårdlösa and the Iron Age Settlement on the Gårdlösa Ridge. Some Reflections based on Historical-Geographical Research in Stjernquist, Gårdlösa 1981.

Higgs, E.S. and Vita-Finzi, C. 1972. Prehistoric Economies: A Territorial Approach. Papers in Economic Prehistory (ed. E.S. Higgs). (Cambridge: University Press).

Hjelmqvist, H. 1979. Beiträge zur Kenntnis der prähistorischen Nutzpflanzen in Schweden. Opera botanica 47.

Hjelmqvist, H. 1981. Grain Impressions from Gårdlösa, in Stjernquist, Gårdlösa 1981.

Jankuhn, H. 1976. Methode und Probleme siedlungsarchäologischer Forschung. Archäologie und Geschichte 1. (Berlin).

Jankuhn, H. 1977. Einführung in die Siedlungsarchäologie. (Berlin).

Kossack, O., Harck, G. and Reichstein, J. 1975. Zehn Jahre Siedlungsforschung in Archsum auf Sylt. Bericht der Römisch-Germanischen Kommission 55, 1974.

Linke, W. 1976. Frühestes Bauerntum und geographische Umwelt. Bochumer Geographische Arbeiten 28. (Bochum).

Mikaelsson, J. and Sandgren, P. 1981. A Geological Survey of the Smedstorp Area, in Stjernquist, Gårdlösa 1981.

Nordström, H.-Å. 1981. Pottery Fabrics at Gårdlösa, in Stjernquist. Gårdlösa, 1981.

Olsson, I.U. 1981. C 14 Dating of the Settlement at Gårdlösa, Smedstorp Parish, Scania, Sweden, in Stjernquist, Gårdlösa 1981.

Plog, F.T. 1974. The Study of Prehistoric Change. Studies in Archaeology. Academic Press. (New York-London).

Skansjö, S. 1981. Landowners, Tenant Farmers and Cottagers. An Investigation of the Village of Gårdlösa and the Parish of Smedstorp in the Oldest Written Records, in Stjernquist, Gårdlösa 1981.

Stenberger, M. 1974. Eketorp. Entwicklung und wirtschaftliche Bedeutung. Vor- och Frühformen der europäischen Stadt im Mittelalter II, (eds. Jankuhn, W. Schlesinger und H. Steuer). (Göttingen).

Stenberger, M. and Klindt-Jensen, O. (Eds.) 1955. Vallhagar. A Migration Period Settlement on Gotland, Sweden. (Stockholm).

Stjernquist, B. 1951. A Scanian Grave with a Rune-inscribed Brooch. Meddelanden från Lunds universitets historiska museum. (Lund).

Stjernquist, B. 1955. Simris. On Cultural Connections of Scania in the Roman Iron Age. Acta Archaeologica Lundensia, Series in 4° N° 5. (Lund).

Stjernquist, B. 1961 Simris II. Bronze Age Problems in the Light of the Simris Excavation. Acta Archaeologica Lundensia, Series in 4°, N° 5. (Lund).

Stjernquist, B. 1964. New Light on Spring-Cults in Scandinavian Prehistory. Archaeology 17:3.

Stjernquist, B. 1970. Das Problem der Grubenhäuser in Südschweden. Jahrbuch des Röm.-Germ. Zentralmuseums Mainz 14. 1967.

Stjernquist, B. 1971a. Zur Frage der Siedlungskontinuität der Völkerwanderungszeit. Meddelanden från Lunds universitets historiska museum 1969-1970. (Lund).

Stjernquist, B. 1971b. Einige Gesichtspunkte zu vorgeschichtlicher Eisenverarbeitung. Meddelanden från Lunds universitets historiska museum 1969-1970. (Lund).

Stjernquist, B. 1971c. Archaeological Analysis of Prehistoric Society. Scripta Minora Regiae Societatis Humaniorum Litterarum Lundensis 1971-1972:1. (Lund).

Stjernquist, B. 1973. Skeppssättningar i Gårdlösa. Honos Ella Kivikoski. Finska fornminnesföreningens tidskrift 75. (Helsingfors).

Stjernquist, B. 1978a. Approaches to Settlement Archaeology in Sweden. World Archaeology, Volume 9, No. 3. (London).

Stjernquist, B. 1978b. Studies of Structure, Continuity and Change in Iron Age Settlements in Sweden. Lowland Iron Age Communities in Europe. Papers presented to a Conference of the Department for External Studies held at Oxford, October 1977 (eds. B. Cunliffe and T. Rowley). BAR International Series (Supplementary) 48. (Oxford).

Stjernquist, B. 1981a. Gårdlösa. An Iron Age Community in its Natural and Social Setting. I. Interdisciplinary Studies by B. Stjernquist, S. Skansjö, J. Mikaelsson and P. Sandgren, T.S. Bartholin, B.E. Berglund and N. Malmer, H. Hjelmqvist, N.-G. Gejvall, H.-Å. Nordström, I.U. Olsson. Comments. Appendix: C 14 Datings by I.U. Olsson and S. Håkansson. Acta Regiae Societatis Humaniorum Litterarum Lundensis LXXV. (Lund).

Stjernquist, B. 1981b. The Gårdlösa Research Project, in Stjernquist, Gårdlösa 1981.

Vita-Finzi, C. 1978. Archaeological Sites in their Setting. (London).

THE IDENTIFICATION OF TRIBAL HIERARCHIES

Hans Lundmark

1. Introduction

Recently the concepts of "tribes" and "tribal society" have become increasingly more important in contemporary European archaeology (e.g. Kristiansen, 1982). This is partly due to influences from American, anthropologically oriented, archaeology, but is mostly an effect of the rising interest in analysing the function and behaviour of past societal systems. Although it has been somewhat "taboo" since pre-war times to deal with and study remains of "real" tribes, i.e. to identify the different archaeologically defined cultural groups and influence areas as reflections of functioning societies, such studies are prerequisite to explaining prehistoric relationships in any detail. The problem is to bridge the gap between data and theory, between the artifacts and the explanation of complex societies. This can only be done by identifying and studying the networks of social and economic relationships which determines the character of social system.

Different features discovered by archaeologists, are resulting from different levels of the previously existing system, and understanding of these contexts desires an elaborate study of the function and meaning of these levels.

Thus, the explanation of past human culture as such, presupposes a detailed study of "cultures", i.e. the remnants of the previously existing societies (Kleijn, 1973, p. 701, cp. Daniel, 1976, p. 246).

This does not mean that one should follow in the footsteps of the nationalistically oriented school of e.g. Kossina, attempting to trace the "history" of existing peoples and match the identified cultural groups with tribes named by different classic writers, e.g. as Tacitus (Kristiansen, 1981, p. 273, Trigger, 1980, p. 28). The present interest is not so much directed towards tribes as historical realities but rather as objects for research, serving as laboratories in a study of more general regularities.

The tribe is, however, a somewhat floating concept, its composition varying in time and space. Each level of organization, e.g. families, kinships, clans etc., may have different meanings and functions within different societies. In a similar way, artifacts, the mainstream of our source material, circulate within different distribution channels depending upon the level at which it functions (cp. Kristiansen, 1982, p. 259, also Larsson this volume). Relationships such as these make it difficult to identify the remains of past social behaviour; especially the distinct functioning groups and their composition.

In this paper a comprehensive framework that solves all of these problems will not be presented. Instead, a method of analysis is presented which may be of some assistance in such a study. It is based upon a spatial approach. By discerning the spatial behaviour of different levels of a society a better and more detailed understanding of the functioning of the system may be reached.

Previously a method has been presented (Lundmark, 1984) in which cluster analysis is utilized to identify regularities and hierarchies in spatial groupings. Its application is based upon a number of propositions. Thus, if a specific social system is based upon a certain social group, e.g. familes, or kinships, and these are spatially separated, then there exists a possibility that they can be identifiable within a geographical context. A self-dependent group within a society, not protected or subdued by a central authority, would be expected to develope social "bufferzones" against neighbouring groups in order to avoid unnecessary tensions. If the tribal groups are composed of similar units, then their populations will tend to be of the same size. This should result in similar demands for territory within a homogenous economy. A regular pattern of settlement clusters separated by "bufferzones" indicates that such an arrangement has existed. Therefore the purpose of this method has been to identify clusters of roughly the same size in order to discern different levels in the organizational pattern.

A strict segmentary tribe, as outlined by Sahlins (1968, p.20) may well represent the archetype of this behaviour in which each group may also function as a member of higher constellations, depending upon the circumstances. This might be reflected geographically through a clustering of groups, similar to the way that settlements cluster on a lower level. This unrestricted cluster hierarch should also be discernable within the distribution of settlements. Even more complex societies may behave in a similar manner, at least in relation to neighbours of similar status, although, their internal organization could be more complex and organized, possibly with the retardation of previously existing internal bufferzones. A marked hierarchy between groups may indicate a dependent situation where the larger configurations represent a concentration of power, necessary to uphold authority. A few such relationships are mentioned in the following examples. Groups of similar size and magnitude infer self dependent units, probably existing in a competitive situation.

Higher levels of contact, influence and cooperation, e.g. trade, religion etc., might not follow the above route. Similarities in artifacts, circulating in different exchange cycles and locations of religious and other centres can, however, provide information of such relationships, covering these more vague contexts of levels.

In addition to analysing the structures of different levels, we are also able to gain insight into developments over time, by applying such a method structures from different time periods can be compared and indications of structural processes can be traced within a specific group.

A final, clear-cut result can not be produced using this approach. Society is an organic system of relations and our findings must be ordered within static structures. This, combined with problems of representativity, will lead to problems in interpretation of the eventually found structural order. It may, however, be of some value in providing a more explicit framework for detailed study and as a hypothesis generator.

II. The D-curve Method

The method (fully discussed in Lundmark, forthcoming), is based upon the use of detailed density maps, with 70-80% overlapping reference cells used in their construction (figure 1). The picture which emerges, however, is very much dependent upon the cells size or "generalization level". A system of clusters of a given size can only be identifiable within a certain range of cell sizes. Such regularities can be found to exist by analysing a distance matrix containing all distance relations within a specific site distribution.

The degree of change (D) in the density around each point is calculated by expanding a circular area around each of them, by a certain fixed interval. The mean value of this density variation is represented graphically as in figure 2. Eventually, "bufferzones" will be displayed as local minimas in the curve, and the size of the reference cell thereby determined. The minimas occur when the expanding circles include more and more of the less densely populated "bufferzones", which results in a decline in the change of the density. As the expansion continues, the circles begin to include points from neighbouring groups and the relative density rises again. If several levels of grouping exist this will correspondingly result in several local minimas. The generalization levels, thus obtained, are then used in the construction of the density map in which the clusters appear as "hills" or "peaks" (figure 1). Such maps might also be termed "influence" or "gravity" maps which may indicate the relative strengths of social interactions.

The starting value of the D-curve is an indication of the nearest neighbour relationships between the points. A value around 1.0 indicates a random pattern, a higher value a dispersed pattern, and a lower value a clustered pattern, i.e. several small nearest neighbour distances and a few larger ones. The starting value is of special interest if it indicates a regularly dispersed pattern which may reflect a controlled organization within the group. The latter two cases might be of less interest for analytical purposes since they are not correlated with respect to a specific area.

A disturbance, which has been termed a "shadow effect", occasionally occurs in the distribution patterns. Within a regularly clustered distribution there will be a large number of distances within each group but markedly few representing distances towards points which would be situated in the empty areas surrounding the groups, hence the occurrence of minimas in the curve. However, if the clusters are regularly spaced, this will result in a large number of distances just above the value of the local minima, while the relations towards more distant groups will be more dispersed within the next level of organization. The result is a sharp rise and fall in the density producing a peak in the curve and a "false" minima. Some examples (e.g. figure 2) show this special feature. If the distance relations between the clusters are more varied, this effect will not occur (e.g. figure 11).

Three examples follow; one covering a process over time, one comparing factor analysis with spatial analysis and a third discussing spatial hierarchies.

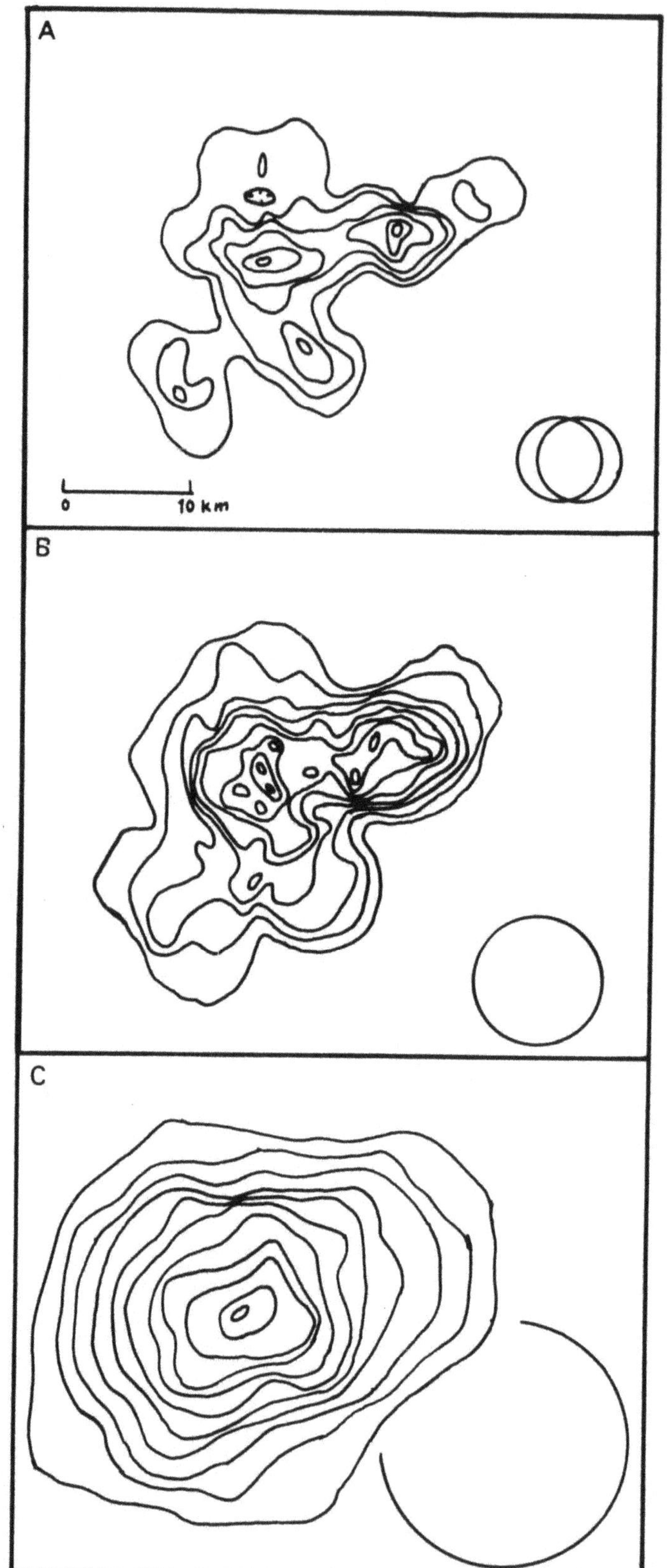

FIG. 1: Density maps of the distribution in Fig. 2. The sizes of the reference cells are indicated. The size of the overlap is seen in A.

III. Development over time - an East Swedish example

Since 1938, the National survey of ancient monuments, administrated by the Swedish Central Board of National antiquities has provided an enormous amount of material for spatial research (Hyenstrand, 1979). The character of the physical landscape in most parts of Sweden has helped to preserve a large proportion of the original monuments. Monuments are often situated on nonproductive till or bedrock implements and threatened little by farming activities, except for occasional construction etc. Some exceptions exist, e.g. in southern Scania, where intensive agricultural activity has destroyed a large part of the visible remains. However, the majority of the monuments, mostly cemeteries, have been preserved although many have been excavated by the antiquity authorities in areas of urban expansion during the past thirty years. This has lead to a situation in which most of the artifact material still remains buried in the soil as contrasted with the situation in e.g. Denmark, where possibly (cp. Kristiansen, 1981, p. 242) most of the finds of certain groups have been discovered. As one compensation Sweden still have their monuments left, visible at the places where they were once built. Grave monuments from prehistoric times are relatively insensitive as "time-calenders" when compared to different types of artifacts. However, since most of the country has been surveyed we do have good opportunities for large-scale studies, both spatially and over time (Hyenstrand, 1979). This example will not cover a large area, but instead it will trace the development of the spatial behaviour of a certain population over time. In this instance, the study will only cover the distribution of monuments. Later, a comparison between artifact distributions and spatial groupings will be performed, using a French example.

The investigated area, Vikbolandet, in the county of Ostergötland, is situated on the east coast of Sweden (figure 3). It is a relatively homogenous area with respect to land use potential which makes it especially suitable for this kind of spatial analysis. Four main horizons can be identified among the monuments. The Late Bronze Age horizon is represented by sites with heaps of fire cracked stone (figure 4A) (also discussed in more detail in Lundmark, 1984), that strongly indicates settlement activity. The others consist of different key-grave types. Consequently, they are only an indirect reflection of settlement structure. The nature of these relationships will briefly be discussed for each case.

The cemeteries of this area can be subdivided into two easily recognizable major groups; early Iron-age (up to about 400-500 A.D.) and Late Iron-age (500-1000 A.D.). The former period is characterized here by relatively small grave groups (at least the visible parts) containing several distinguishable grave-types. Combination analysis suggest a division into two main horizons, probably reflecting a slight time difference. Erected stones are present on some sites while others contain flat, wide, circular graves, mostly with a concentration of larger stones, or earth mounds in the central part. (By local archaeologists often referred to as "fried eggs"). The latter type regularly occurred during the roman period while the erected stones might be placed somewhat earlier in time. It is difficult to discern the earliest Iron-age (early La Tēne) in the monument distribution. However, this continuity problem might be solved by studying the structures from the periods before and after the early La Tēne. In this context, the erected stone distribution will tentatively be viewed as the earliest Iron-age structure. This question needs, however, much more careful study and is a major problem in the large scale analysis of this period.

FIG. 3: The position of the Vikbolandet, county of Ostergötland, Sweden.

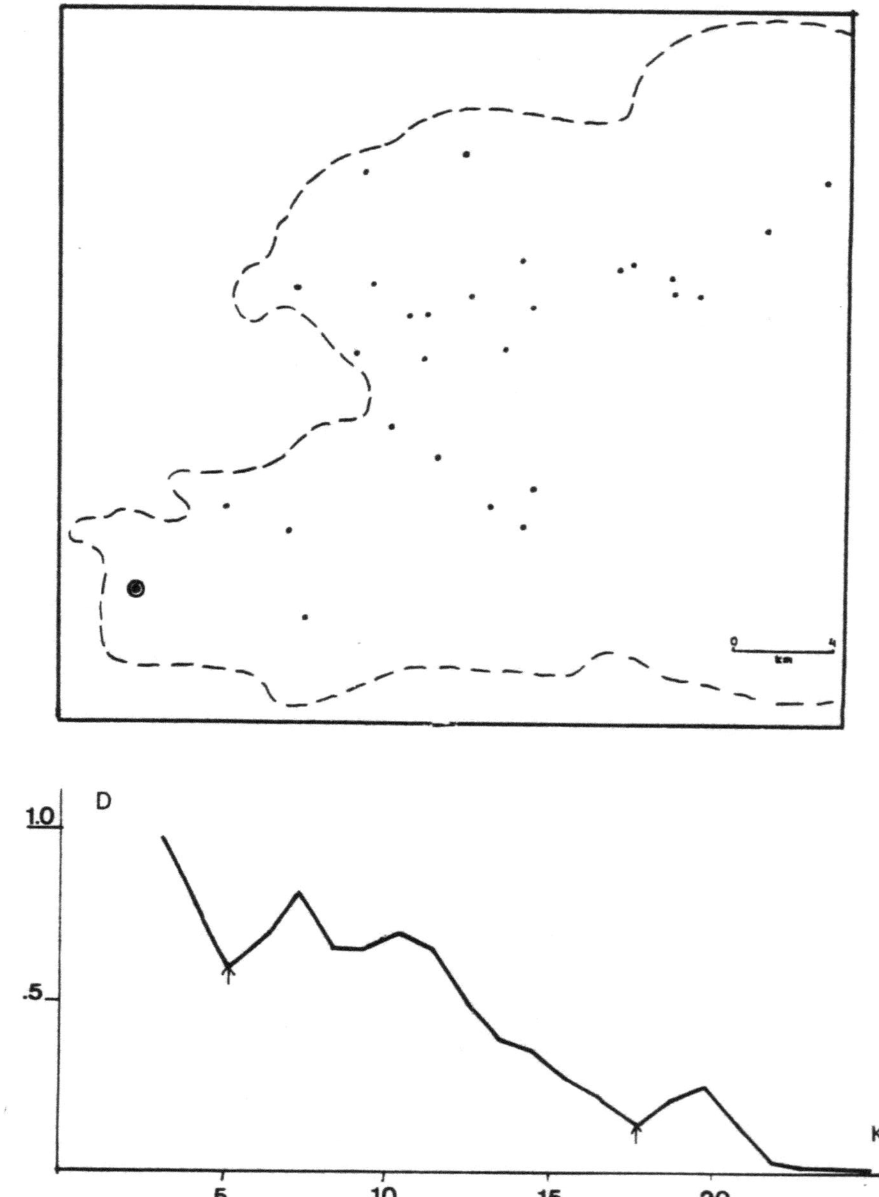

FIG. 2: The distribution of long barrows in western Salisbury plain in England (after Renfrew) and the corresponding D-curve. Dashed line indicates the border of the chalkland.

A marked difference between the two groups can be seen in their spatial distributions (figure 4B and 4C). In general, the erected-stone sites are evenly distributed, suggesting a direct correlation with the settlement pattern. In contrast, the circular graves ("fried eggs") occasionally form clusters in small areas that are not especially suitable for settlement. These areas also include the largest cemeteries in question. We might therefore expect a certain deviation from a one to one relationship between settlements and cemeteries, where a tendency towards central burial areas occurs. Aside from these cases there are no other significant signs that large central places or concentrations existed during these periods. Additionally, a rather local style in both gravetypes and other features e.g. the stone fence systems, (cp. Widgren, 1979) indicate that a relatively decentralised independent tribal area existed and probably included the central area of the county, stretching from the east coast, to lake Vättern in the west (cp. maps in Hyenstrand, 1979).

The late Iron age period shows a clearly different picture. The cemeteries are often larger in size and mostly include gravetypes of less varied character. These gravetypes are characterized by small barrows and turf-covered, round graves of moderate height (up to 0.3m) which are mostly flat versions of the barrows (cp. Hyenstrand, 1979, p. 144). Occasionally, triangular graves with concave sides occur. 1 Later versions of these triangular monuments, (treudds) also of moderate height, are mostly turf covered. There exist another variant primarily with a stone surface, but their location suggests an earlier dating.

The "treudd" seems to hold a specific position within the Late Iron age burial system. The cemeteries of the period are mostly situated adjacent to the farms and settlements of the time (ibid. 145) and a significant variation in size between the different units is therefore of interest since most of the "large" units include the "treudd" while it is rarely included in the smaller units. Since the relative numbers of each type of grave within a given unit are similar, regardless of the units' size, differences in unit size may probably reflect differences in their population.

Thus, the pattern of sites with "treuddar" (figure 5) indicates a well organized system where some units (characterized by their large size and this peculiar grave type), may serve a central function. The largest cemetary (Gullestad) in this part of the county, is twice the size of any other site. It includes 15 "treuddar" as compared with the second largest value of eight. This is obviously a central place of some kind and is parallelled by the largest site in the county, near Tift in Linköping. "Tift" is about twice the size of "Gullestad", both in number of graves and number of "treuddar". "Birka" the largest cemetery in Sweden, contains more than 2000 graves and about 70 "treuddar". A hierarchy of central places, "Birka" - "Tift" - "Gullestad", may be indicated; the latter controlling an area of small territories as shown in figure 5. These territories are indicated in the figure by Thiessen-polygones between the hypothetical central units. Some alterations had to be arbitrarily made due to the occurrence of pares of sites (mostly in the northeast) where one site in each pare usually has an older character than the other. A picture emerges showing a territorial

---

1) Named in Sweden by the Swedish word for trident, "treudd", which, for convenience will be used in this discussion.

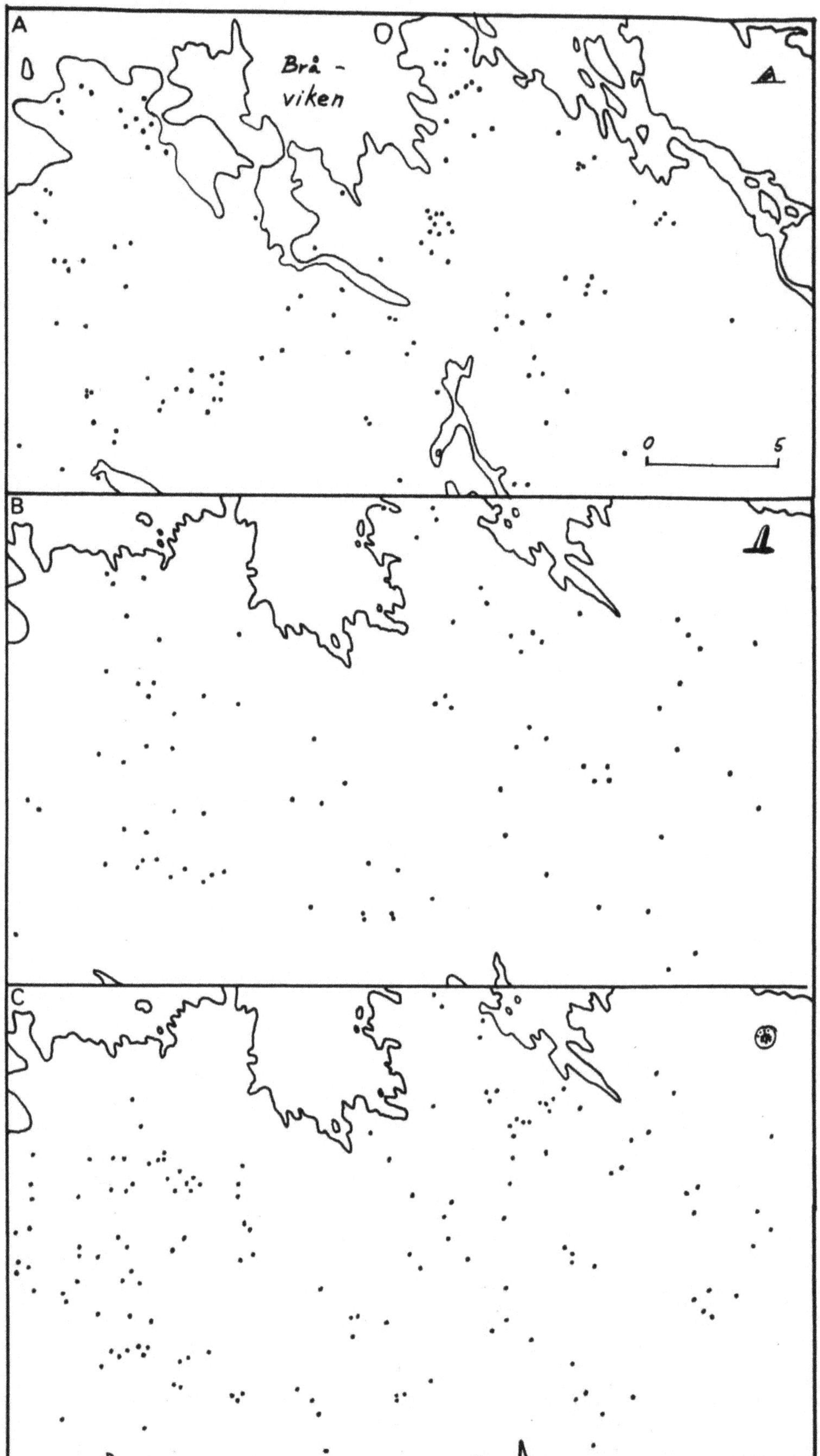

FIG. 4: Distributions of certain ancient monuments in Vikbolandet (after the National Survey of Antique monuments).
A. Sites with heaps of fire-cracked stone.
B. Sites with erected stones.
C. Sites with "fried eggs".

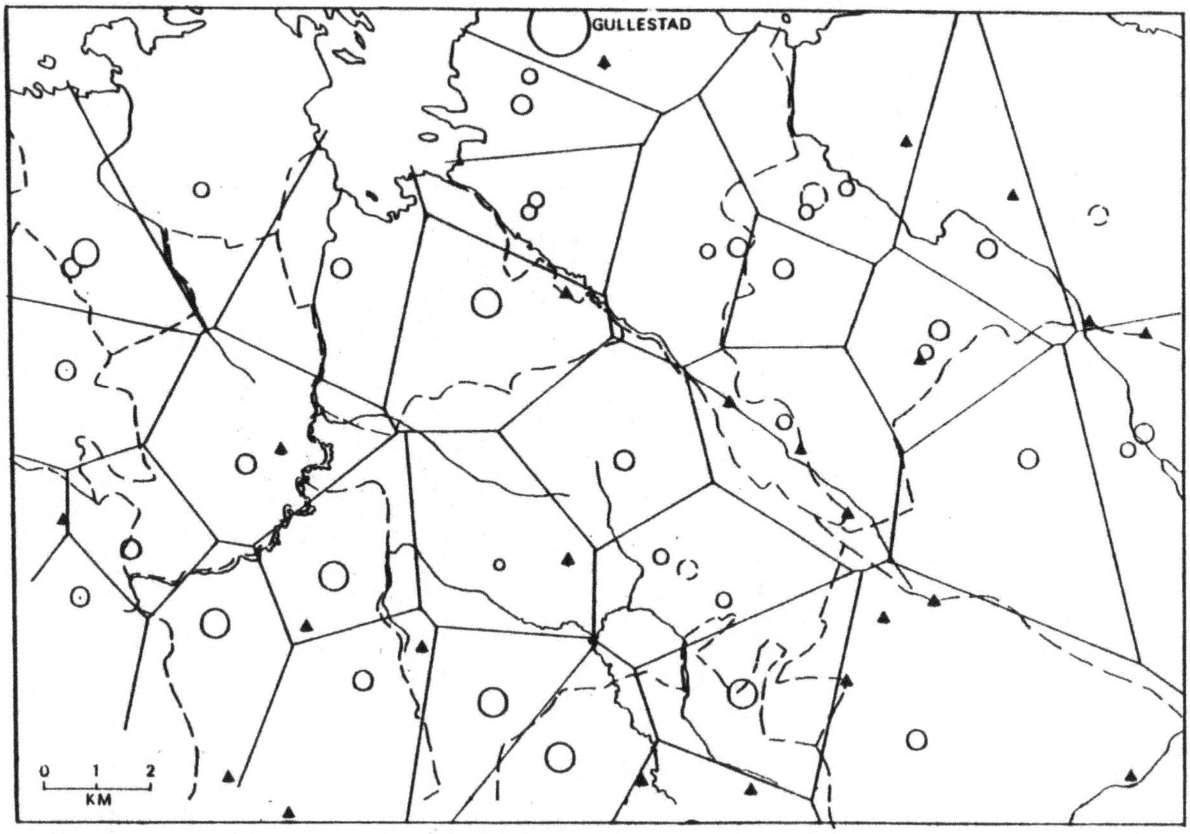

FIG. 5: Distributions of certain ancient monuments in Vikbolandet (after the National Survey of Antique monuments).
Circles: Sites with "treuddar" (Size proportional to the total number of monuments).
Triangles: Hill-forts.
Straight lines: Hypothetical unit boundaries.
Dashed lines: Present day parish boundaries.

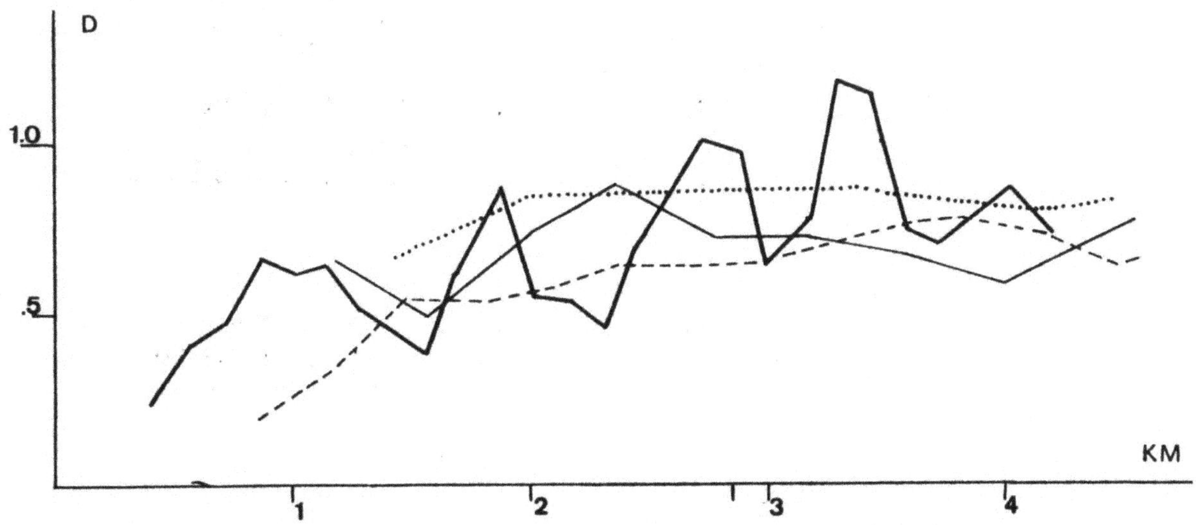

FIG. 6: D-curve calculated on the distributions in Fig. 4 and 5.
Heavy line: Bronze age (heaps of fire cracked stone).
Thin line: Early Iron age (erected stones).
Dashed line: Roman Iron age ("fried eggs").
Pointed line: Late Iron age ("treuddar").

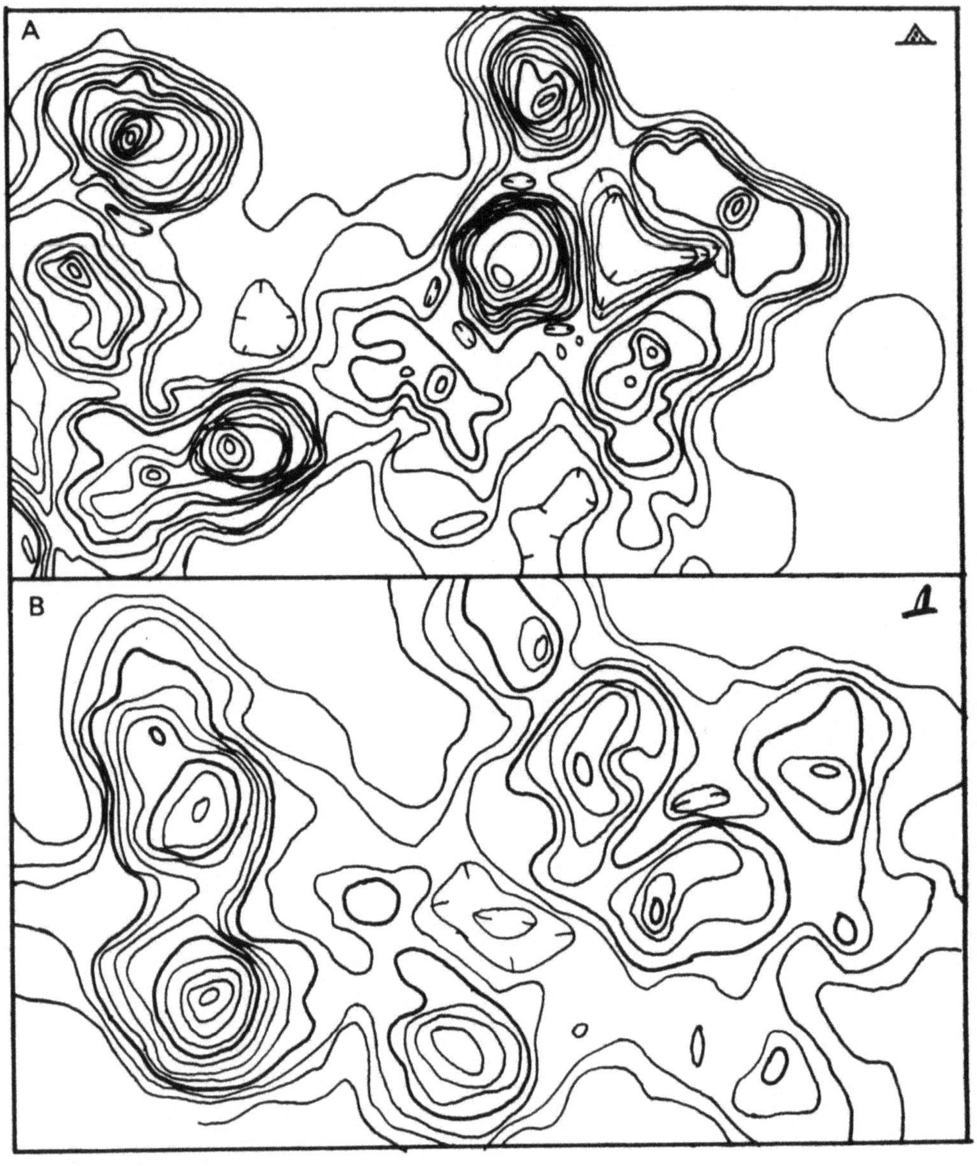

FIG. 7: Density maps of the distributions in Fig. 4A and B.
A: Heaps of fire cracked stone. Reference cell size: 3.2 km.
B: Erected stones. " " ": 4.0 km.

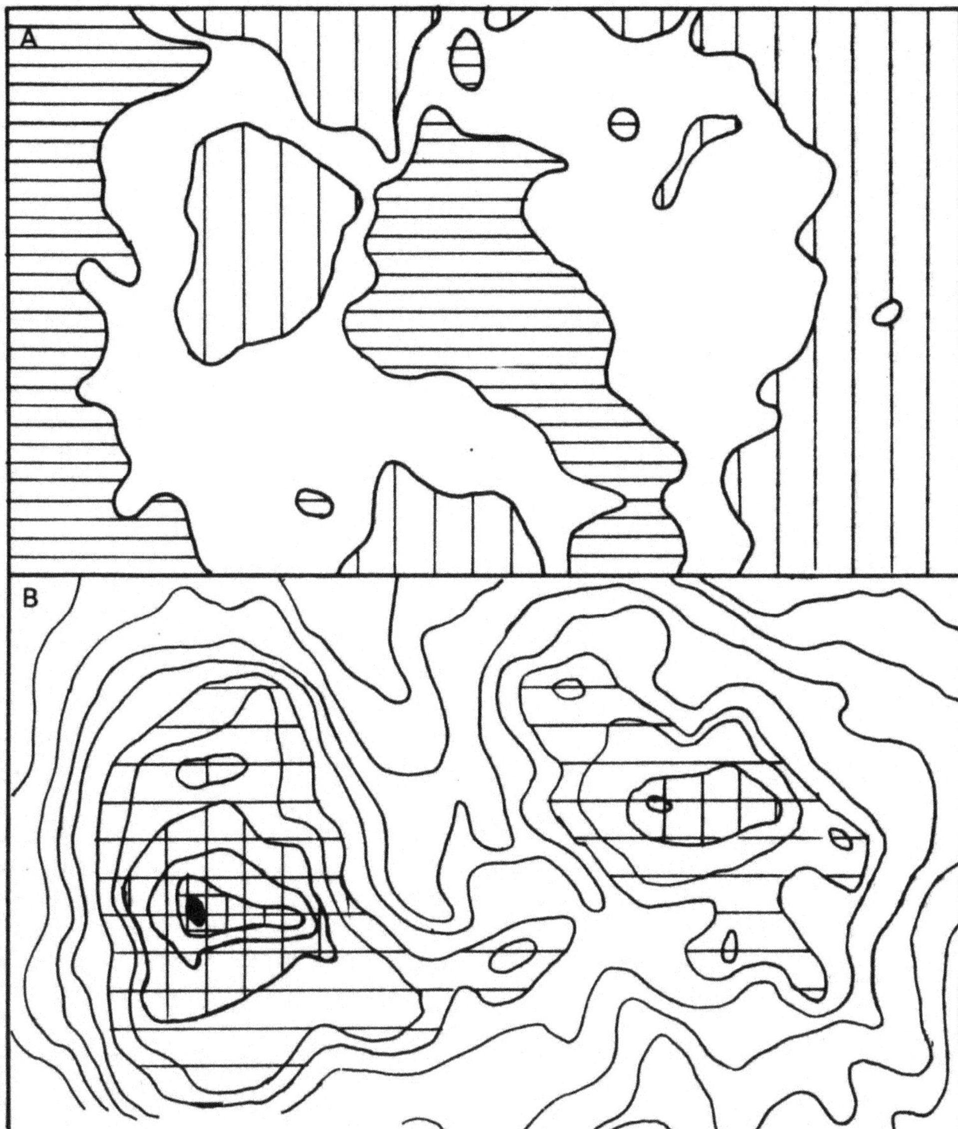

FIG. 8: A: Change of density between Bronze age and Early Iron age.
Horizontal hatching: lower density; Vertical hatching: higher density.
B: Density maap of the distribution of erected stones.
Reference cell size: 7.5 km.

organization that may have provided a pattern upon which the later Parish organization was based (dashed lines in figure 5).

The distribution of hill-forts in the area also fits well into this settlement system. With some exceptions they are located in the border areas. Several of these have been excavated and dated to the migration period (the transition phase between the early and late Iron ages in this region). Perhaps an indication of the time of introduction of this new system. In short, the whole picture shows signs of a centralized authorative system in sharp contrast with the earlier periods.

The method presented earlier was applied to each of these four distributions and the result is presented in figure 6.

The figure illustrates a development over time. It leads from a marked spatial grouping in the bronze age, towards less differentiated structures in the later periods. This could be a result of an increasing emphasy on central authority and control. Thus the importance and function of the "bufferzones" decreases. Instead, a more complicated internal structure developes, including site hierarchy, as shown in the above discussion.

The Late Bronze Age & Early Iron Age

A comparison between density patterns of two adjacent time periods is shown in figure 7. The picture is similar for both of the periods, at this level, but a slight reorganization seems to have occurred. The relative positions of the cluster have been altered and a tendency towards a size hierarchy has developed (manifested in the relative number of sites within each group)[1]. The reason behind this transformation may be indicated in figure 8A which shows the relative change of density between the two time periods. The figure illustrates the emergence of a central "bufferzone" dividing the area into two distinct, larger groups (figure 8B). This, combined with the indications of internal hierarchy within them, may suggest a tendency towards a more centralized organisation. The importance and meaning of the different levels has changed and the patterns show that this is probably a result of internal reorganization, since several properties of the structures are preserved over time.

This kind of analysis comparing different spatial structures from different time-periods may, as shown, give further information about the character of their respective internal organization.

IV. A comparison between two approaches - The Marnian La Tene example

In 1971, a short study was published concerning multivariate analysis of burial assemblages (Rowlett & Pollnac, 1971). One object was to determine if regional variations occurred within the rather homogenous Marnian La Tene culture. A factor analysis was performed with rather significant results, dividing the area into three regional groups (figure 9B). The authors believed that these groups resulted from differences in communication flow, at least partly due to social factors (ibid. p. 56).

---

1) A Chi-square test strongly confirms this (excluding the extreme one-point group at the eastern most part in figure 7A).

I consider this study suitable for a comparison between the pattern of local variations in cultural traditions and the spatial behaviour of a distinct cultural group. A published point pattern (ibid. p. 47) was used in the calculations (also figure 9A). Since the map probably was not produced to underly a more detailed spatial study of this kind, some distortion is expected at the most detailed scale (cp. p. 13). While the use of exact coordinates is preferable, the general trend should still be significant (in this case). A notable difference in density between the southeast and northwest areas is of special interest. It may have resulted from different levels of investigative activities in the two areas. Alternatively, it may reflect differences in burial ritual (ibid. p. 46), i.e. the western area tends to have free lying cemeteries while burials in the east are situated within the settlements. Such relationships/differences will also effect the methods' behaviour at lower levels. A revaluation of each major grouping is therefore recommended as a second step in the analysis as examplified in p. 13.

The D-curve of this total distribution is shown in figure 9C. The first significant minima appears at about 16.8 km. This is followed by the occasionally observed "shadow effect" and then by a moderate minima at 28.5 km. The overall low profile indicates a relatively weakly differentiated structure but with the groupings still distinguishable. The density maps (figure 9; D,E) show the two identified levels. The lower grouping level (figure 9D) is not especially conspicuous except in the northern area where a dominant group is surrounded by a couple of small groups. The next level is however more interesting. Figure 9E corresponds strikingly well with figure 9B although the western (factor II) area is divided into two well separated groups.

This coincidence lends validity to the results from both approaches and also offers a further, enlarged framework for more comprehensive studies. A revaluation of each major group can now be undertaken examining regional variations within the groups by way of similar factor analysis. The division of the western group would be a particularly interesting feature in such an investigation. The lack of differences between these two apparently separated areas may be a result of distortion in the factor analysis, due to the large mass of the eastern groups which may "hide" tendencies in the west.

If they are considered to be closely related groups, then the partition in space must be explained in some way. This partition could simply be a result of ecological constraints i.e. the landscape does not allow room for a closed group, thus it must be divided into two. Alternatively, we may be observing the traces of an expansion, either from west to east or, conversely, from east to west. The new settlements would then be situated preferably in those areas, that were formerly cultivated by the previous inhabitants. During the initial period of expansion, the old border area would appear unexploited and unpopulated. Such a hypothesis can only be tested in a time-space framework, i.e. structures from earlier and later periods must be evaluated. (e.g. as in part III).

As compared with the following example, the "bufferzones" are not so obvious at either level which suggests a relatively homogenous and integrated system including all groups within some sort of authorative system. This agrees with the notion that this culture was an important independent socio-cultural unit within the La Tēne world (ibid. p. 46).

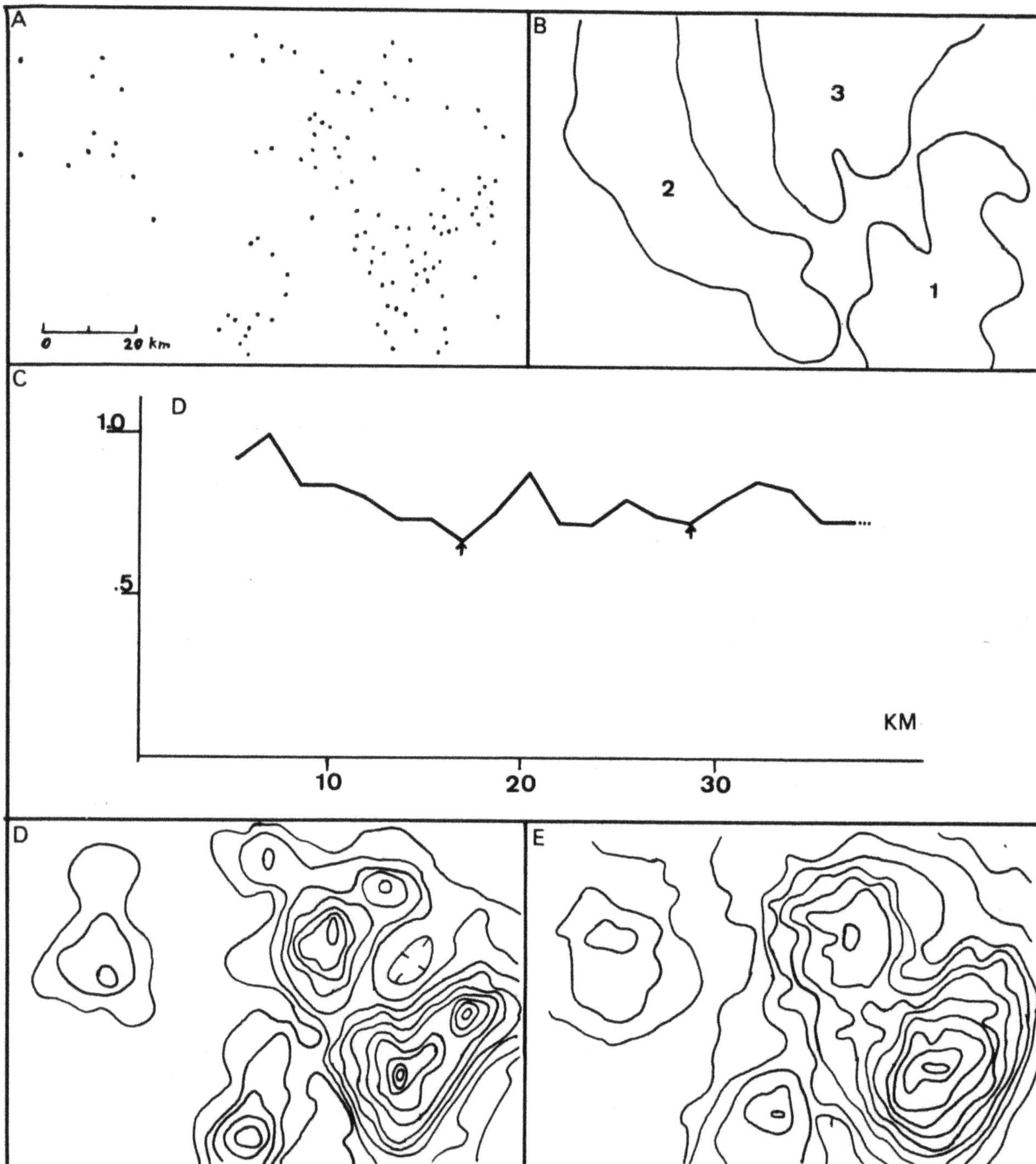

FIG. 9: A: Distribution of the earliest Marnian La Tène culture (after Rowlett & Pollnac).
B: Major cultural groups according to a multivariate factor analysis (after Rowlett & Pollnac).
C: D-curve calculated on the distribution in A.
D: Density map, reference cell size: 16.8 km.
E: Density map, reference cell size: 28.5 km.

V. The chiefdom approach - comments on a hypothesis

The following example is based upon a study published in 1973. It proposes that the emergence of chiefdoms was prerequisite to the construction of large monuments in neolithic Wessex (Renfrew, 1973:1). A major part of his discussion is based upon distribution patterns of neolithic long barrows concentrated into five main groups (as identified by Ashbee) and interpreted as tribal units. Renfrew convincingly uses this framework to explain the possible factors underlying the construction of these large monuments.

His figures clearly show that groupings with very marked bufferzones exist also in ecologically attractive areas (ibid. p. 546). Consequently, this area should be suitable for testing the spatial approach.

The published point pattern was, once again, used in the calculations (figure 10). As expected, the result (figure 11) is clear, with one evident minima at about 15 km. Thus, 15 km was used as a basis for the construction of the map in figure 10.

This figure displays the general picture outlined in Renfrew's paper where the five major groups stand out as separate units. Additionally, small periferal groups were identified surrounding the major ones. Their existence is of interest because several of them are not situated on chalk ground.

The frequency of monument building may vary, depending upon different subsistence strategies or different social systems and could explain the lower density of monuments in these areas. In such a case, the pattern would not reflect actual variations in the population density. Another interesting hypothesis is that smaller groups expanded into marginal lands, perhaps as a result of overpopulation. In a similar discussion (Renfrew, 1973:2), monument construction in certain overpopulated areas is explained as a way of releasing internal tensions through peaceful competition. This occurred on islands but it can perhaps be applicable to the chalkland area in the present study. The marked "bufferzones" between the clusters apparently indicated a competitive situation which inhibited full utilization of the chalklands and may have eventually forced colonization of less attractive areas.

Renfrew interpreted the large monuments, e.g. causwayed enclosures or henges, as central places within a chiefdom system (Renfrew, 1973:1, p. 549). Each tribal group was served by one enclosure and one henge. However, their location also suggests, that they may have functioned as rendevous points for several neighbouring groups, since, in several cases, they are situated in the border areas or in periferal positions. As an example the area between the three northern groups contains three major monuments; Marden, Rybury and Knap Hill. These monuments cannot be attributed to any specific tribal unit. It may therefore be assumed that these monuments functioned mainly as inter-group cooperation points. These relationships reflect an intertribal level of interaction especially in the northern area, which manifests itself in these impressive constructions. I.F. Smith proposed that the causwayed enclosures functioned as cult <u>centers</u> (e.g. Smith, 1971, p. 100). This may be parallelled with the rock-carving centers in Sweden which often are situated in periferal positions with respect to settlement clusters (c.p. Larsson, 1984). External contacts are also discussed by Smith who presented a table, which listed imported artifacts found in the causwayed enclosures. This indicated two exchange cycles including 1) the central and

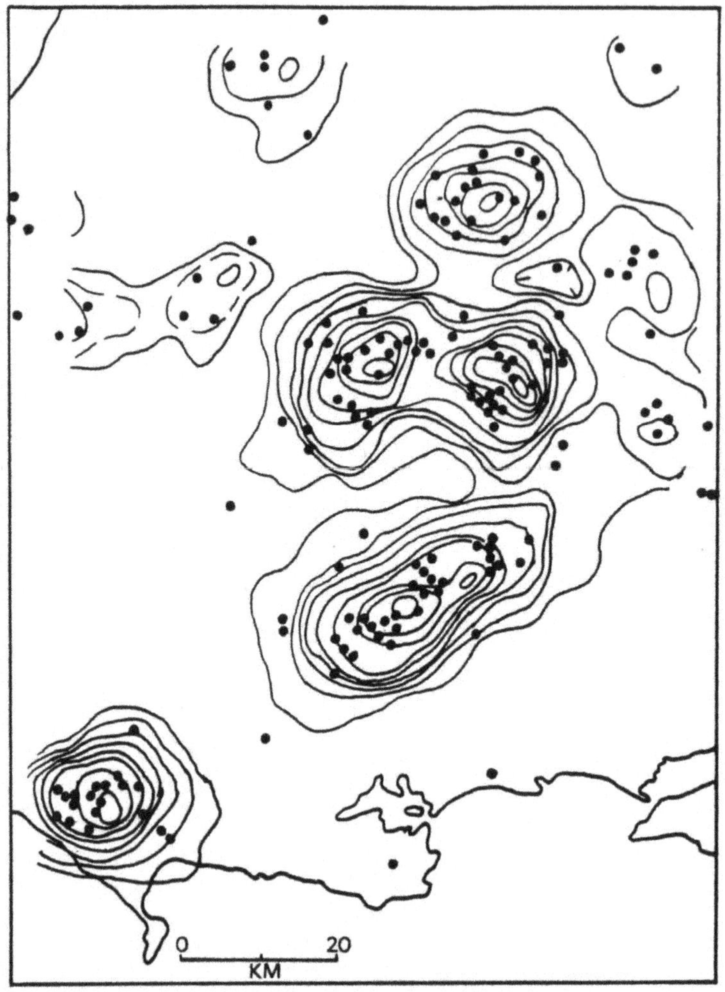

FIG. 10: Distribution of neolithic long barrows in a part of Southwestern England (after Renfrew) and corresponding density curves; reference cell size: 15 km.

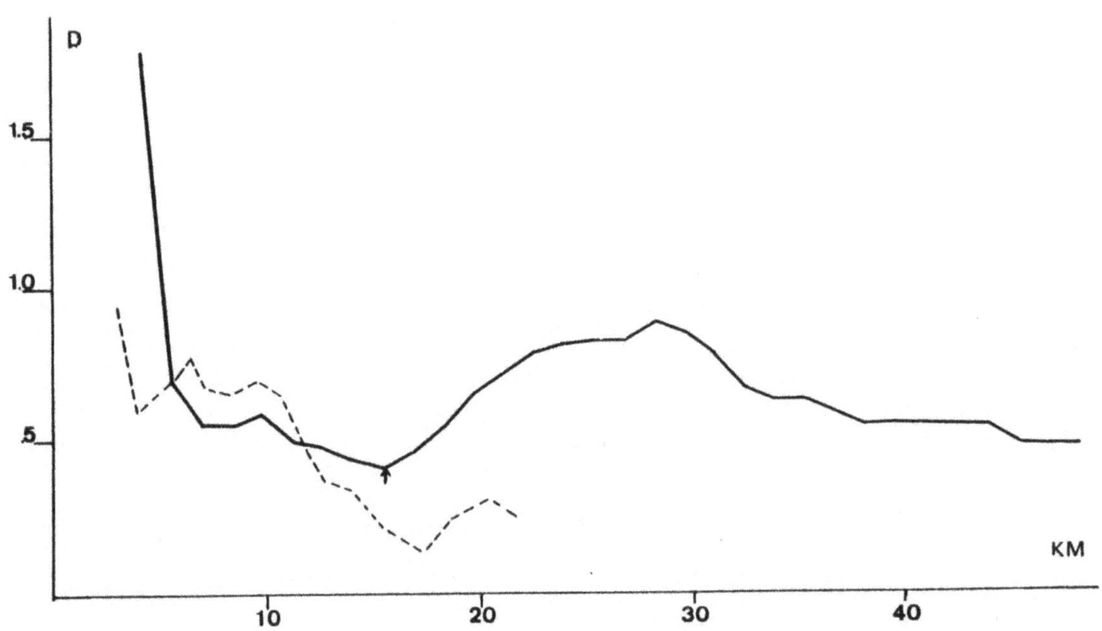

FIG: 11: D-curve calculated on the distribution in Fig. 10.
Dashed line: same as Fig. 2.

northern part of this study area and 2) the southwestern part (Dorset Downs). This division in contact spheres is also reflected in the size of the "bufferzones", which may reflect social distances. The northern groups appear to have had a high degree of social interactions culminating in the construction of Stonehenge, a central monument uniting several tribal units (Renfrew, 1973:1, p. 552).

The spatial organization within these "tribal groups" also is of importance. The high starting value in figure 11 indicates a dispersed pattern. I suggest, however, that this dispersion may have resulted from a slight generalization on behalf of the mapdrawer in order to make the map more readable (compare with the more detailed mapping (figure 2) of part of the total distribution). The distribution in figure 2 was therefore re-analysed to get a better close-up view of the details of the system. Renfrew interpreted this distribution as an example of dispersed land use, each long barrow serving a definite territory. He illustrated this distribution with Thiessen-polygons (ibid. p. 545). A more complicated situation is reflected in the D-curve of figure 2 where cluster levels appear at 5 km and at 17 km.

Figure 1 shows these two generalization levels along with an intermediate, non significant, density map. The curve in figure 2 is also shown in figure 11 (dashed line) to compare it with the overall structure. The accordance is fairly good except for the starting values.

Since the number of sites within each "group" is rather low in this latter system, the result must be viewed with some caution. However, the tendency towards clustering does not really contradict Renfrew's above proposal. Within each of the above groups, there exist a regularity in the distance-relations which does not oppose the idea that long-barrows were central-places within small territories.

The distribution patterns discussed in this example shows signs of four or five hierarchical levels within this particular tribal system. A basic one is represented by individual long barros which are organized into segments of 2-10 sites and together constitute the major, dominant, third level. The five main groups, as defined by Ashbee, show a coherent picture both in size, area, and weight, i.e. number of units (a Chi-square test shows no significant deviation from the null hypothesis). This indicates that these groups are independent units of equal status, perhaps functioning as separate tribes. In contrast, their internal structures shows a hierarchy with one large group and several smaller ones. The fourth and fifth levels represent the inter-tribal relationships manifested by large monuments in the borderzones in the northern part of the area. The main central monument, Stonehenge, indicates the highest level, possibly incorporating the majority of groups in question within its sphere of influence.

6. Concluding remarks

In the previous discussions a social origin for the cluster patterns has been assumed for the reason that ecologically determined clustering should not behave in the same manner. The more random ecological processes would probably not order themselves in such a way that they could be identified in the distance matrix. However, this is theoretically possible; therefore the results of the method must be compared with the results of other approaches (e.g. as in part 4 above).

Another disturbing point is the representativity problem. Doubts have often been expressed that detailed spatial studies of prehistoric remains could never give significant results since we can never be sure to what degree the monuments have been disturbed. However, if we approach the problem as a matter of scale, it can be partially solved. At the most detailed scale, we can of course never be sure of the accurancy of our results. Instead we must search for more general patterns over larger areas which give a higher degree of confidence in our findings. Large scale destruction can of course destroy groups or patterns but it cannot change their basic character over large areas. These general patterns therefore provide a framework which helps in evaluating the result from more detailed structures.

Acknowledgements

My thanks to Dr. David Tilles for editing the English and Miss Birgit Andersson for typing, additionally editing and patience.

BIBLIOGRAPHY

Daniel, G. 1976. 150 years of archaeology. (Harvard University Press).

Hyenstrand, A. 1979. Ancient monuments and prehistoric society. (Central Board of National Antiquities. Stockholm.

Kleijn, L.S. 1973. Marxism, the systematic approach and archaeology. In Colin Renfrew (ed.). The explanation of culture change. Models in prehistory. (691-710). Duckworth, London.

Kristianssen, K. 1981. Economic models for bronze age Scandinavia - towards an integrated approach. In Sheriden, A. & Bailey, G. (eds.). Economic Archaeology, towards an integration of ecological and social approaches. (239-303). BAR International Series 96 Oxford.

Kristianssen, K. 1982. The Formation of Tribal Systems in Later European prehistory: Northern Europe, 4000-500 B.C. In C. Renfrew, M. Rowlands, and B. Segraves (eds). Theory and explanation in archaeology. Academic Press (271-80).

Larsson. T. 1984. Structure and function of social institutions - a social anthropological approach. In Archaeology and Environment 2, Umeå University.

Lundmark, H. 1984. A method of analysing hierarchical organization in settlement patterns. In Archaeology and Environment 2, Umeå University.

Renfrew. C. 1973:1. Monuments mobilization and social organization in neolithic Wessex. In Renfrew (ed). The explanation of culture change . Models in prehistory - 539-58. Duckworth, London.

Renfrew. C. 1973:2. Before Civilization: The radiocarbon Revolution and prehistoric Europe. London: Jonathan Cape.

Rowlett, R.M. & Pollnac, R.B. 1971. Multivariate analysis of Marnian La Te'ne cultural groups. In Hodson, F.R., Kendall, D.C. and Tautu. P. (eds). Mathematics in Archaeological and Historical Sciences. University Press. Edinburgh.

Sahlins, M.D. 1968. Tribesmen. New Jersey: Prentice Hall.

Smith, I.F. 1971. Causewayed enclosures. In Simpson, D.D.A. (Ed.) Economy and settlement in Neolithic and Early Bronze Age Britain and Europe. 89-112. Leicester University Press.

Trigger, B.G. 1980. Gordon Childe. London, Thames & Hudson.

Widgren, M. 1979. A simulation model of farming systems and landuse in Sweden during the early Iron Age c. 500 B.C. - A.D. 550 In Journal of Historical Geography. 5.1. (1979) 21-32. London, Academic Press.

MULTI-LEVEL EXCHANGE AND CULTURAL INTERACTION IN LATE SCANDINAVIAN BRONZE AGE

Thomas B. Larsson
Sweden

> "...cycles of exchange, both within and between tribal groups, take place not primarily for economic reasons but as a basic mechanism of social integration." (Sherratt 1972:506).

Society and symbols [1)]

Every activity in human society can be explained in relation to the two major functional spheres governing social ife; i.e. the symbolic and the practical spheres.

The word 'symbolic' refers to objects and activities which embody non-utilitarian functions, and the word 'practical' is used to define phenomena where the utilitarian dimension dominates (see Binford 1972: 23-25 and Hodder 1982: 11-12).

If we take a look around in our own (modern) society it is easy to point out some institutions or objects which could be classified in these terms. Marriage rituals, wedding rings, jewellery, and, for example a flag, are typical representatives of 'symbols'. To harvest a wheat-field or to put coins in a parking-meter, are two activities which in contrast relate to the 'practical' sphere. Though, most objects and social activities contain both a symbolic and a practical function, and the scale between these two poles is smooth, fluctuating from the extremly symbolic to the extremly practical (see Figure 1, the transition from empty to filled circles). The need for symbolic social action in a society is integrated with ideology and with the magnitude of social relations prevailing between the participants.

The emergence of symbols, and symbolic action in a society, is caused by the "epistemic attitude" (Tilley 1981b:141) within the social formation. This results in:

Individual feelings of solidarity

Collective, ritual behavior

Objects which represent the group

(cf. Lévi-Strauss 1969a:79)

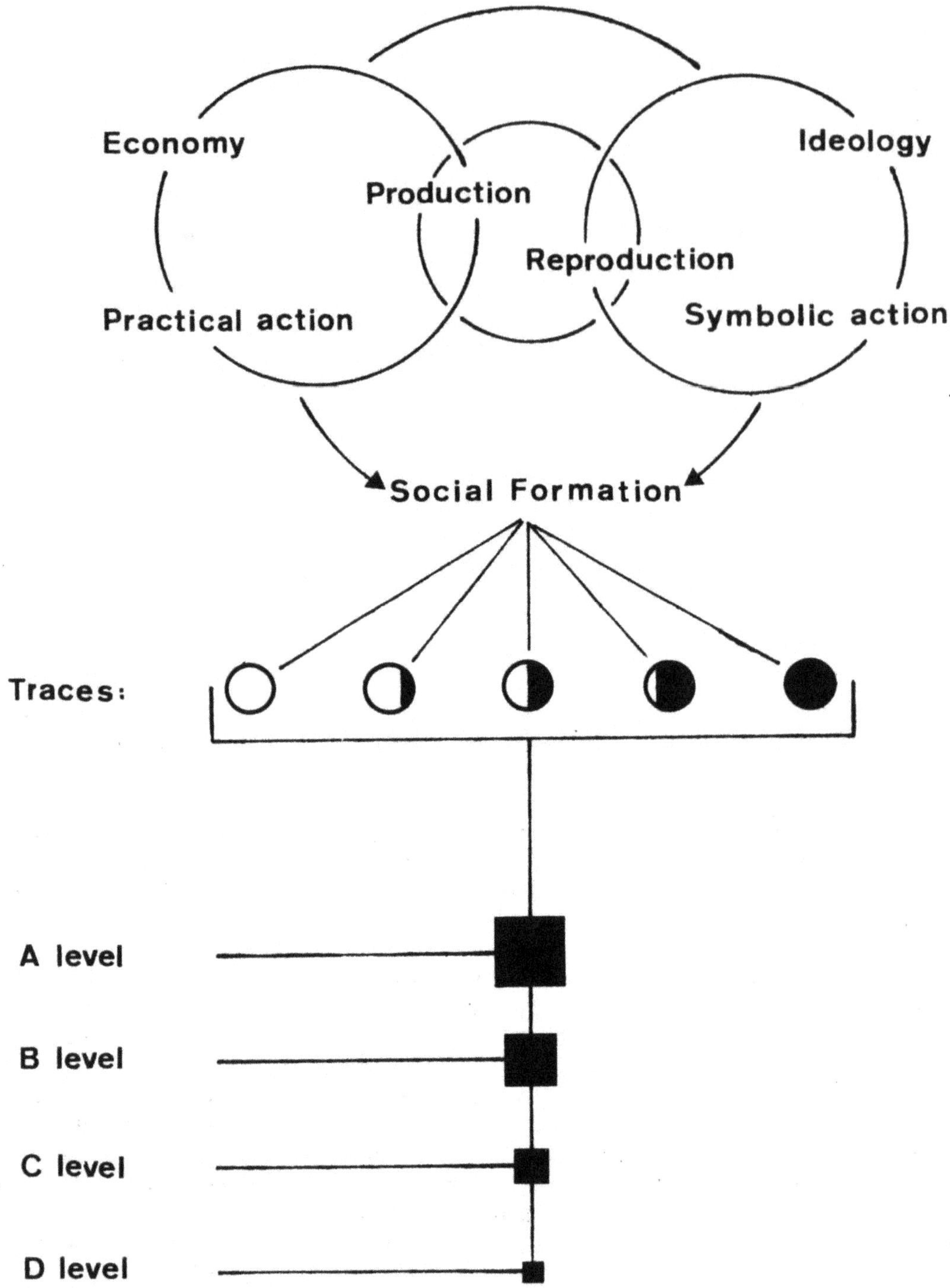

Figure 1. Dialectrical relationship between instances forming the Social Formation and its Traces, recognizable at every 'level' in a society (here A to D).

The main function of the symbolic dimension can also be viewed as a form of social communication; a language uniting families, clans, local sodalities etc., within the total social formation. In this way symbols contain coded information about the social until it represents, in the same way as a DNA-molecule embodys the life-code. This affects everything in a society, from the linguistic dimension to clothing and pottery decoration (cf. Wobst 1977). Therefore, it is in the exchange and communication flow, horizontal and vertical within a social formation, that the symbolic functions are most active (see Johnson, 1978). Social institutions and symbolic objects in 'tribal' societies, active in the 'tribal level' (A-level in Figure 1), tend to unite all members under mutual 'flag' which expresses the ideology of the system. Objects and activities mainly connected to this general superstructural 'flag' function are solely a 'tribal' (A-level) matter, and therefore not in the hands of commoners.

Extremely symbolic objects and activities (rituals), are therefore, more likely to occure at the 'top level' in the society, even though, ideological expressions and manifestations can not only be seen as a superstructural phenomenon but also as an integrated part in everyday life (Godelier 1977).

Individuals in a society can survive without the 'tribal flags' in times of social change (compared to the system itself, which is being transformed), but they can hardly be active in this revolutionary process without a strong foundation (self-identification) in the lower spheres of the social structure. It is in these 'bottom levels' that the roots of the individuals existence is founded. Social action in everyday life, and objects mutually connected to such activities, is an essential basis for the relationship between individuals and groups in a social formation (c.f. Levi-Strauss 1969b:32). Phenomena belonging in the lowest social levels are those which are deepest founded in the mind of the individual, and therefore most resistant to change; inversely, the 'tribal flags' are the first institutions collapsing in a societal transformation phase (Sahlins 1968:16).

Figure 1 is a model of the relationship between economy, ideology, practical and symbolic functions, and how this governs the obsevable traces (archaeological data). The circles indicate a dialectical relationship between all instances forming the totality (social formation). The variation in this relationship through time constitute the historical background as well as the future trajectory for this formation. The variation in traces, as archaeologists may observe, is a result of the dialectical processes operating in prehistoric times. This theoretical model is applicable to collective as well as individual human action.

Empirical 'wisdom' suggests, after studying the spectrum of preserved remnants, that models of social formations must take into consideration both individual and collective social action (Tilley 1982:26:27). It is not only the structures themselves, but also the individuals and groups forming the structures that are of interest when discussing dialectics and social change.

However, the focus of this paper is not to present an elaborate analysis of theoretical perspectives on social formations, but to apply such concepts to an analysis of exchange networks during Late Scandinavian Bronze Age.

When looking at the distribution of different artifacts in the archaeological record some questions spontaneously arises: (1) their function in the economic/ideological context, (2) at which level(s) in this context did they operate. The word 'level' refers to the organizational levels (hiearchies) of production and reproduction of a social formation (Figure 1). In a settlement hierarchy, from household to 'tribe', both production and reproduction are performed at every level, but the proportions and intensity of these activities vary according to internal and external conditions. Fishing and hunting, for example, and the reproductive aspects of this kind of subsistence production, may involve two or three villages (B-level in Figure 1) due to the very nature of this activity. Such expeditions can be seasonal, while the basic unit during the rest of the year is the household. Also, internal conflicts between groups with conflicting interests may change the structural balance and the emphasis on different organization levels.

Before I proceed to the empirical section of this paper, I would like to mention the discussion concerning archaeological inference. How do I know that the results of my analysis of archaeological data really reflect real 'pattern of the past'?

This positivistic search of an ideal theory which link together archaeological data with 'firm knowledge' has been presented recently by Sullivan (1978). He suggests "a model of past information transmission", consisting of three interlinked theories: Formation theory, recovery theory and analytical theory (ibid. p. 192-210). In studying these aspects in archaeology, one should, according to Sullivan, be able to bridge contemporary reality and past reality. This problem has been discussed earlier by Binford (1962; 1968; 1975), Clarke (1968), Deetz (1968), Hill (1970; 1972), Longacre (1970) and Plog (1978). It is obvious that the American school of archaeology during the last decades has taken a positivistic position. I believe that this question is rather irrelevant because we can never hope to explain a past phenomenon and prove that our explanation is valid. The only thing we can discuss is the logical relationship inbuilt in our theories, and how these can be rejected or verified by alternative theories, and further "'Facts' are not in themselves sufficient to disprove theories, since our theories decide what is or is not a 'fact'" (Tilley 1981b:138).

Knowledge is not anything absolute, nothing universal, but a product of a specific social formation at a specific time. Therefore, the whole positivistic inference discussion may only, at its best, produce subjective knowledge of the past, because nothing else exists.

The primary reason that objects have different symbolic, non-utalitarian functions is caused by their active participation in different positions in the social formation; i.e., the ideological expressions require a common language, uniting individuals and groups. When a society transforms from a simple to a complex form of organization, caused by the dialectical relationship between structures, new institutions and functions emerge which require a modified network of information chanels, maintained partly by the circulation of new symbols.

The channels in which goods are distributed may also be the chanels used in the exchange of people by marriage. An exogam exchange system is of great social importance because it "provides the means of binding men together" (Levi-Strauss 1969b:480), and also creating new alliances. Therefore, a highly organized system requires a complex exchange network which can manage to keep us an efficient circulation of objects (people and goods), as a positive response to the ideological and economic 'demands', stimulating and securing production and social reproduction.

Turning to Scandinavia, one artifact group of special interest are the bronzes, which occur with a striking concentration in Denmark, rapidly decreasing in number the further north one moves. In Eastern Götaland in Sweden, for example, only about 100 bronzes are found, compared to Denmark were thousands are registrated.

When speaking about bronzes in this paper, I am refering to bronze objects dated to the Bronze Age, particularly the Later Bronze Age (B.C. 1000-500). Then, why do we have so relatively few bronze finds in Sweden compared to Denmark? Most likely the middle Swedish region was located in the periphery with regard to the major circulation-sphere of bronze objects.

Social structure and wealth during the Bronze Age, as reflected by the fluctuating amount of bronzes, have been discussed particularly by Kristiansen (1977; 1978; 1979) and Randsborg (1974) for the Scandinavian area. The consumtion of wealth (bronzes) was not so developed in the middle Swedish region, due to distance from the major copper and bronze trade.

Middle Sweden probably was at the end of the line for the trade routes; therefore, there was no way that the bronze trade could create any significant increase in wealth. Instead, one hypotheses is that bronzes were used in this marginal area mainly as circulation gifts of symbolic (and secondary practical) value for the inter- and intratribal relations. So in this marginal area the exchange did not produce surplus comparable to that in Denmark and northern Germany.

Assumptions and Methods

Now, if bronzes were objects circulating within different social levels as a symbolic language, then we might do some predictions about their presence in the archaeological record:

A1 Objects with mainly a practical function, and with only a slight temporary symbolic value, should be distributed throughout the total area under study.

A2 Further, one should expect great stylistic variation within each object group, due to local, regional manufacturing.

B1 Extreme symbolic objects are expected to be rare and are located to places functioning at the top-levels (A-level in Figure 1) in the exchange system, or in specific areas where these symblols were manufactured, which might be the same.

B2 A limited stylistic variation (sub-types), compared to A2 above, are to be expected within this group, mainly because most items are manufactured at a small scale for an articulated symbolic purpose, in specialist workshops before entering the 'A-level' circulation.

The two major groups (A and B above) are the extremes; all other contemporary objects can be placed in a discrete, step-by-step succession on the scale between these two, regulated by their status in the exchange network.

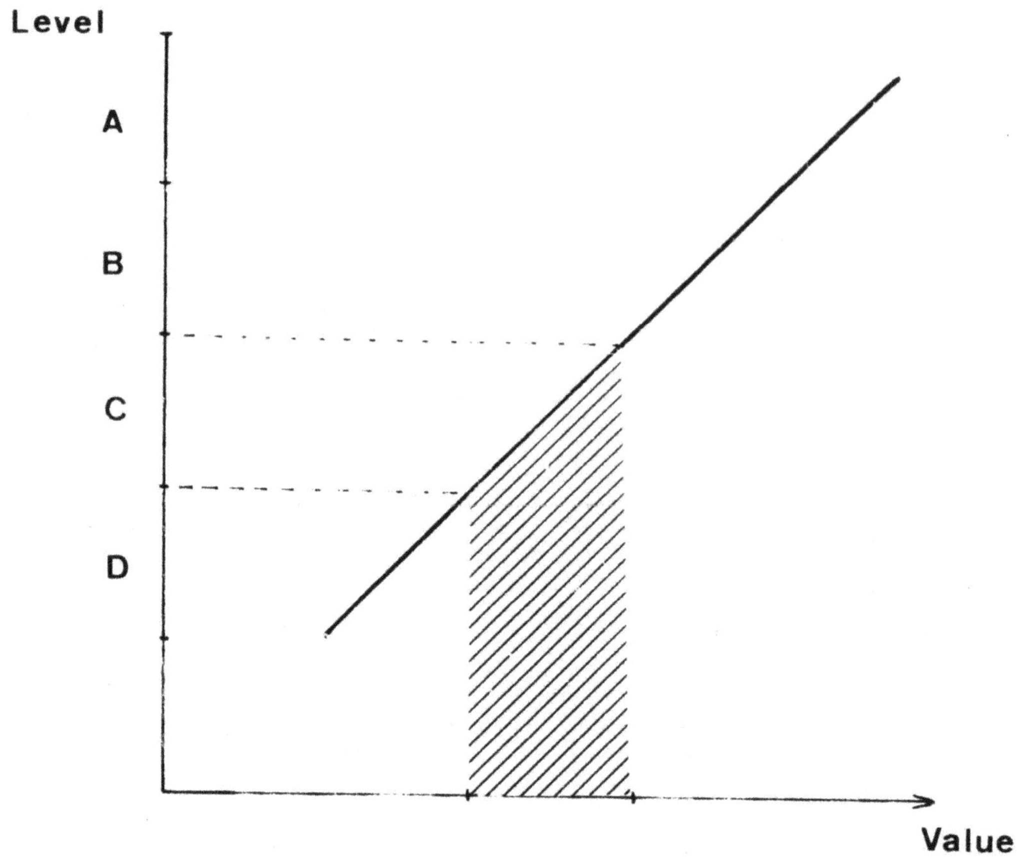

Figure 2. Correlation between value (objects, activities etc.) and level in a hierarchal system.

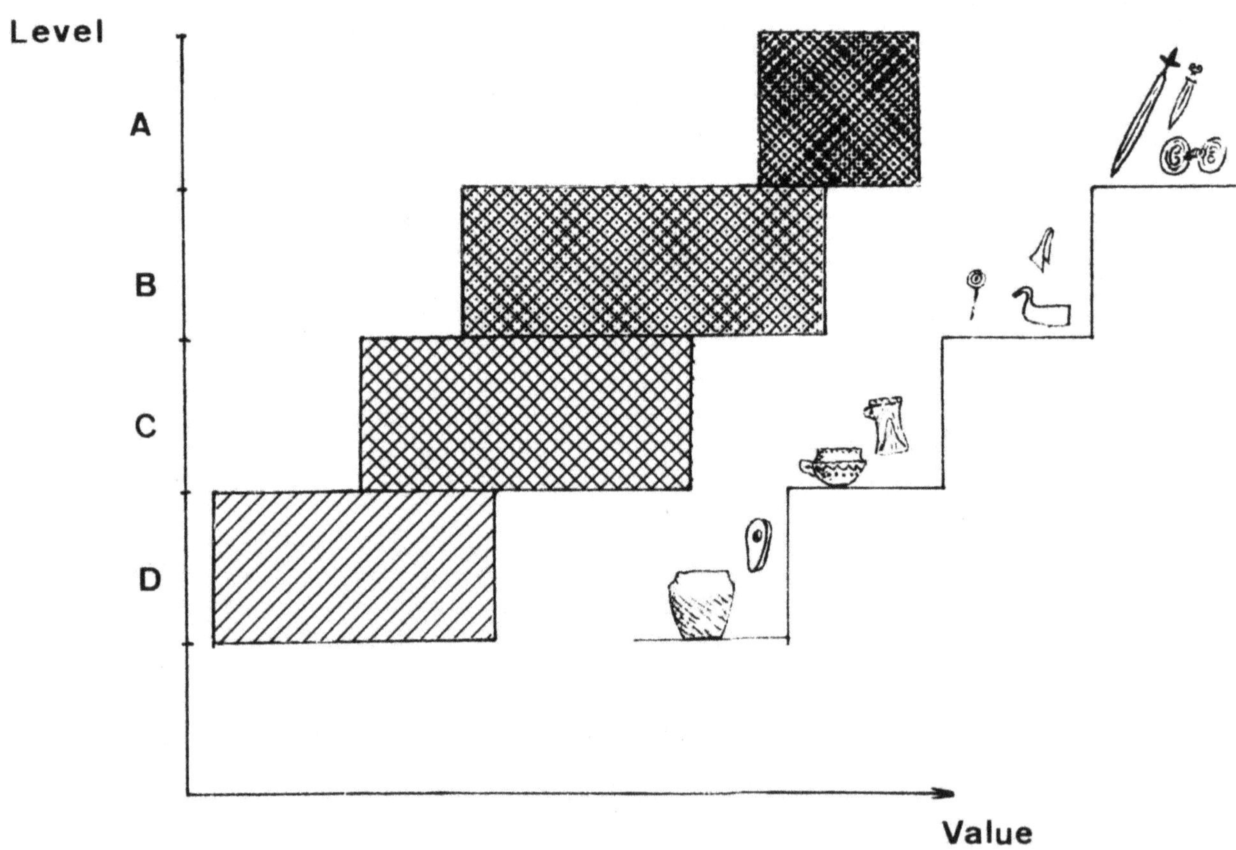

Figure 3. Different circulation levels (A–D) with regard to increasing value, in an overlapping relationship.

To test the four predictions above, nine types of bronzes were selected for analysis. Table 1 below shows the types, total number and number of sub-types within the Scandinavian region: Norway, Finland, Sweden, Denmark and North Germany.

Table 1	Total number	Number of sub-types
Swords	271	5
Mini-swords	119	4
Daggers	18	1
Celts	2605	20
Razors	1590	16
Tweezers	751	9
Neck rings (Wendel type)	304	4
Needles	1837	24
Spearheads	97	4

(All figures are taken from Baudou 1960)

Two models are considered for the bronze circulation within four hypothetical levels (A to D) in a social structure. The A-level is the highest in the hierarchy, in which top-level symbols are distributed between units and areas. Conversely, D-level circulation contains mainly objects of a low symbolic status and utilitarian goods. The first model (Figure 2) shows a perfectly linear correlation between higher symbolic value and higher position in the social structure. There are slight differences within each strata due to internal variations in the exchange flow of goods, requiring different objects. But as the symbolic value of the goods increases, and the value passes certain thresholds, the goods are used in a higher level. No B-level objects are used, or can be used, in A-level exchange, as they are seldom or never used in the lower C-level exchange.

This model is a strictly theoretical one, based on a total separation of the hierachical segments, and therefore I believe that it may only be valid in systems with sharp boundarys between distinct social groupings, such as developed chiefdoms or states.

In Figure 3, the different levels are overlapping each other; which means that important B-level occations may render an exchange of objects traditionally of A-level status, and so forth.

The different levels are not necessarily equivalent only to groups such as workers, local chiefs or paramount rulers, but can also reflect the regional status of particular trades, missions etc., appurtenant to individuals as well as institutions.

In this model artifacts, individuals and institutions can temporarly occur in more than one segment of the structure, in a co-ordinate, multivariate relationship.

Also, the more centralized the economic and political functions are, the more level-bound circulation emerges to explain and manifest the present state of the social formation. This is caused by the dialectical mechanism involving primarly economy, ideology and symbolic action (Figure 1), which at the same time embodies the embryo to the future state of the formation. Fluctuations in political power between regions as within social systems can also be expected to cause changes in the circulation network, and disrupt intra-social dialectics.

If the regulation of a socio-economic system relies on, for example redistribution, then the communication network of vertical and horizontal channels in which the redistributed goods are passed are maintained by a circulation of goods of different symbolic value. In more decentralised political systems, as in segmentary tribes (Sahlins 1968: 20-24; 50-52), the reason for exchange of symbols is somewhat different. Here the main purpose of symbols is to define a particular group against others, and also to strengthen group solidarity, e.g. by expressing rights and obligations of individuals due to age etc., (Hodder 1982: 75ff). Anyhow, one can ascertain that gift exchange keeps the wheels of social life in motion (Mauss 1954), and further that it plays an active role in production and reproduction of the society.

Analysis and Interpretations

Returning to the Bronze Age Scandinavia Celts are one type of bronze artifact that are commonly distributed throughout the entire survey area. More than 2600 celts are found, with a marked concentration to South Sweden and Denmark. Their regional distribution and chronological aspects have been analysed and discussed by Baudou (1953; 1956; 1960), who discerns different culture provinces within the Scandinavian area (1953: 259; 1960: 128 ff. see also Kristiansen 1978; 1981: 269). In his major work on the Late Bronze Age (1960), Baudou records 20 sub-types of celts during periods IV to VI (B.C. 1000-500), (ibid. p. 16-26, Taf. IV-VII), in which some are contemporary and some not. During this period also bronze swords, mini-swords, daggers and spearheads, to take a few types, occur, but much more sparsely compared to celts. Only 505 of these items have been found in the area. This is almost six times less than the celts, and only 6.6% of the total number of bronzes found.

The amount of sub-types are also less for weapons: swords 5; mini-swords 4; daggers 1; spearheads 4 (Table 1).

Here we notice a significant difference between on one hand celts, numerous in total number and in sub-types, relatively eavenly spatially distributed, and on the other hand the rest of the weapons, few in both total number and sub-types, and with a more heterogenous spatial distribution (Baudou 1960, Karte 1-3; 8-16). I think one possible answer to this is to be found in the four predictions earlier made; namely the relations between the character of a phenomenon (practical - symbolic) and its active role in the social context. This relationship is in a state of continuous transformation. "In human systems both 'change' and 'stability' relate to processes. As such we should regard both in terms of a continous trajectory without clearly defined beginnings or ends" (Tilley 1981a: 363-364).

The regional variation in stylistic design of celts is an obvious indication of local manufacturing. Their quantitative dominance during periods IV to VI is another 'evidence' of their common character. Also, the occurence of celt-moulds signals low level exchange and local manufacturing of this artifact group.

For the swords, mini-swords, daggers and spearheads, which I refer to as 'weapons', the picture is quite the opposite. Therefore, these objects are hardly to be considered as any 'common stuff', manufactured and exchanged on a large scale. Instead, there is reason to believe that bronze items like the weapons were 'words' in a highly symbolic language, 'spoken' by the top level in the social structure; maybe a 'tribal voice' when speaking to adjacent 'tribes' or regions in times of conflict or at mutual manifestations, or when establishing new alliances (Rowlands 1980: 18).

This assumption does not necessitate the existence of a strictly ranked or politically 'top controlled' society with local, regional and paramount chiefs, even if it is a tempting conclusion.

In South Scandinavia, the wealth connected to bronze 'trading' may have initiated the emergence of a chiefdom system (Kristiansen 1978; 1981 and Randsborg 1973; 1974), but it was probably not the same organizational and structural changes that took place in the marginal regions, due to the different function of bronzes in the area. The rich burials, especially in Denmark and Northern Germany, reflecting both east and west European contacts during the Late Bronze Age (Kristiansen 1981: 249-250; Thrane 1975), also emphasise this picture.

Figure 4, shows the correlation between total number and number of sub-types for the nine bronze types presented in Table 1.

There is an almost perfect one-to-one correlation (r= 0.935) and the types are divided into three clusters (A, B and C), corresponding to three hypothetical levels in a social structure. Cluster A contains five 'top-level' artifacts: swords, mini-swords, daggers, neck-rings and spearheads. Cluster B: razors, tweezers and needles. Finally, cluster C: celts. This simple analysis indicates that it is possible to divide into three groups the bronzes due to differences in total number and in number of sub-types.

However, one can of course expect to find a 'natural' high correlation between the two variables, but in a random simulation one would also expect to find a more continous relation, and not a discrete one made up of clusters.

If there existed distinct levels in the social structure in which the bronzes circulated between 'tribes', clans, sodalities etc., then, the different types, when sorted in a decreasing sequence, should have a good fitting to a logarithmic curve ('rank-size-rule', Hagget et al. 1977; 111 ff; Hodder & Orton 1976).

Figure 5, shows the 'rank-size test' on the selected bronzes. The clusters are the same as in Figure 4, and the curve fitting to a logarithmic curve is high (r= -0.924). It is clear that cluster B forms a rather significant grouping compared to cluster A and C. Figure 4 and 5 indicate

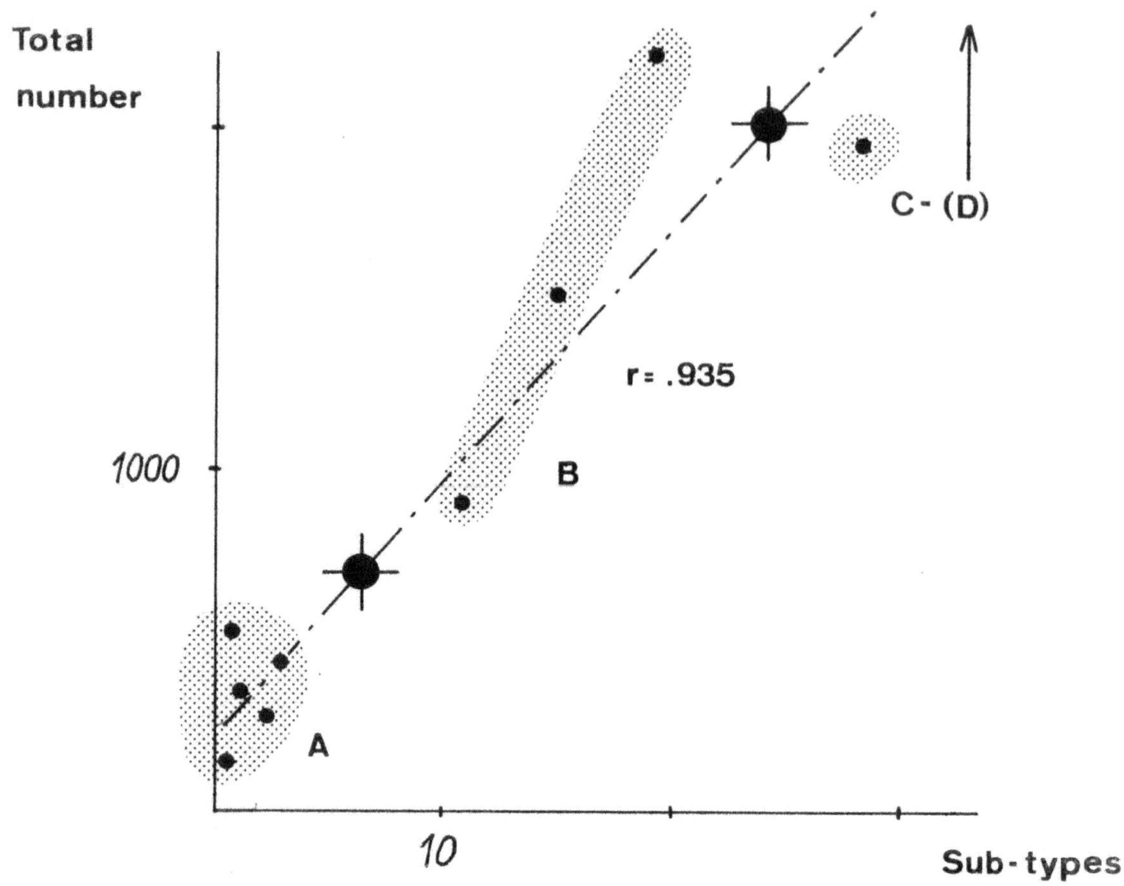

Figure 4. Correlation between total number and number of sub-types for nine groups.

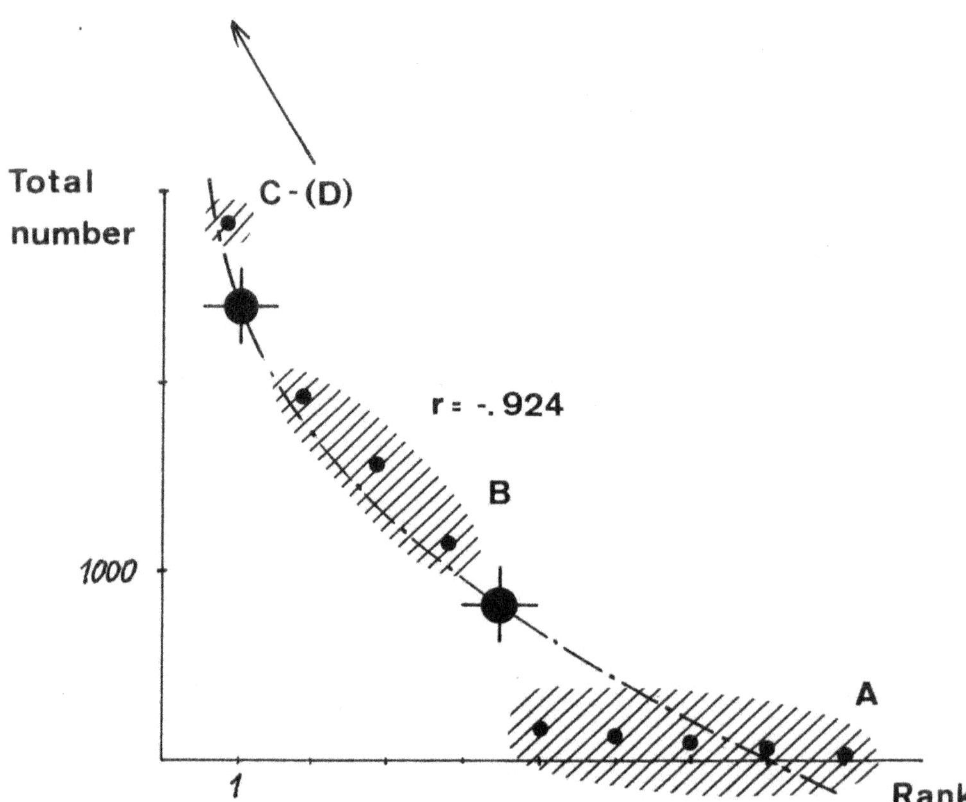

Figure 5. The nine bronze objects placed in a decreasing sequence according to total number. Curve fitting to a logarithmic curve is r= -0.924.

that the bronzes may have circulated within three partly separated levels. As I pointed out earlier, in Figure 3, the levels are not thought to be totally separated from each other; so cross-level exchange can also occur in a limited way. The three levels reflect the main trend in the material during a period of c. 500 years. Therefore, it can not be used to identify fluctuations of economic and social significance within this period. Also, in smaller regions within this Scandinavian area there are of course deviations from this 'average picture'.

One of the main points made by Baudou (1960) is the relationship between stylistic variation in bronze manufacturing and variation in cultural contact. The regional groups discussed by Baudou, based on the celt distribution in Scandinavia, shows a basic pattern of social and cultural interaction. I use the word basic because I think of the stylistic language expressed by the celts as being closely connected to the lowest level in which bronzes did circulate, and therefore it expresses the practical and symbolic action exercised by familes, households, local groups etc., all participating at a low level in the social hierarchy (see Figure 3). To grasp the low level pattern it is of importance to deal with objects functioning at the 'household sphere'. If different exchange cycles existed during the Late Bronze Age, then, the regional variation for celts is not to be expected to be similar to variations in, for example, sword or dagger distribution. Conversely, if we are dealing with a non-hierarchical exchange system, ie. if all objects were distributed in the same channel, we would expect a high degree of similarity and covariation for all studied objects. In spite of the discussion above, I argue that there might have existed different interacting regions at the same time, partly separated due to the nature of the social formation. Different objects with a different symbolic function circulates through exchange in a complex network of information channels. Luxury objects like swords and daggers, manufactured in a small scale by craftsmen in, for example, Germany and Denmark, are distributed in a 'top-level' exchange to certain areas of interest. The distribution of these items show the interaction on another level compared to celts.

The total picture of this multi-level exchange structure reflects the range of cultural interaction and alliances in Scandinavian Late Bronze Age. Some regions may be interlinked at every level, while other have a more dispersed profile. When discussing the social and economic systems in prehistoric social formations it is of importance to be aware of this complexity in artifact distribution, because it indicates the magnitude of the social structure and organization.

The distribution of bronzes and pottery have been studied by Rowlands (1976) and Elison (1975; 1980). Ellison has identified different levels of metalwork and pottery distribution during the Middle Bronze Age in southern England, and she states that: "The spatial patterning of the weapons (spearheads and rapiers), which mainly occur as single finds, shows a marked contrast with that of the tools or ornaments" (Ellison 1980: 132). This fact is extremely interesting in comparing with the Scandinavian area and the above discussion.

One way of analyzing the exchange network, and to define the regional similarities, is to study artifacts belonging to different levels in the structure (Figure 3). Starting with the celts one can compare the variance in quantitative representation of sub-types in different regions through time. The following analysis is concentrated to Sweden, mainly because my

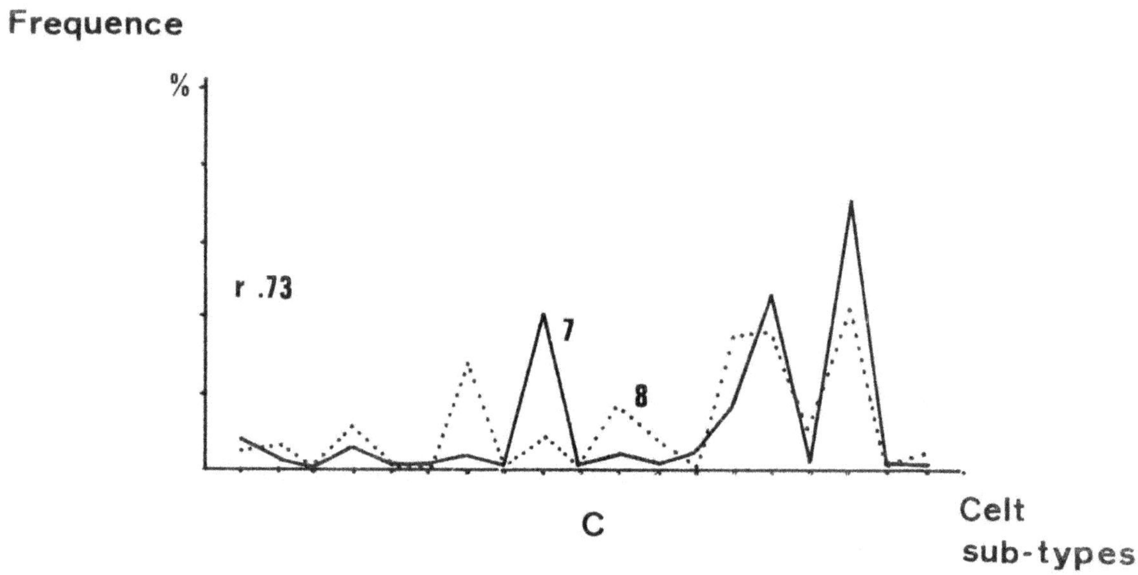

Figure 6. Procentual frequence of celt sub-types in two regions (7 & 8), and the degree of similarity expressed in a correlation coefficient.

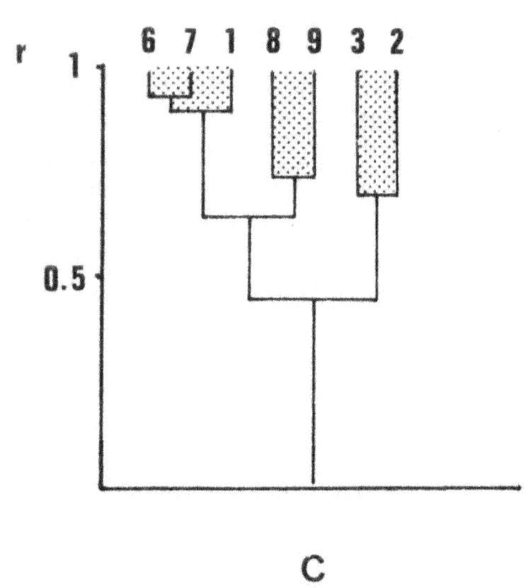

Figure 7. Dendrogram illustrating the C-level similarity (celts) between seven Swedish regions.

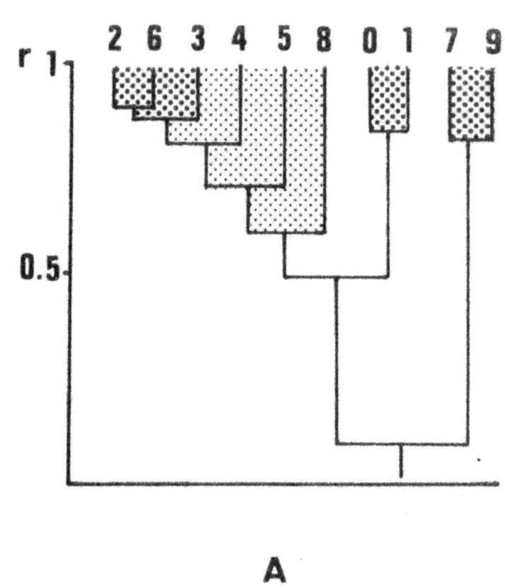

Figure 9. Dendrogram illustrating the A-level interaction between eight Swedish regions and Denmark.

research work has dealt with this area. Figure 6 shows the degree of similarity between two Swedish regions, Småland (7) and Ostergötland (8). The x-axis represents the celt sub-types, and the y-axis the procentual occurence. The similarity is expressed in a correlation coefficient, which in this case is r= 0.73.

To grasp the total picture in the entire Swedish area, a cluster analysis was carried out. The matrix below (Table 2) shows the correlation between seven Swedish regions.

Table 2

	1	3	2	6	7	8	9
1	-						
3	37	-					
2	70	73	-				
6	93	24	68	-			
7	87	28	62	94	-		
8	60	34	43	72	73	-	
9	47	21	35	51	41	74	-

The numbers represent Swedish regions (see Table 3 below) and all figures are to be $x10^{-1}$, to get the correlation coefficient.

The correlation coefficients for the three basic pairs are encircled (for an elaborate description of cluster analysis see Johnson 1972: 309 ff, and Orton 1980; 47 ff).

The fact that there are 721 celts found in one region (1) and only 32-175 celts in the other regions (Baudou 1960: 140-141) does not bias the result of the cluster analysis when using weighted (procentual) values. Instead of drawing 21 frequence diagrams, as Figure 6, to compare all seven regions, which anyhow give a rather scattered picture, a dendrogram was used to illustrate this (Figure 7).

The dendrogram indicates that we are dealing with three major areas with an internal similar variation in celt variation during some 500 years. The map (Figure 8) shows these areas marked by different hatching. The borderlines between the three areas divide southern Sweden into a northern, a western and a south eastern zone, which reflect areas united by an internal dialect in 'celt language'. Of course, the strength of this unity must have altered during a period of 500 years, but the over-all trend is rather distinct (see Baudou 1956: 34-35). A zonal division is possible because the regions linked together are adjacent to each other.

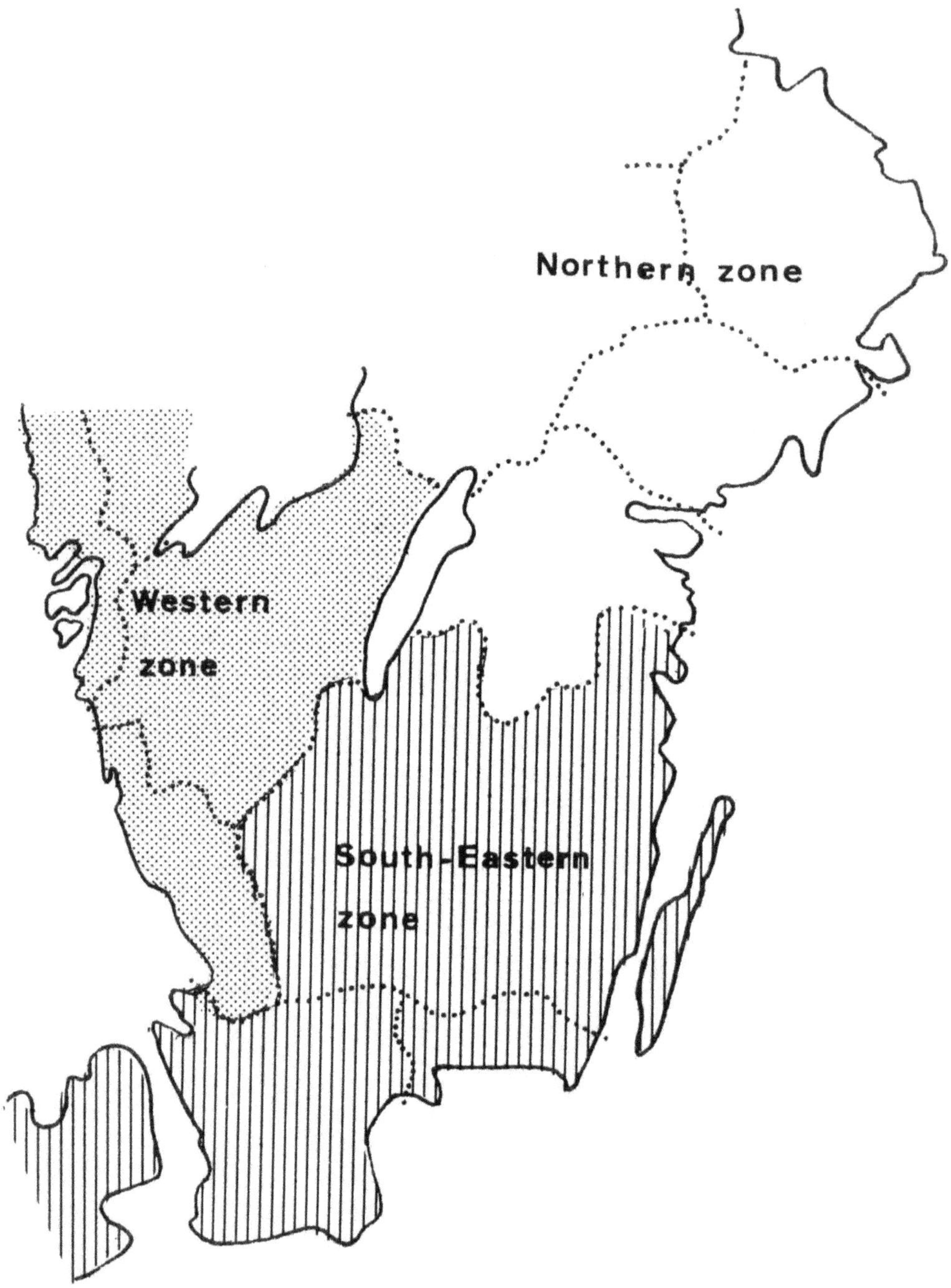

Figure 8. Map showing the zonal division of Sweden into three major areas with an internal co-variation in celt circulation during Late Bronze Age.

Table 3	Swedish region	Number of celts
1	Skåne	721
2	Halland	70
3	Västergötland	175
4	Bohuslän	32
5	Blekinge	37
6	Oland	75
7	Småland	72
8	Ostergötland	65
9	Uppland	87
10	Denmark	627

Turning to the A-level items (the weapons) the picture is more complex. Here, the regions with a high degree of similarity are not adjacent to each other. Figure 9 shows the result of the cluster analysis of this artifact group. When comparing Figure 7 and Figure 9, it is obvious that there is a significant difference.

This is not surprising if the goods are exchanged and spread within partly separated levels, as suggested in Figure 3. In contrast, it would be very suprising and hard to explain the observed difference as being a product of a non-hierarchial system. As I pointed out earlier, the regional variations in celt distribution are not expected to be similar to the variation in weapon distribution, if different levels of bronze exchange existed.

Halland (2) and Oland (6) are two regions that form a basic unit with an almost exactly similar variation in weapon-pattern. Västergötland (3) is a region with a strong connection to this unit. Skåne (1) and Denmark (0) forms a separate cluster, and so do Småland (7) and Uppland (9), which are two areas with a close internal coordination, but with an almost total separation from other regions or cluster of regions. Skåne (1) and Småland (7), for example, form a homogenous group together with Oland (6) when looking at celt distribution (Figure 7), with a high correlation (r=0.87); and now, with regard to the weapons, the correlation is almost non (r= 0.02). If the exchange cycles between these regions were the same, independent of the nature of the goods exchanged, this dissimilarity would never emerge.

In the same way we have an opposite relation between Västergötland (3) and Oland (6); the correlation for celts is r= 0.24, and for the weapons r=0.89. Regions separated in social interaction on the 'celt-level' suddenly express a high degree of interaction on the 'weapon-level'. Further, Oland (6) and Småland (7), closely tied together at 'celt-level', are being separated in the weapon circulation; celts r= 0.94; weapons r= 0.11.

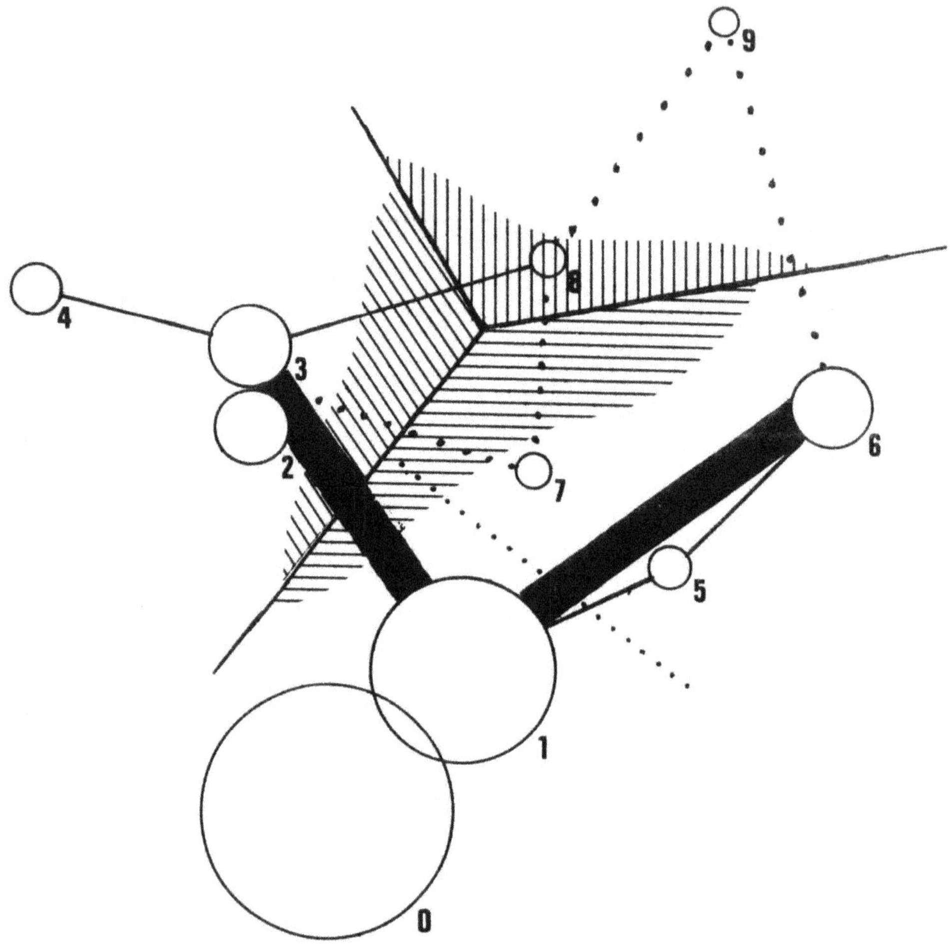

Figure 10. A-level exchange pattern between the studied regions as indicated in Figure 9, and the basic zonal division (C-level exchange) as shown in Figure 8 marked by hatching.

All together, these differences are strong indications of the existance of a multi-level exchange system in Scandinavian Late Bronze Age. Such an exchange system can also reflect a social formation made up of hierarchally organized structures, with different functions within the system.

Figure 10 is a model generated from the analysis and discussion above. It shows the zonal division described by the celt distribution, and the 'top-level' exchange pattern as indicated by the weapons. Together, Denmark (0) and Skåne (1) forms a rather distinct cluster in which 78% of the weapons are being distributed (67% in Denmark and 11% in Skåne). One reason to the high density in these regions must be connected to the intense land exploitation. If turning the entire Småland (7) into 100% farming land, which would require a good portion of hard work, one would naturally expect an increasing amount of finds. But even if we calculate with the relative land exploitation, and the total land area in all regions, the relative bronze density is still higher in Skåne and particularly Denmark.

Table 4 below shows the relative celt density in the Swedish regions. A is the total land area, B is procentual land exploitation, C is celts per km^2, D is the index value (celt density).

Table 4

Region	A 1)	B	C 2)	D 3)
1	10.970	53.7%	65	3.00
2	4.770	28.6%	14	1.00
3	16.670	32.5%	10	0.67
4	4.450	24.5%	7	0.52
5	2.920	22.1%	12	0.93
6	1.340	63.3%	55	2.00
7	29.320	11.0%	2	0.18
8	9.990	24.5%	7	0.52
9	12.670	24.3%	7	0.53

1) Area in km^2

2) All figures are to be $x10^{-3}$

3) D is (100-B)xC

The weapons may have been manufactured and exchanged mainly in the most southern parts of the survey area, but due to the presistence of a social system with an exchange participation in the northern regions too, some objects were distibuted to areas of particular economic or social interest, such as Halland (2), Västergötland (3) and Oland (6). This may explain the similarity between Halland/Västergötland and Oland, even if the distance between the region is 340 km. Put in other words, certain objects were sparsely but evenly distributed from Denmark/SkåN along one western and one eastern exchange route (Figure 10), which stopped in Västergötland in the west, and at Oland in the east.

It is especially interesting to note Olands (6) position in the top-level circulation of bronzes. Traditionally, this region is not considered to be any major Bronze Age 'central-place' in Sweden, especially not in comparison to Småland (7) and Uppland (9) (Hagberg 1978; Hyenstrand 1979: 219 and 241).

But if Oland really was an important region in the 'top-level' exchange during Late Bronze Age, as suggested in this paper, we might also expect to find other rare and 'symbolic' artifacts here, and this is exactly what we do! Two magnificent bronze lurer are found here, in a bog at Långlöts Norregård. These kind of lurer are extremely rare in the whole european area, and other are found in Denmark, Skåne and Västergötland (Bronsted 1939: 169).

Also, the characteristic two-piece fibula (glasögon-fibula) is a type which is concentrated to Denmark/Skåne, Västergötland in the west and Oland in the east. This emphasises the polarisation between a western and an eastern center-place in Late Bronze Age. Probably this east-west division, with internal socio-political centers, has its roots way back at least in the Early Bronze Age. A recent study by the author (not yet published) of the Early Bronze Age flanged axes in Sweden (see Oldeberg 1974; 1976) points clearly in the same direction. A Factor analysis (Principal Component) was carried out, which discerned two general types of flanged axes, one 'common type' and one 'special type', with significant attributes such as decoration, bow-formed edge etc. The 'special type' had its highest Factor scores for Västergötland and Oland.

Concluding remarks

The major aim of this paper has been to describe a possible way to identify and explain differences in the distribution of Late Bronze Age artifacts. This has been accomplished in relation to a theory of social action and exchange. The circulation of goods is sub-divided into partly separated levels which are thought to be a reflection of a hierarchally designed social formation.

The brief study presented here deals with regions that are equivalent to countys, and this may disturb the spatial picture.

A more refined analysis of the spatial distribution of the finds may also give a more distinct pattern and a better perspective on cultural interaction during the Late Bronze Age. Such a method has been suggested recently by Lundmark (1984).

Another aspect on the Bronze Age are the monuments: graves, settlements and rock-carvings. A structure analysis of the Bronze Age social systems in Scandinavia must deal with all possible data at the same time before a clearer picture can be drawn. When studying only a limited part of the total spectrum one is doomed to fail both in description and in explaination of complexed social formations. The study in this paper focus only on the bronzes and must therefore be supplemented with other analysis as mentioned above. The total summary of such a multi-structural approach can only be evaluated in connection to a defined theory of the dialectics of social formations. I believe that this is an important point in forthcoming archaeological work, at least for archaeologists commited to societal studies.

NOTES

1) Part of this chapter originates from a paper entitled "The structure and function of prehistoric social institutions - a social anthropological approach". (Larsson 1984).

BIBLIOGRAPHY

Baudou, E. 1953. De svenska holkyxorna under bronsåldern. Fornvännen.

Baudou, E. 1956. Regionala grupper i Norden under yngre bronsålder. Fornvännen.

Baudou, E. 1960. Die regionale und chronologische Einteilung der jüngern Bronzezeit im Nordischen Kreis. Studies in North European Archaeology 1. (Stockholm).

Binford, L.R. 1962. Archaeology as Anthropology. American antiquity 28: 217 - 225.

Binford, L.R. 1968. Some comments on historical versus processual archaeology. Southwestern Journal of Anthropology 24: 267-275.

Binford, L.R. 1972. An archaeological Perspective. (Seminar Press N.Y.).

Binford, L.R. 1975. Sampling, judgement and the archaeological record. Sampling Archaeology. ed. J.W. Mueller. (University of Arizona Press); 251 - 257.

Brøndsted, J. 1939. Danmarks oldtid II. (Copenhagen).

Clarke, D.L. 1968. Analytical archaeology. (Methuen. London).

Deetz, J.F. 1968. Cultural patterning as reflected by archaeological materials. Settlement archaeology, ed. K.C. Chang. National Press Books; 31-42.

Ellison, A. 1975. Pottery and Settlement of the later Bronze Age in southern England. PhD thesis, (University of Cambridge).

Ellison, A. 1980. Settlements and Regional Exchange: a case study. Settlement and Society in the British Later Bronze Age, eds. J. Barret and R. Bradley. B.A.R. (Oxford).

Godelier, M. 1977. Politics as 'infrastructure'. The Evolution of Social Systems, eds. J. Friedman and M.J. Rowlands. (London. Duckworth); 13-28.

Hagberg, U.E. 1978. Tiotusen år på tio sidor -ett försök till sammanfattning. Kalmar län.

Hagget, P., Cliff, A.D. and Frey, A. 1977. Location analysis in Human Geography. Vol. 1. Second edition. (London).

Hill, J.N. 1970. Prehistoric Social Organization in the American Southwest: Theory and Method. Reconstructing prehistoric Pueblo socities, ed. W.A. Longacre. (University of New Mexico Press); 11-58.

Hill, J.N. 1972. The methodological debate in contemporary Archaeology: A model. Models in Archaeology, ed. D.L. Clarke. (London. Methuen); 61-107.

Hodder, I. 1982. Symbols in Action. New Studies in Archaeology. (Cambridge).

Hodder, I. & Orton, C. 1976. Spatial Analysis in Archaeology. New Studies in Archaeology. (Cambridge).

Hyenstrand, A. 1979. Arkeologisk regionindelning av Sverige. Riksantikvarieämbetet. (Stockholm).

Johnson, G.A. 1978. Information sources and the development of Decision-making Organizations. Social Archaeology: Beyond subsistence and Dating, eds. C.L. Redman et al. (New York Academic Press); 87-112.

Johnson, L. 1972. Introduction to Imaginary models for Scaling and Clustering. Models in Archaeology, ed. D.L. Clarke. (London. Methuen); 309-379.

Kristiansen, K. 1977. The circulation of ornaments and weapons in Bronze Age Denmark. Arch. Baltica 2.

Kristiansen, K. 1978. The consumtion of wealth in Bronze Age Denmark. A study in the dynamics of economic processes in tribal societies. New Directions in Scandinavian Archaeology, eds. K. Kristiansen & P. Müller. (Copenhagen); 158-190.

Kristiansen, K. 1981. Economic models for Bronze Age Scandinavia - Towards an integrated approach. Economic Archaeology, eds. A. Sheridan & G. Baily. B.A.R. International series 96; (Oxford) 239-303.

Larson, T.B. 1984. The Structure and Function of Prehistoric Social Institutions - A Social Anthropological Approach. Archaeology and Environment 2. (University of Umeå).

Lévi-Strauss, C. 1969a. Totemismen. (Uppsala).

Lévi-Strauss, C. 1969b. The Elementary Structures of Kinship. (Boston. Beacon Press).

Longacre, W.A. 1970. Archaeology as Anthropology: A case study. (University of Arizona).

Lundmark. H. 1983. A method of analyzing hierarchial organization in settlement patterns. Archaeology and Environment 2. (University of Umeå).

Mauss, M. 1954. The Gift. (London. Routledge & Kegan Paul).

Oldeberg, A. 1974. Die ältere Metallzeit in Schweden I. Kungliga Vitterhets Historie och Antiqvitets Akademiens Handlingar. (Stockholm).

Oldeberg, A. 1976. Die ältere Metallzeit in Schweden II. Kungliga Vitterhets Historie och Antiqvitets Akademiens Handlingar. (Stockholm).

Orton, C. 1980. Mathematics in Archaeology. (London. Collins).

Plog, S. 1978. Social Interaction and Stylistic similarity: A reanalysis. Advances in Archaeological Method and Theory, vol. 1., ed. M.B. Schiffer. (New York Academic Press); 143-182.

Randsborg, K. 1973. Befolkning og social variation i eldre bronzealders Danmark. Kuml: 197-208.

Randsborg, K. 1974. Social stratification in Early Bronze Age Denmark: a study of the regulation of cultural systems. Prähistorische Zeitschrift 49: 38-61.

Rowlands, M. 1976. The Production and Distribution of Metalwork in the Middle Bronze Age in Southern Britain. B.A.R. (Oxford).

Rowlands, M. 1980. Kinship, Alliance and Exchange in the European Bronze Age. Settlement and Society in the British Later Bronze Age, eds. J. Barret & R. Bradley. B.A.R. (Oxford); 15-55.

Sahlins, M. 1968. Tribesmen. Foundation of modern Anthropology series. (New Jersey).

Sherratt, A. 1972. Socio-economic and Demographic models for the Neolithic and Bronze Ages of Europe. Models in Archaeology, ed. D.L. Clarke. (London. Methuen); 477-542.

Sullivan, A.P. 1978. Inference and Evidence in Archaeology: A discussion of the Conceptual problems. Advances in Archaeological Method and Theory, ed. M.B. Schiffer. (New York. Academic Press); 183-222.

Tilley, C. 1981a. Conceptual frameworks for the explaination of sociocultural change. Pattern of the Past, eds. I. Hodder, G. Isaac & N. Hammond. Cambridge. (Cambridge University Press); 363-386.

Tilley, C. 1981b. Economy and Society: what relationship ? Economic Archaeology: Towards an Integrated Approach, eds. G. Baily & A. Sheridan. B.A.R. (Oxford); 131-148.

Tilley, C. 1982. Social formation, social structures and social change. Symbolic and Structural Archaeology, ed. I. Hodder. (Cambridge). New Directions in Archaeology; 26-38.

Thrane, H. 1975. Europaeiske Forbindelser. Nationalmuseets skrifter. (Copenhagen).

Wobst, M. 1977. Stylistic behaviour and information exchange. University of Michigan Museum of Anthropology, Anthropological Paper 61; 317-342.

"CELTIC FIELDS" AND PREHISTORIC AGRARIAN LANDSCAPES

Approach, methods and results from a human geographical study of reasons for the development of the agrarian society at Vinarve in Rone parish on Gotland, Sweden.

Bengt Windelhed

INTRODUCTION

In Sweden, agriculture has been the dominant way of life for the majority of the population from early prehistory until the late 19th century.

Agrarian production has left behind traces, so-called form elements, a term defined by Lindquist (1968:9) as: "The agrarian landscape's morphological components, formed as a result of man's activities and arranged into definable patterns." These ".... geographical patterns are the end product of a large number of individual decisions made at different times for often very different reasons." (Harvey, 1973: 119). Thus, the agrarian landscape represents an empirical material well suited for analysis of important trends of prehistoric societies lacking written records.

In the area that is treated here, Vinarve in Rone parish on Gotland, an island in the Baltic Sea, the long-term development of the agrarian landscape has been studied from a geographical perspective. Research has been directed towards the spatial aspects of prehistoric societies. This provided a theoretical framework that to some extent diverged from the social and economic theories formulated within the so-called 'new archaeology'.

In the first stage of field work at Vinarve, traces from two agrarian phases were discovered (Lindquist, Carlsson and Windelhed 1973). A large number of connected fields over an area of c.130 hectares were interpreted as an older and systematically laid out field system of the "Celtic field" type here excavated for the first time in Sweden. Such fields, which appear in corresponding forms in Denmark, Northern Germany, the Netherlands and England, have been generally dated to the Pre-Roman Iron Age (see Fig. 1).

The Celtic fields were stratigraphically covered by form elements from the Roman Iron Age - Migration Period. This younger agrarian landscape was built up around single farms which had arable lands and meadow lands within enclosed, so-called infields. From the dwelling areas cattle paths lead out through the stone fenced infields into the surrounding pasture lands.

Based on these form elements, agricultural development during the Early Iron Age has been interpreted as a change from an extensive to an intensive exploitation of the landscape both at Vinarve and on Gotland (Lindquist 1974). This interpretation has served as a general hypothesis for a regional analysis (Carlsson 1979) and for my own detailed analysis of the

215	Field-wall, line indicating top of enclosed field-boundary
	ditto, uncertain
	Terrace
BN	Edge of tilled field (survey)
ML	ditto (air photo interpretation)
22	Stone fence (disused)
	ditto, uncertain
	Modern fence
	ditto stone fence
33:4	House foundation (Iron Age)
R 124	Burial cairn
R 32	Monolith
R	Ancient remain
	Modern stone heap from field cleared for cultivation
	Stone, stone heap
	Road
	Field road
GK,33,727	Codes for area description
	Air photo interpreted area
	Moderna edge of field
	Ditch
	Boundary without fence between modern field and grassland
	Difference in land height
	Marsh, depression
	Marsh, with water
	Water-hole

Fig. 1. Part of the fossilized agrarian landscape at Vinarve in Rone parish on Gotland. The map covers c 60 hectares, which is approximately half of the fossilized agrarian landscape in the RA.

PREHISTORIC FIELDS AT UGGÅRDE - VINARVE
Rone parish
Gotland
AREA K
AREA AB
AREA O
AREA A

Vinarve area.

The form elements here have morphological and stratigraphical similarities with other areas on Gotland, for example Anningåkra, Stånga and Sjonhem (Carlsson 1979: 65 ff, 71 ff and 94 ff).

The purpose of my work has been a chronological and functional interpretation of the location of productive lands and dwelling sites and an explanation of their change during the Early Iron Age.

This approach has social implications without claiming to capture the entirety of the prehistoric society. My analysis of the agrarian landscape will be limited to the basic units of society: the farm and its relationships to other farms, along with land use and production.

In the following, land use refers to areas which were created for agricultural purposes, and production refers to the agricultural output from these areas.

Those parts of the agrarian landscape which are directly included in this analysis are dwelling sites along with arable lands and stone fences which give indirect indications concerning meadow and grazing lands.

The agrarian landscape on Gotland is rather relatively simply organized. Since the Roman Iron Age it has been characterized by single farms. This implies that reorganizations of the agrarian landscape on Gotland is not so devastating for the older form elements, which is why these forms should be able to contribute to an increased understanding of the early agrarian development in Scandinavia.

On Gotland the Early Iron Age has been studied through problems involving the transitional phase from the Bronze to the Iron Age. The empirical material has primarily consisted of a usually poor grave material. However, knowledge concerning the succeeding phase in the Vinarve area is more extensive. It is accounted for in, among others, the literature relating to the international excavations at Vallhagar in Fröjel parish during the late 1940's (Stenberger 1955). On Gotland, the distribution of Migration Period dwellings (so-called giants' graves) is rather well known. This is because both the house foundations and fences are stone constructions which are clearly visible in the terrain. The reason for the abandonment of these dwellings is one of the most discussed problems in Scandinavian archaeology. Hypotheses of abandonment as a result of war, plagues and impoverishment of the arable lands show that our present knowledge of this period, in spite of everything, rests on a weak factual basis which allows for a wide range of interpretations.

The research area

The research area (RA) lies very close to the southeastern coast of Gotland approximately 5 km southwest of Ronehamn.

The prehistoric agrarian landscape lies in attractive meadow environments surrounded by the large and perfectly geometrical fields representative of today's modern agriculture. These modern fields have sometimes been laid out over the prehistoric fields.

From the air it is possible to see how modern fields, established about 20 years ago, "show" the prehistoric field pattern. The ancient field walls, appear in the modern fields as light-colored ribbons and the ancient field surfaces appear as dark-colored ribbons and the ancient field surfaces appear as dark-colored areas. In spite of the influence of modern ploughs, these ancient field traces have not totally erased. The ancient field walls have been too sturdy.

The delimitations for the RA have been centred around the assumed demands that prehistoric agriculture placed upon the natural landscape, primarily with respect of the distribution of soil types and their qualities. Along with studies of land use from land survey maps (one from c 1700 and one from 1875) the RA has been delimited to a square surface of c 3 x 3 km. The RA is then, in the south and west surrounded by barren forest areas, in the north by bog lands, and in the east by soils with low cultivation capacity. Thus, the RA may be seen as an enclave within which settlement and respective cultural lands have been located from early prehistory up until today.

Most noticeable, from a natural geographical aspect, is the flat terrain. The Ancylus wall in the northern part of the RA is the highest area at 21 - 23.7 meters above sea level. The Litorina wall lies 14 m asl and the southern edge of the RA lies at c 5 m asl. The Ancylus and Litorina walls are ancient shore walls from the early developmental phases of the Baltic Sea which are a result of the last glacial recession. Land elevation has meant that the sea has sorted out the soil cover and left a sharp border between the dominating and cultivatable soil types of sandy soils and moraine clay. The sandy soils (Sw "grovmo") appear in the central parts of the RA. These are surrounded by moraine clay while the periferal areas of the RA do not contain any cultivatable soils.

In the central part of the RA, low bands of marshy areas appear between the shore walls formed after the Ancylus period. These smaller shore walls are located between both the Ancylus wall and the Litorina wall and between the Litorina wall and the present-day coastline. The fossil fields are located on these shore walls which are between 50 and 75 m wide and primarily made up of sand. As we shall see later, from the Iron Age onwards, it has been gradually possible to cultivate certain of these marshy areas between the shore walls.

The map (Fig. 1) gives the impression of a well-organized pattern of field surfaces. This has been interpreted as one field system as the result of one planning effort (Crawford, 1928, Hatt, 1949, Bowen, 1963, Lindquist, 1974, Brongers 1976).

The field surfaces, which lie on easily drained sandy soils are often 30 x 40 and 40 x 50 m large. They have a slightly concave surface framed by four ridge-shaped field walls of sand. The walls are 4 - 8 m wide and 0.5 - 1 m high. They are crowned by a 0.2 - 0.4 m thick cover of turf (raw humus layer in podsoil).

In the RA there are six known dwelling sites from the Roman Iron Age - Migration Period, two of these have been relocated through field work. Land use during this period was located in the peripheral areas of the RA. The fossil stone fences, which often lead out from and appear in connection with the house foundations (giants' graves) lie on both sandy soils and moraine clay.

Beyond the central area of sandy soils there are six so-called historical farms. They have been surrounded by their respective fields while their grazing lands have been located out towards the peripheral areas of the RA. The meadow lands were located on the sandy soils in the central part of the RA. Portions of these lands were first cultivated during the 1900's. The fossilized agrarian landscape has thus been preserved through the demands for large meadow lands during successive periods.

THEORETICAL POINT OF DEPARTURE

Change in the agrarian landscape within the RA may be studied against the background of a natural environment with qualities which have attracted farmers for a long time. Through this, reasons for the changes ought mainly to be sought among ideas and possibilities of using the land within the single farms along with ideas concerning how the agrarian production was organized within a given form of society.

Excavations have produced datings of the fossil form elements which lie both earlier and later than the Early Iron Age. In order to understand the agrarian changes during the Iron Age, it has been important to insert the form elements into a longer time perspective. Here a geographical approach has given an analytical foundation which chronologically and functionally orders the form elements.

The field of human geography involves how spatial elements of human activity change through time. The classical investigations involving the spread of innovations is an example of geographical studies often directed towards the complex relationships between how different processes influence spatial form (Harvey 1973: 127, and Abler, Adams and Gould 1972: 60). Through studies of innovation processes the term "process" has been described as the transfer of innovation and acceptance and the term "spatial form" has received a physical association (Gerger 1978: 31-35).

In the work at Vinarve geographical terms for spatial analysis have been used to study changes in the agrarian landscape via a two-stage interpretation.

In the first stage the agrarian landscape's physical form is analysed, illustrated by a series of spatial models which characterize different time horizons. This static presentation concerns primarily the composition and function of the spatial organization. It is a result of a test of the general hypothesis. This is based upon datings obtained in the field as well as functional information concerning the form elements.

This descrete division provides a foundation for the dynamic interpretation stage. This is directed towards the continual process which, through time, physically form and change the agrarian landscape. Process becomes a collective term for the activities which give spatial consequences, achieved by social and economical ideas, techniques, activities and organizational forms. In the following, the term "process" concerns agrarian land use and the cultivation techniques.

The static presentation originates from the related terms for spatial analysis which Wärneryd (1968) calls element, pattern, structure and system (see Fig. 2).

Form element (for example fields, dwelling sites, enclosures) have a defined location and a certain character (for example, age and function). The form elements' location in space create a pattern. The different connections between the form elements in the pattern create a structure which "....refers to the internal location organization of a distribution in space" (Abler, Adams and Gould 1972: 60). In the following, the relationships consist of functional relationships between the central form element dwelling site (farm or agricultural unit) and its respective production surfaces. One example of functional relationship is the size relationships between fields, meadows and pasture lands in traditional Swedish agriculture. With a given land resource the field area stood in relation to manure from the cattle that obtained fodder from a certain meadow area and pasture lands.

Wärneryd uses system as a general term which is built upon ideas from systems theory. It gives a convenient abstraction of a complex reality and an isolation of certain events in time and space (Norrbom 1973: 13 and Harvey 1973: 448-50).

Systems theory provides the point of origin for the static division of the agrarian landscape. These time horizons, here called production systems shall characterize the type of agriculture during a certain period. How that agriculture was organized, primarily spatially but even with respect to agricultural technology and socially, has been interpreted from the spatial models. The production systems may be seen as open systems which are influenced by and influence their surroundings (Norrbom 1973: 44 ff). The production system's surface area is defined by the delimitation of the RA as presented above. This surface is populated at a certain point in time by a group of people who carry out a production which creates a spatial organization. The production demands and forms a certain combination of form elements.

Changes in production may be registered through the abandonment of form elements, their reformation or through new form elements which arise (Lindquist 1968: 9 and Prince 1971). A new production system is built up.

The different production systems give a series of constructed "snapshots", where their differences invite a dynamically-directed interpretation of the more general and long-range processes which influenced change in the agrarian landscape.

Empirically speaking we are interested in a local production system, but our intention is to there seek components and relationships which contribute to the understanding of a general regional system (Harvey 1973: 484-5).

The production system constitutes, in this way, a point of departure for an interpretation of how one lived and organized his existence during the prehistoric period in the area. With our present day knowledge it is hardly possible to more closely capture the entire surrounding social system. The purpose here has been to provide a theoretical basis for the interpretation of the agrarian landscape's development where the physical and abstract terms make up the point of departure for a geographical synthesis (Harvey 1973: 127).

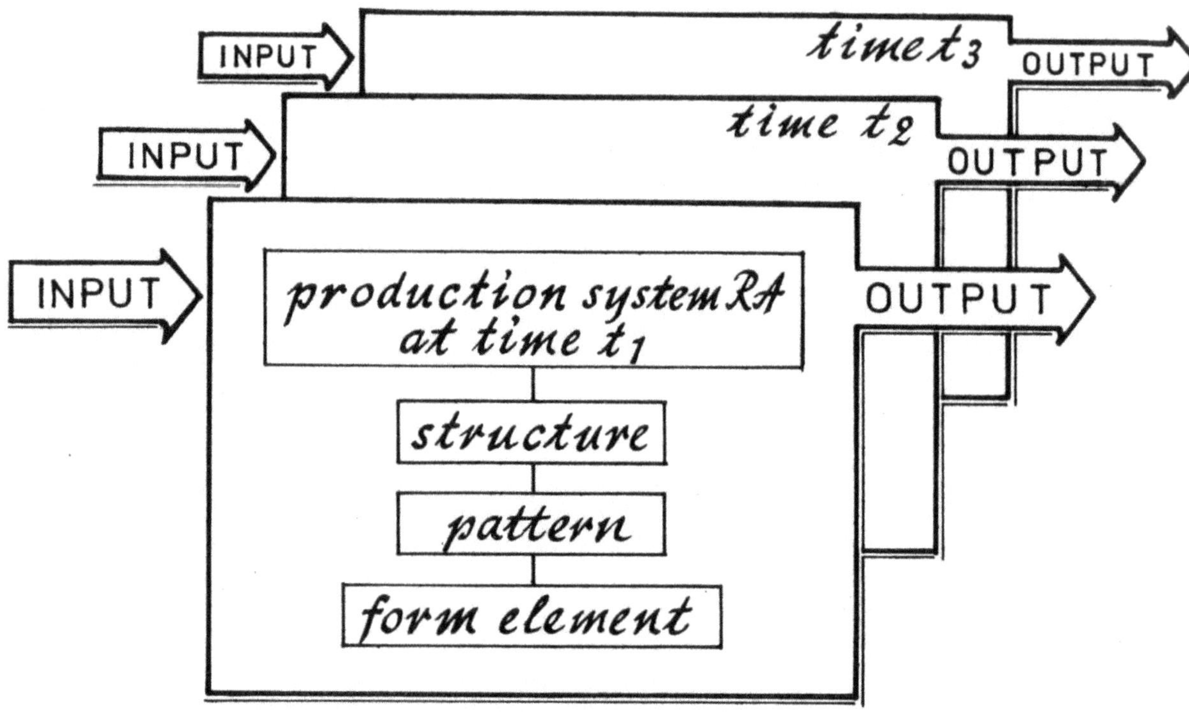

FIGURE 2: General sketch of approach and terms used in the analysis of the agrarian landscape's development. The model will show how the analysis takes place through a layering of the agrarian landscape in so-called production systems. The interpretation of the dynamics in the development takes place within the concept process.

TESTING THE HYPOTHESIS

Above we have created a foundation for an analytical method where the general hypothesis through partial-hypotheses may be tested by excavations. Within a number of smaller areas in the RA, the fieldwork has ranged from general investigations to a detailed conclusion. To the general methods belong mapping of the form elements, phosphate mapping, systems of test holes and levelling. The results of these methods form the basis for the detailed investigations with total excavation of meter-wide trenches of various lengths. The trenches have been excavated in layers, the earth sifted and the finds have been collected within each square meter. The final interpretation of the smaller areas has been made after combination of the results from the fieldwork. Important information has been the field formations visible in the terrain, the height, relationships, stratigraphy and datings.

In the following, I have limited the presentation of the results to two smaller areas. These shall exemplify the method, its relation to the theoretical formation along with the basis for a presentation of a development model over the change in the agrarian landscape at Vinarve.

AREA AB

In the meadow area around the cattle path in the eastern part of the RA there are a large number of prehistoric fields along with fences and a cattle path (see Figs. 1 and 5). The cattle path has been cut off in the south when the modern field was established. The cattle path has been cut off in the south when the modern field was established. The mouth of the cattle path to the north faces lands which, at least during historical times, have been pasture lands.

The purpose of the investigations in this area has been to study the stratigraphical and chronological relationships between the fields and the fences.

Hypothetically, it was assumed that the fields primarily belonged to the Pre-Roman Iron Age field system. These were covered by fences and the cattle path which have been judged to belong to a Roman Iron Age - Migration Period population investigated in area O.

Stratigraphy

The more general stratigraphy in the area appeared relatively early in the investigations. One of the fences in the cattle path had been laid out on the field walls 104 and 131, the other had been laid out on the field west of these walls. Another fence lies on the walls belonging to the field BH. Ard marks were found lying in the field surfaces and under the field walls which were covered by the fences and the cattle path. Under the ard marks were simpler types of dwelling remains.

The interpretation of the field areas' development shall first be directed towards a relative chronology in order to show in which succession the fields were established. The empirical material does not allow an interpretation of how later cultivations used these earlier fields.

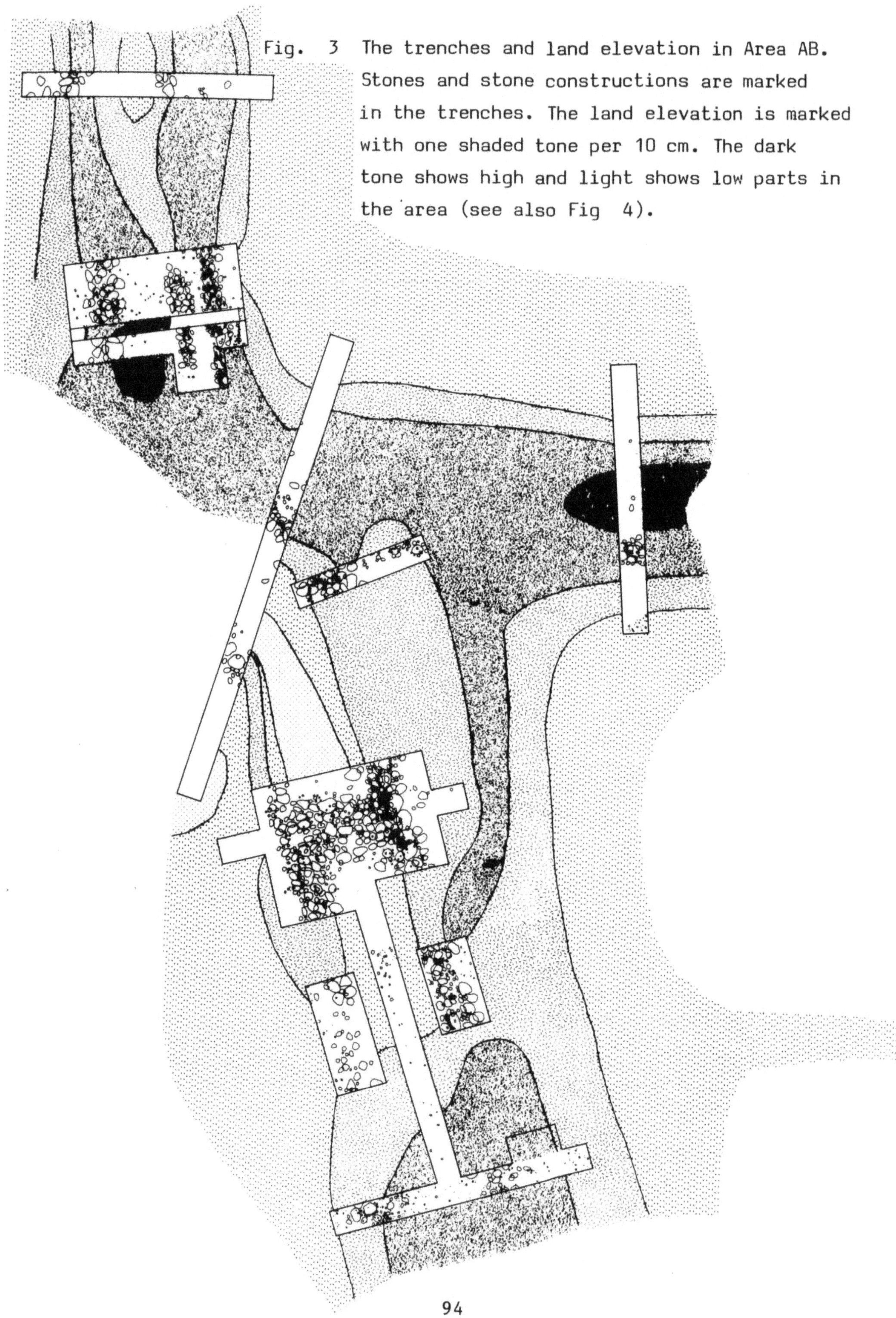

Fig. 3 The trenches and land elevation in Area AB. Stones and stone constructions are marked in the trenches. The land elevation is marked with one shaded tone per 10 cm. The dark tone shows high and light shows low parts in the area (see also Fig 4).

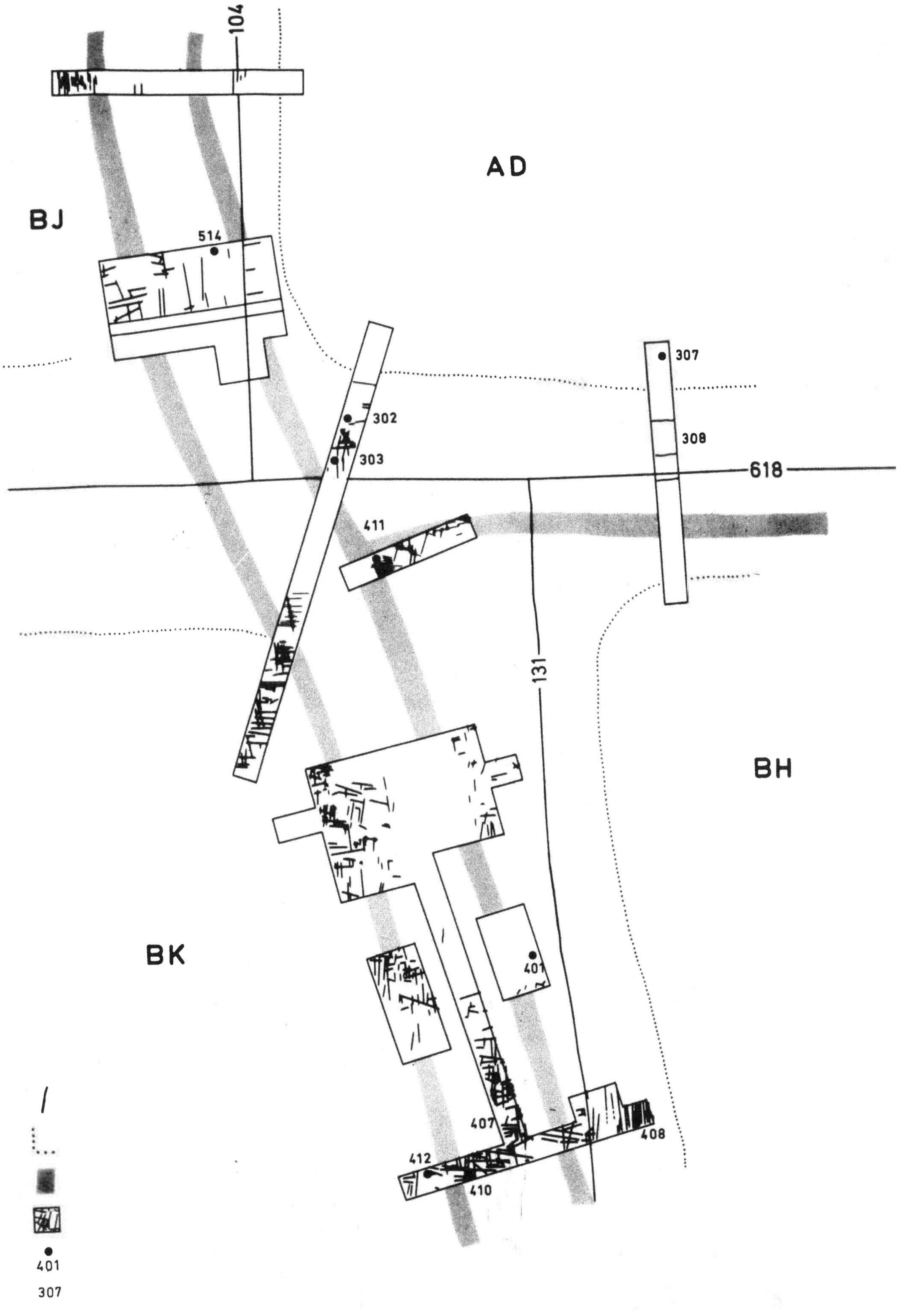
104
AD
BJ
514
307
302
308
303
618
411
131
BH
BK
401
407
408
412
410
401
307

Interpretation of ard marks and field forms

The relative chronology of the fields shall, in the following, be analysed from the ard marks. Analysis is based upon the pattern which the marks create, the pattern's location in relation to the delimitations of the field surface along with the height relationships of the ard marks. This allows a judgement as to how the fields' form have appeared and how they technically have been cultivated.

In the trenches ard marks appear in the bottom of the dark grey layer here called "the culturally influenced layer". In that layer a poor find material appears, consisting of small rounded bits of among other things bone, charcoal and pottery. The layer, which has been interpreted as a cultivated layer, lies immediately above the sub-soil. The ard marks have been created when the ard deposited the dark culturally influenced layer in the light yellow coloured sub-soil.

The exposure of the marks in the trench means that we create a level with ard marks. It is that level where the contrast between the ard marks and the stratification below is the greatest. We can study the pattern only after having scraped the marks as clearly as possible in a flat surface. At first glance, the marks give the impression of being contemporary.

As seen in Fig. 4, the ard marks created both a criss-cross, almost rhombical pattern along with a pattern of parallel marks.

The principle for how ploughing with an ard (Sw "ärja") took place still exists with the older farmers even today. At each cultivation in the nearly square fields a regular pattern of ard marks is created. One begins by ploughing a criss-cross pattern (Sw "korsplöjning"). These marks are parallel respectively perpendicular to the field walls. A band c 2-3 meters wide is saved, however, alongside the field edges, where the draught animals and the ard are turned. When the central part of the field is finished an edge-plowing (so-called Sw "förplöjning") is done. The remaining band alongside the field edges is then ploughed with parallel ard marks. Investigations have shown that levels with criss-cross ploughing lie, with respect to height, lower than edge-plowing. This criss-cross plowing has eroded the underlying stratigraphy more which has meant a depression of the level containing the ard marks.

For each cultivation we ought to assume that each ard mark was drawn approximately at the same depth in the field. If earlier ard marks shall be preserved, they must be drawn at such a depth so that the later marks are unable to erase them. The ard marks which appear in the trench ought then to be those deepest drawn and <u>mainly the latest</u>. On the other hand, the marks do not need to be contemporary with the latest <u>cultivation</u> of the fields. On several occasions in the Vinarve area, later prehistoric indications of cultivation have been found above the ard marks which we shall come to below.

In addition to the fact that the field walls are very clearly visible in the terrain in this area, they even appear in the study of ard marks. The ard marks appear under the crown of the field walls, where they lie somewhat higher than out in the field surfaces. In addition, the field walls appear where the ard marks are parallel with the walls.

During cultivation the walls have gradually been formed by agricultural tools and, perhaps even the wind has moved up the light sandy soils against a simple, marked field delimitation. Cultivation has given the field surface a concave form where criss-cross ploughing has lowered the field surface and material has been moved up to the field edges. The cultivation soil decreases in thickness and more and more sub-soil in the cultivated layer has made the field poor in nutrition.

The earliest datings of cultivation traces within the RA belong to the end of the Bronze Age. From this period on through the Pre-Roman Iron Age, we have no evidence that the number of livestock should have been so large that it could have made possible a more extensive manureing of the fields. The probable access to land was then so good that the fields could most easily regain nourishment through long periods of fallow (Lindquist 1974). The demand for greater production, for example, as a result of the increase in population, meant that even with the cultivation technique of fallow fields, there was an eventual deterioration of the soil.

We can, in conclusion, constitute that "the ploughing technique", which brought the subsoil up into the cultivated layer, the practice of fallow fields along with perhaps even wind transportation of soil has meant that the earliest fields in the RA have very easily been impoverished. Obviously the need for new cultivation appeared. The new fields have probably been located alongside the old fields.

Even with the demand for a changed field form an effort was made not to disturb the old field pattern. New fields have not been established out over the earlier field walls, and since the field walls contain so much soil they have, therefore, been resistent. The modern fields within the RA, which have recently been established on the prehistoric fields, show that it takes c 20 years with modern ploughing techniques in order to flatten out the prehistoric field walls.

In analysing the development of the fields we must even touch upon the possibilities and restrictions which the natural landscape set for cultivation (see Fig. 5).

The fields lie in an area of homogeneous sandy soils, but the marshy bands between the shore walls mentioned in the introduction give certain restrictions for cultivation. The possibility of establishing fields in, among other places, the area AB has been influenced by the c 10-20 meter wide depressions between the low and wide shore walls. Above the depressions lie fossilized fields, in spite of the fact that even today they are filled with water after the winter's snow melting. These fields ought to have been relatively speaking, established at a late stage. According to the datings obtained from area AB, the fields here have been laid out during c 1500 years. During this long span of time the land elevation must have brought about a certain dehydration of these depressions which gave access to new cultivatable land.

As the demand for new fields increased, larger and larger parts of the sandy soils were taken over by both cultivated and abandoned fields. It is only an illusion that a functional and at one time laid out field system was created. The fossil fields of the type "Celtic fields", ordered in a chessboard formation, ought instead to be seen as a sum of the fields laid out in the area during a long period of time.

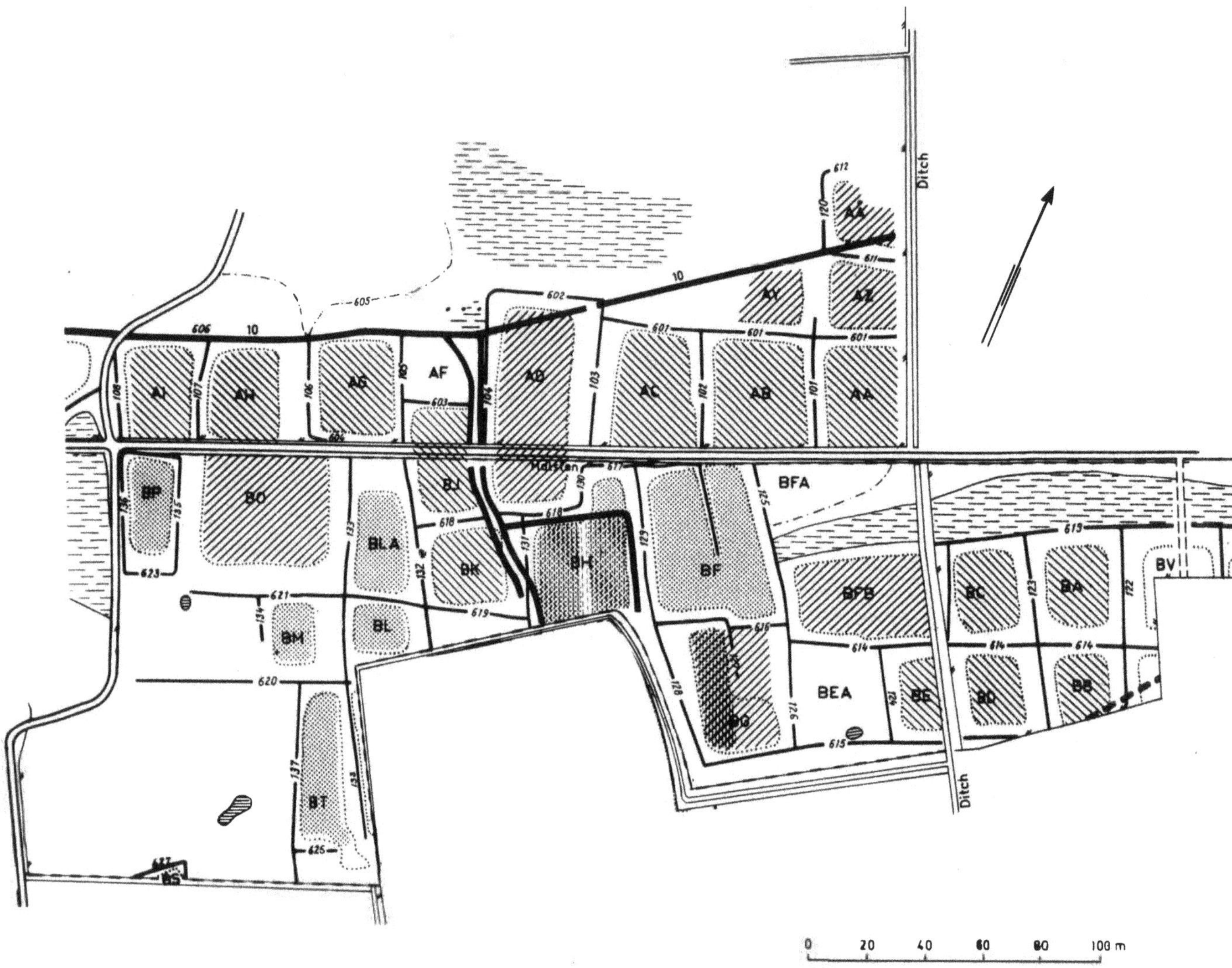

Fig. 5. Map of Area AB

Field pattern 1. Established at the end of the Bronze Age and beginning of the Pre-Roman Iron Age.
Dated directly by C-14 datings 401, 410 and 514 (see Table 1)

Field pattern 2. Established during the Pre-Roman Iron Age.
Dated indirectly by C-14 datings 302, 303 and 307.

Field pattern 3. Established during the Roman Iron Age- Migration Period. Dated directly by the C-14 dating 407.

Field pattern 4. Established during the Vendel Period-Viking Age. Dated indirectly by C-14 datings 411 and 412.

The extensive form of cultivation has obviously spread throughout the whole area of sandy soils in the central part of the RA. For the farmers who lived in the area around the Birth of Christ, continued existence demanded a new direction in production with an intensified form of cultivation along with manureing of the fields.

In order to test this argument we shall arrange the development of the fields and fences in an absolute chronology. The datings which have been described here from both of the areas AB and A are supported even by other datings from the RA. The interpretations below come from an evaluation of the argument carried out above concerning the development of the fields, their location on the shore walls, their morphology along with the relationship between the fields and the fences.

TEXT TO FIGURE 5 and TABLE 1

FIELD PATTERN 1

Under the ard marks indications of settlement from the Bronze Age appear in the form of dark colourings, patches of soot, single post holes and hearths. The earliest cultivation datings from the culturally influenced layer comes from the C-14 samples 410 and 514. Fields with these early datings from the Bronze Age are found on the highest and driest parts of the shore walls. These fields, which are relatively small and almost square, are placed side by side in groups and lie very near the above mentioned settlement indications. The ard marks under the field walls may possibly belong to the beginning of this period. These fields have successively acquired a more defined shape, the field walls and the concave field surface have been formed.

FIELD PATTERN 2

Gradually new fields may be established above the dehydrated depressions between the shore walls. Morphologically these square fields distinguish themselves from the preceeding period through size. The field forms are C-14 dated to the Pre-Roman Iron Age through samples 303 and 308, both from the culturally influenced level. In the field south of the cattle path (area O, see below) there are settlement indications from this period.

FIELD PATTERN 3

Continued dehydration of the depressions makes the establishment of new fields possible (C-14 dating 408). Morphologically they diverge from the preceeding periods through their rectangular form.

FIELD PATTERN 4

The foundation stones in both the cattle path and the fence which surrounds field BH lie very close to (1-10 cm above) the ard marks. This implies that the fences were laid out directly on the earlier fields since the ard probably at most reached c 10 cm below the ground surface. The difference in height ought then to imply continuity in the area's agrarian exploitation. In one of the trenches contemporanity between the cattle path and the fence which surrounds field BH were shown, since the construction's foundation stones lie on the same level. A C-14 sample

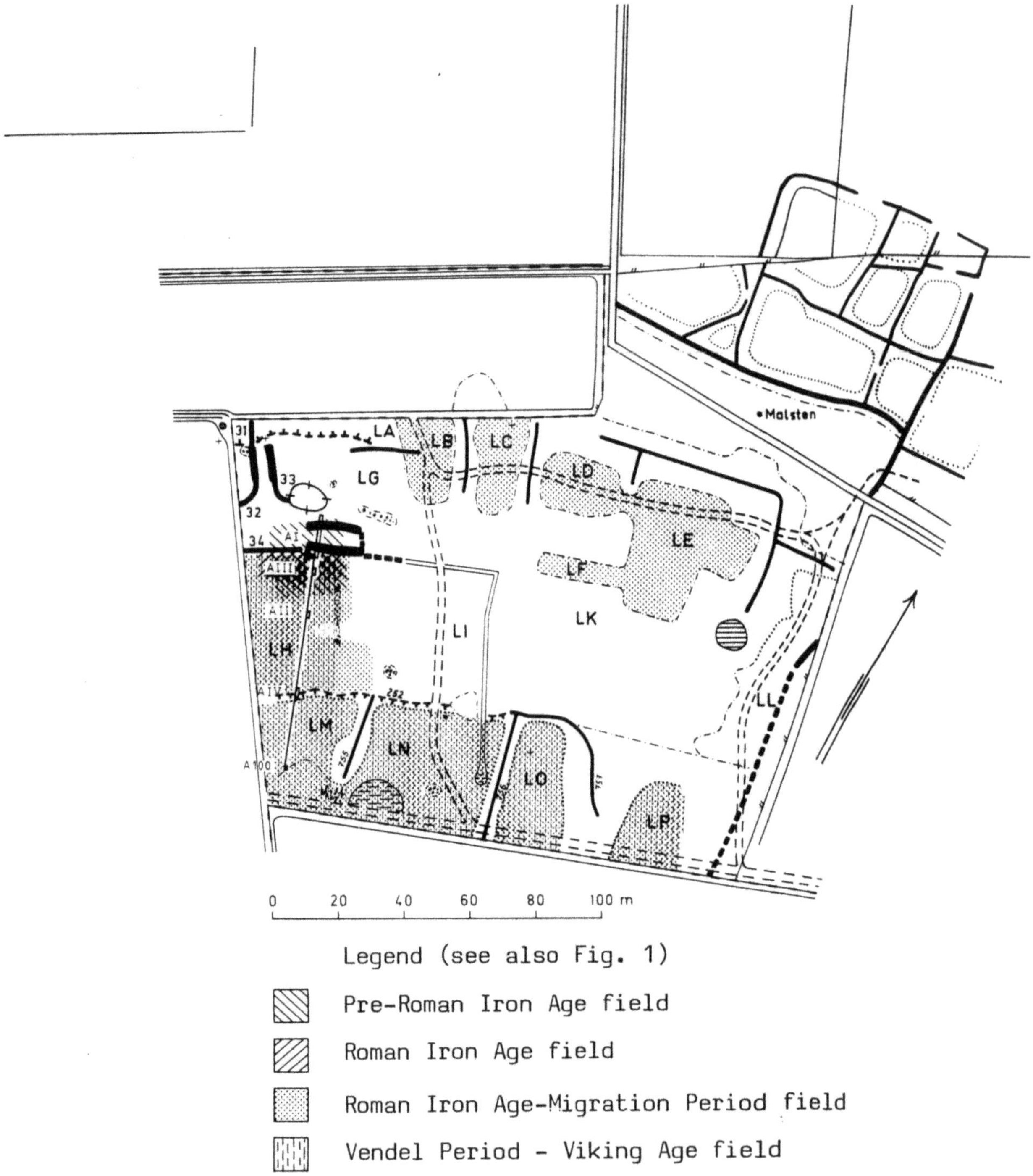

Fig. 6 Map of Area A. The visual form elements in the area are shown on the map. The shaded tones show the datings of the fields.

A I, A II, A III and A IV are excavated trenches and A 100 is a test hole. The trench A IV passes through the terrass, named in the text.

(411) here gave AD 1194 ±119 a dating comparable with a C-14 (412) dating of AD 1041 ± 105 from the bottom of the western fence in the cattle path. The age of the cattle path is implied even through C-14 dating 407 from a cultural layer which lies stratigraphically below the cattle path. The fence and cattle path are then clearly later than originally assumed. In field BH, which was cultivated at the time the fences existed, there is, among other methods, through C-14 dating 408 evidence for a secondary cultivation of an earlier field.

The cattle path leads out from the above described settlement in area O. Through excavations a complicated stratigraphy has been evidenced here with, among other things rich settlement remains from the Roman Iron Age - Migration Period. In addition, there are indications of a continued settlement contemporary with the fences.

The infields belonging to the giant's graves settlement here can only with great difficulty be reconstructed. The modern field has erased its fences. The cattle path and fences north of the settlement site show a great change in land use during the Vendel Period - Viking Age.

AREA A

In a meadow in the southwestern part of the RA there is a relatively well preserved dwelling site from the Roman Iron Age - Migration Period. The settlement lies in the sandy soil area which continues in towards the RA's central parts. South and west of the meadow is moraine clay (see Fig. 6).

The settlement site consisted of two houses (so-called giants' graves), which, judging from their size and fences, have been interpreted as a dwelling house in the south and a cattle shed to the northwest. A cattle path leads out towards the pasture lands west of the settlement site. The fences which lead out from the settlement site imply a common enclosure with the contemporary dwelling sites in the north (area K) and in the northeast (area O). The infields can have been located immediately southeast of the settlement. Here on the sandy soils there are definite traces of cultivation in the form of a terrace and some low field walls.

Field analysis of the area began from the hypothesis that the traces of prehistoric land use were contemporary with the giants' graves settlement. The fields were assumed to have been located south of the terrace edge while the other parts of the area were meadow lands. A test of the hypothesis was begun by establishing a system of test holes (25 test holes were dug in layers and the material sifted), mapping and levelling. From these results the object collection was complimented by four trenches.

In this sandy soil area, which at one time was formed by the sea's surge, almost every stone can be seen as an artifact, transported there by man. A quantification of object and stone frequency has been an indicator of the kind and character of land use. The test holes show, namely, a variation in both the vertical and horizontal distribution of object and stone intensity within the area. In Fig. 7, for the sake of simplicity, only the stone frequency is shown since it correlates with the object frequency. The quantifications showed that in several of the test holes south of the settlement site there was a <u>lower</u> cultural level. Two C-14

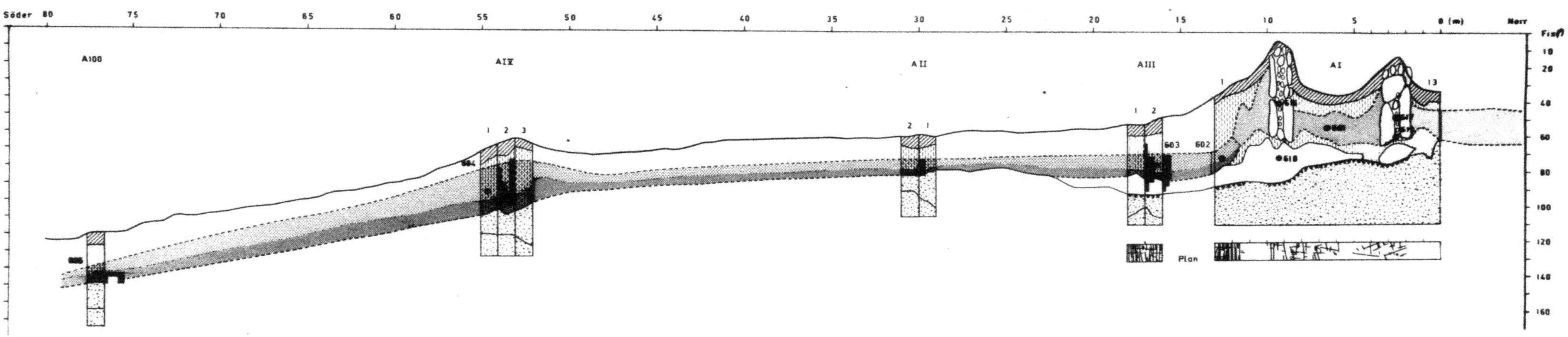

Fig. 7 Profile of land elevation and the trenches in Area A. The numbers refer to the C 14-datings in Table 2.

datings imply a large chronological span for that layer 1814 ± 127 BC and AD 282 ±162).

At a depth of 20-30 cm below the ground surface an upper cultural level was evidenced with a varying find frequency. This level was found again in connection with the settlement site and in the cultivated slope south of the terrass edge. The level, which contained a relatively large amount of bone, charcoal, pottery and small fire-cracked stones can not be related to the dwelling constructions. They have been interpreted as a result of manureing of the fields with household waste. This type of manure level, which even exists within other parts of the RA, distinguishes itself from the find material from the dwelling area itself. It is dominated by charcoal, and pottery in clearly defined cultural levels.

The test holes showed a complicated stratigraphy in the area which was studied more closely through four trenches placed in a line from the dwelling site to the terrass edge.

A trench 13 meters long was dug across the settlement site's dwelling house. Two C-14 datings and stratigraphical evidence implies that the house was established c AD 300. The house was abandoned about AD 500 according to four C-14 datings. In a carefully defined stratigraphical level below the house, two different patterns of ard marks were evidenced. In the northern part of the trench, the ard marks made up a criss-cross pattern, and in the southern part the marks were parallel to each other. Through the earthern layer along with the pattern of ard marks and height, it has been possible to establish two phases of cultivation before the house's establishment. Only one C-14 dating (618) implies the age of the stone-free culturally influenced layer (see Table 2). The dating (AD 234 ± 167) which refers to the parallel ard marks implies, for the RA, a late age of the ard marks. With information from the trench and test holes, the related fields have been possible to reconstruct. The field ought to have been rectangular, c 10 meters wide with ard marks parallel with the field surface's length. From experience from the other trenches within the RA the older and underlying cultivation ought to have taken place during the Pre-Roman Iron Age in a square field c 25 x 25 m large.

The house foundation lies at the same depth as the upper cultural layer in the area described above. This manureing layer can be followed from the house's southern long wall, over the flat surface and down to the cultivated slope south of the terrace edge. Two C-14 samples (AD 582 ± 93 and AD 552 ± 93 AD) imply an age of this level which allows the following interpretation of the cultivation development. At the time the dwelling site was being used two fields of the same size, between the dwelling site and the terrace edge, were being cultivated. The delimitation between these fields appear, among others, as a slight rise in the ground. One C-14 dating (621) in one of the test holes supports this interpretation. From the trench in the terrace edge the upper cultural layer has given the dating AD 853 ± 135 (604). This dating, together with both of the above named datings from the 500's, establishes the latest cultivation phase in the area. During the Vendel Period - Viking Age a change took place in the area between the house and the terrace edge, at which time a larger field was formed. In addition, during this time the fields south of the terrace edge were cultivated.

In the area east of the settlement, there are several flat surfaces of varying size, sunken in under the surrounding podsoil-rich land. These surfaces could, through find and stone frequencies along with slight ard

Fig. 8 A static model of the development of the agrarian landscape at Vinarve.

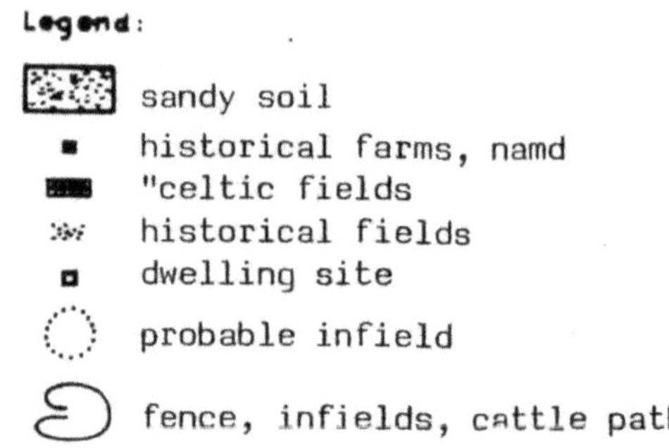

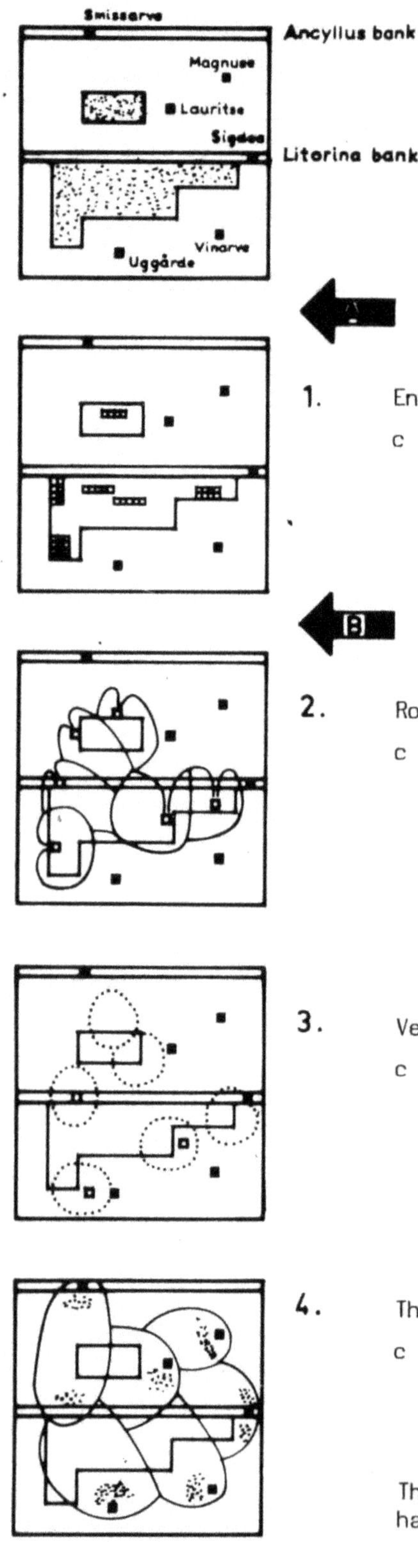

1. End of Bronze Age - Pre-Roman Iron Age
c 1000 - 0 BC

2. Roman Iron Age - Migration Period
c o - 500 AD

3. Vendel Period - Viking Age
c 500 - 1000 AD

4. The historical farms established
c 1000 - 1200 AD

The decisive stages in the development process have been marked with two arrows (A and B):

A: Introduction of an agrarian production with extensively cultivated fields.

B: Introduction of a more intensive form of agriculture built upon the three land types: fields, meadows and grazing lands.

marks, be interpreted as cultivation surfaces probably contemporary with the dwelling site.

This leads to the following conclusion of the area. The earliest activity in the area is implied by several settlement indications where a hearth has been dated to the transition between the Stone and Bronze Ages (607). During the Pre-Roman to the Roman Iron Age there are traces of two different cultivation phases in the area. This cultivation lies peripherially in relation to the more well-formed fields from this period in the RA. Both of the fields are covered by the agrarian landscape which was created by the farmers who lived in the giants' graves houses during the period AD 300 to AD 500. Cultivation during this period took place even south of the cultivation terrace along with the flat surfaces immediately south and east of the settlement. After the settlement was abandoned the fields were used during the Vendel Period - Viking Age. Then, and perhaps even at the end of the Migration Period, the fields were manured with, among other things, household waste.

The Migration Period settlement was abandoned c AD 500, but its agrarian landscape has been used even at a much later time. The datings obtained show a continual land use in the area, at least from the Pre-Roman Iron Age up until today.

CONCLUSION

In the following short conclusions, the results presented above shall be set in relation to the interpretations of the production system within the RA (see Fig. 8).

The production system during the Pre-Roman Iron Age

The production system has resulted in a large number of fields over a large area. Obviously the fields have been established in sparcely-lying groups. They have been worked extensively with long periods of fallow.

The fields and grain production does not necessarily need to mean that grain, for example, dominated the diet. Instead, agriculture ought to be seen as the only form of production during this period which placed demands on a more organized land use.

The system has its roots in the late Bronze Age. The simple settlement indications imply dwelling sites of mobile character, determined by movements in and with the practice of fallow.

With increased needs of produce from grain production, the land was cultivated more intensively. Field walls were formed. New fields were laid out on less fertile soils (in the depressions and in the sandy soils' outer edges). Different cultivation techniques were perhaps tested along with new field forms within the framework of fallow practice. Gradually the earlier and abandoned field surfaces covered larger areas and the mobility of extensive agriculture was reduced. Settlement and fields became more stationary. The demand for new forms of production increased when the then extensive practice of fallow fields did not yield sufficient produce.

The production system during the Roman Iron Age - Migration Period

The production system has a differentiated land use with permanent settlement. Grain and livestock production were combined with the land types of fields, meadows and pasture lands. This made possible the annual cultivation of relatively small fields through manureing. The settlements' location, on the border between sandy and clayey soils, meant that infields could be located on the sandy soils and pastures on the clayey soils and the non-cultivateable soils. Between the neighbouring farms common fences appear.

The production system Vendel Period - Viking Age

Even if the form elements are of the same kind as during the preceeding system, their location and character have changed. Settlements have been moved out towards the peripheral areas of the RA. Parts of the preceeding production system's form elements have been used. New fences changed parts of the earlier fence pattern. The fields were manured with both animal and household waste. The increased need of manureing of the fields initiated the exploitation of more clayey soils, which were not as easily drained as the sandy soils.

The historical production system

Even during this period the land types fields, meadows and pastures dominate. The tendency to gradually exploit the clayey soils for fields continues. Settlement locations are changed which, among other things, means that new fences are constructed. The sandy soils are used for meadows.

Summary

I see the development from the Roman Iron Age up until the historical farm as a process which was directed towards adjusting the land use and the production against the possibilities offering of the available technique and the natural landscape within the RA. Even if there are reasons, still hidden for us the traces in the field show that the used technique led to critical situations which necessarily claimed for greater changes of the agrarian landscape. Within the area which one controlled, it was possible to find solutions to, for example, the size relationships between the land types fields, meadows and pasture lands, their location on the most suitable kind of soil, and their location with respect to transportation distances between the land types in relation to the farm. Among other things, this process resulted in the abandonment of the old form elements and the creation of new ones.

The development from the Pre-Roman Iron Age to medieval times has changed from a mobile and simple to a stationary and differentiated land use. This process resulted in large connected but privately owned and enclosed meadow lands on sandy soils. In the RA these made up the central parts of a change between dry (shore walls) and damp (the depressions between the shore walls) lands, which ought to have insured winter fodder both during dry and rainy years.

At the end of the Pre-Roman Iron Age the shore walls gradually became difficult to cultivate. The earlier field surfaces and marshy areas hindered continued cultivation. In addition, the long-range effect ought to have been the difficulty of retaining the nutritional contents in the easily drainable sandy soils. The fields were for that reason established on the RA'S lighter clayey soils during the historical production system.

A part in this process has been the consideration taken and dependency upon earlier form elements. These have surely made the task of carrying out new ideas within agriculture difficult, but they could even have been used as an investment already made. The Early Iron Age agrarian landscape can, in this way, be interpreted as a step in a changing process. There is a contrinual adjustment of the agricultural production and land use to the local population's production demand against the background of availability of land and the natural landscape's characteristics within the territory which one controlled and had the possibilities to work and live.

I am grateful for the translation made by Phyllis Andersson, Stockholm.

BIBLIOGRAPHY

Abler, R., Adams, J.S. och Gould, P. 1972. Spatial organization London.

Bowen, H.C., 1963. Ancient Fields. British Association for the Advancement of Science.

Brongers, J.A. 1976 Air Photography and Celtic Field-Research in the Netherlands. ROB Amersfoort.

Carlsson, D., 1979. Kulturlandskapets utveckling på Gotland Kulturgeografiska institutionen. Stockholms Universitet. Meddelande B 49. Visby.

Crawford, O.G.S., 1928. Air Survey and Archaeology. Ordnance Survey Professional Papers Nr. 7.2 in ed. Southampton.

Damon, P.E., Ferguson, C.W., Long, A. och, Wallick, E.I., 1974. Dendrochronologic Calibration of the Radiocarbon Time Scale. American Antiquity Vol.39, Nr 2.

Gerger, T., 1978 Utbildning och samhälle. Kulturgeografiska inst. Stockholms Universitet Meddelande B 41. Stockholm.

Harvey, D., 1973. Explanation in Geography. London.

Hatt, G., 1949. Oldtidsagre. Köpenhamn.

Lindquist, S.-O. 1968 Det förhistoriska kulturlandskapet i östra Ostergötland. Acta Universitatis Stockholmiensis. Studies in North-European Archaeology 2. Stockholm.

Lindquist, S.-O., Carlsson, D. och Windelhed, B., 1973. Gotländskt kulturlandskap under äldre järnålder. Ett forskningsprojekt. Gotländskt Arkiv.

Lindquist, S.-O., 1974. The Development of the Agrarian Landscape on Gotland during the Early Iron Age. Norwegian Archaeological Review Vol. 7, No. 1.

Norrbom, C., 1973. Systemteori - en introduktion. Stockholm.

Prince, H.C., 1971. Real, imagined and abstract Worlds of the past. Progress in Geography. Vol. 3. London.

Stenberger, M. och Klindt-Jensen, O., 1955. Vallhagar. A Migration Period Settlement on Gotland/Sweden. København-Stockholm.

Wärneryd, O., 1968. Interdependence in Urban Systems. Göteborg.

Table 1 C 14 datings in Area AB

Dating of	Sample number	Age corrected	Age obtained	Taken from
Settlement remains under the ard mark layer	302 307 401	1062 ± 104 BC 1332 ± 155 BC 1494 ± 123 BC	870 ± 100 1080 ± 145 1205 ± 110	Hearth Hearth Hearth
Culturally influenced layer	303 308 408 410 514	607 ± 175 BC 296 ± 158 BC 496 ± 122 AD 1267 ± 331 BC 1474 ± 169 BC	505 ± 140 245 ± 125 475 ± 120 1030 ± 330 1190 ± 160	
Cultural layer	407	475 ± 181 AD	455 ± 180	Under the cattle path and above the culturally influenced layer
Construction of fence/cattle path	411 412	1194 ± 119 AD 1041 ± 105 AD	1200 ± 115 1035 ± 100	Bottom of these form elements Bottom of the cattle path's western fence

The C 14 datings have been analysed by Laboratory of Isotopegeology, Museum of Natural History, Stockholm. The obtained datings have been corrected according to Damon et al. (1974).

Table 2 C-14 datings in Area A (corrections see table 1)

Dating of	Sample number	Age		Taken from
		corrected	obtained	
Settlement remains under the ard marks	607	1814 ± 127 BC	1450 ± 120	hearth
Giant's graves settlement	601	475 ± 93 AD	455 ± 90	floor level in the house
	616	516 ± 93 AD	495 ± 90	southern long wall
	617	334 ± 108 AD	320 ± 105	northern long wall
	619	287 ± 138 AD	275 ± 135	under the northern long wall
	608	459 ± 93 AD	440 ± 90	hearth west of the house
	609	334 ± 94 AD	320 ± 90	hearth west of the house
Culturally influenced layer	618	234 ± 167 AD	225 ± 165	under the giant's grave house
Later cultivation layer	602	582 ± 93 AD	560 ± 90	
	603	552 ± 93 AD	530 ± 90	
	604	853 ± 135 AD	835 ± 125	
	605	42 ± 248 AD	50 ± 245	
	621	282 ± 162 AD	270 ± 160	

THE SETTLEMENT AND FARMING SYSTEM IN OSTERGOTLAND, SWEDEN A.D. 1 TO 500.

Mats Widgren

A deserted landscape - with field lynchets, stone walls and deserted farmsteads - is powerful evidence of prehistoric agriculture. The relics are all direct evidence left over from the agrarian production and indicate the level of exploitation of nature that was possible. But even if we had established a perfectly dated cross-section of a prehistoric landscape and tackled all the chronological problems, we would still only have reached the same point as the agrarian historian when he gets the old cadastral map out of the archives. The map or the relics of prehistoric landscapes give only the physical framework within which the agrarian production took place. The functioning system and the farming practice, of which the spatial arrangements on the map are only <u>one</u> aspect, remains to be interpreted by the student.

In summing up a book on field systems, Alan Baker and Robin Butlin called for a systems approach to the study of field systems. This requires

> "a search for answers to questions about the basic properties common to all systems: structure, function, equilibrium and change. It is necessary to ask of each system: what was its structure; how did it function; what degree of stability did it have; how did it evolve through time; how might it be expected to develop in the future." (Baker & Butlin 1973:628).

In the process of seeking explanations of prehistoric phenomena, we should not refrain from asking all these questions even if the answers will at best only be assumptions and at worst false speculations. The first section of this paper is aimed at the reconstruction of the agrarian landscape during the period A.D. 1 to 500 in the eastern part of the Swedish province of Ostergötland. In the second section, I seek answers to the crucial questions of how the farming system functioned and what were the weak links and the possibilities of development? In the third section, some evidence of the changes over time is presented and in the final part I ask questions about how we might expect this farming system to function in the subsequent centuries.

THE AGRARIAN LANDSCAPE IN EASTERN OSTERGOLAND, A.D. 1 TO 500

The inconsiderable surface features of the Early Iron Age house foundations on the Swedish mainland have hampered research, as compared with the developments on the islands of Oland and Gotland. At the time when Stenberger was discussing farming on Oland during the early Iron Age (Stenberger 1933), the corresponding evidence of prehistoric stone walls and fields in Östergötland was discussed in terms of <u>cult</u> or <u>fortifications</u> (Edlund 1926, Nordén 1930, 1942). The following survey will be based on

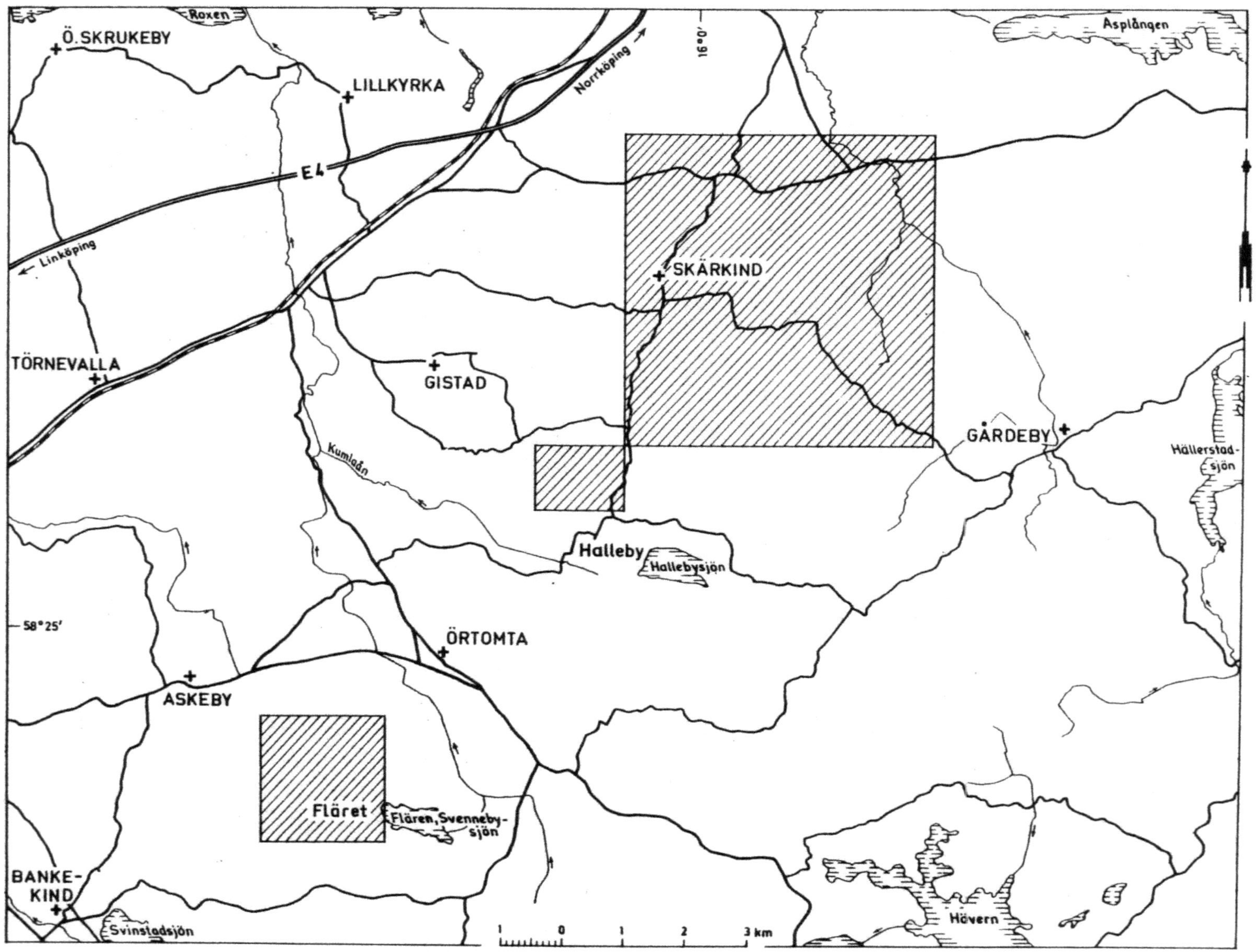

FIG 1: A part of the plain south of lake Roxen, Ostergötland. Areas mentioned in the text are shaded.

investigations carried out in the 1960's by Sven-Olof Lindquist (1968) and Evert Baudou (1973), as well as on my own material (Widgren 1977, 1979 and unpublished manuscripts).

Halleby

The work of Lindquist was to a large extent based on investigations in the deserted settlement at Halleby (Figs. 1 and 2) but also included mappings of three other localities in Östergötland, as well as a regional analysis. Lindquist discerned two types of field walls:

(1) Stone walls serving as barriers between different types of land-use (Sw. hägnad. In this paper the phrase stone walls will be used for this type.).

(2) Field walls with other functions: earth banks, lynchets, field walls with one row of stones. Most of the field walls of this type have been boundaries within the arable area (Sw. begränsningar) (Lindquist 1968:12).

On the basis of excavations of the settlements and field walls, Lindquist dated the deserted agrarian landscape in the Roman Iron Age:

> "The settlement was loosely grouped, but functionally united to villages (Sw. by) through the development of the physical structure of the agrarian landscape. Common greens, cattle paths and infields (Sw. gärden) are created in this connection." (Lindquist 1968: 155, transl. by M.W.).

The excavations of the settlement at Halleby showed that the settlement had been deserted at the end of the fifth century, resettled during the sixth century and finally deserted during the seventh century A.D. (Baudou 1973, Lindquist 1968). The datings of the stone walls were however questioned by Baudou. The settlement and the arable land were directly dated by Lindquist through excavations, while no stratigraphic datings of the stone walls, enclosing the arable land and functionally uniting the settlement to a village-like type of community were made.

Baudou felt it to be most likely that

> "as fences at Halleby the field walls date from historical times, chiefly medieaval times or the end of the Iron Age at the earliest" (Baudou 1973:131).

He considered the field walls at Halleby to be a conglomeration of vestiges from different periods and with different functions. The spatial connection between the farmsteads, the arable land and the associated system of stone walls is, of course, in itself a very strong circumstantial evidence of the contemporaneousness - a method of dating the stone walls that has been accepted on Gotland and Oland (Klindt-Jensen 1955:836, Stenberger 1933:104). The fact that similar kinds of stone walls were incidentally in use later does not change this dating. Recently some stratigraphical datings of stone walls in the Roman Iron Age have also been made (Nilsson 1976a; see also below).

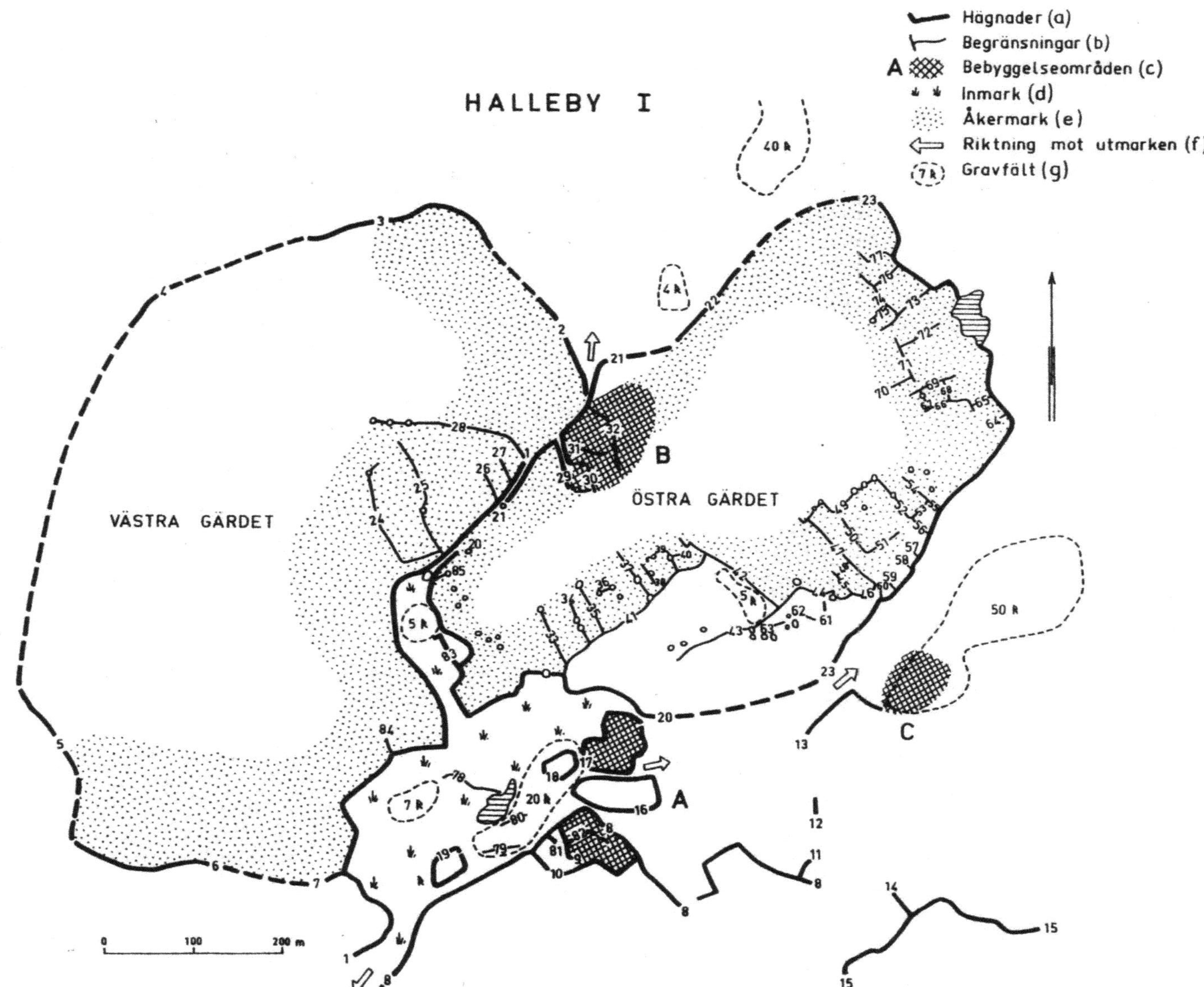

FIG. 2: The Halleby area. (a) barriers, (b) other field walls (c) settlement areas, (d) green, (e) arable land, (f) towards the common pasture, (g) burial ground (from Lindquist, 1968:39).

Thus the research results so far point to a parallel development in Östergötland, on Gotland and in the south-western part of Norway. An agrarian landscape with fixed boundaries between areas of land with different land uses has been established in the first few centuries A.D. It is based on a combination of arable farming and cattle-breeding and the fields have probably been manured. In the sixth century the landscape was restructured and a number of farms were deserted (Carlsson 1979, Stenberger 1933, Myhre 1979).

Skärkind

The problem of the farming system was never explicitly dealt with by Lindquist. The layout of the fields at Halleby, and the model of the agrarian development presented by Lindquist, suggest a structure very similar to that recorded in the seventeenth century maps. The settlement consisted of three or four farms united in a village. Only in the settlement localisation does the structure dating from the Roman Iron Age that Lindquist presents differ from the seventeenth century structure. But the Halleby site is in that respect unique. It forms an enclave in an area of outlying lands. An area of more intensive, prehistoric land-use is situated only some few kilometres north of Halleby. The abandoned stone walls and settlements in that area present another picture. They show a fully occupied landscape, where the proportion of enclosed land might have been the same as during historical times. In that area - the eastern part of Skärkind parish - the fossil traces of the early Iron Age landscape have been compared with the historical landscape (Fig.3). Cadastral maps from the period 1696 to 1769 form the basis of the reconstruction of settlement and land-use during the eighteenth century. Within the area, there were ten vills (Sw. <u>byar</u>) with two to five farms each and five single farms. All the vills and the farms had their fields divided into two enclosures - their tillers were thus practising a two-course rotation. The average area of these farms was 14 ha of arable land and 17.5 ha of meadow land.

In a field survey, all the abandoned stone walls and house terraces in the area were recorded. Two settlements had been recorded and documented earlier (Augustenhill and Skärkinds prästgård, Lindquist 1968, Klang & Widgren 1973). Two more settlements, along with a vast system of stone walls, were found. The four deserted farmsteads have to be considered as a rather small sample of the contemporary landscape. In the area, 20 further sites that <u>might</u> have harboured prehistoric agrarian settlements have been altered to such an extent that the earlier history of the site cannot be assessed from field observations (Widgren 1982).

The prehistoric landscape is characterized by single farmsteads or groups of farmsteads, knit together by the system of stone walls. A certain part of the stone walls can be analysed with regard to their function. Cattle paths leading from large areas of till and exposed bedrock to the settlement sites allow of a reconstruction of enclosed/unenclosed land. Within the enclosed land, signs of stone clearance for tilling can be found on sandy soils while the greater part of the enclosed land comprises former meadowland, mainly consisting of postglacial fine clay, in places covered with different organic deposits.

The system of abandoned stone walls has no connection with the historical landscape. The property boundaries of the vills with prehistoric names often cut across the system of stone walls. Two of the settlement

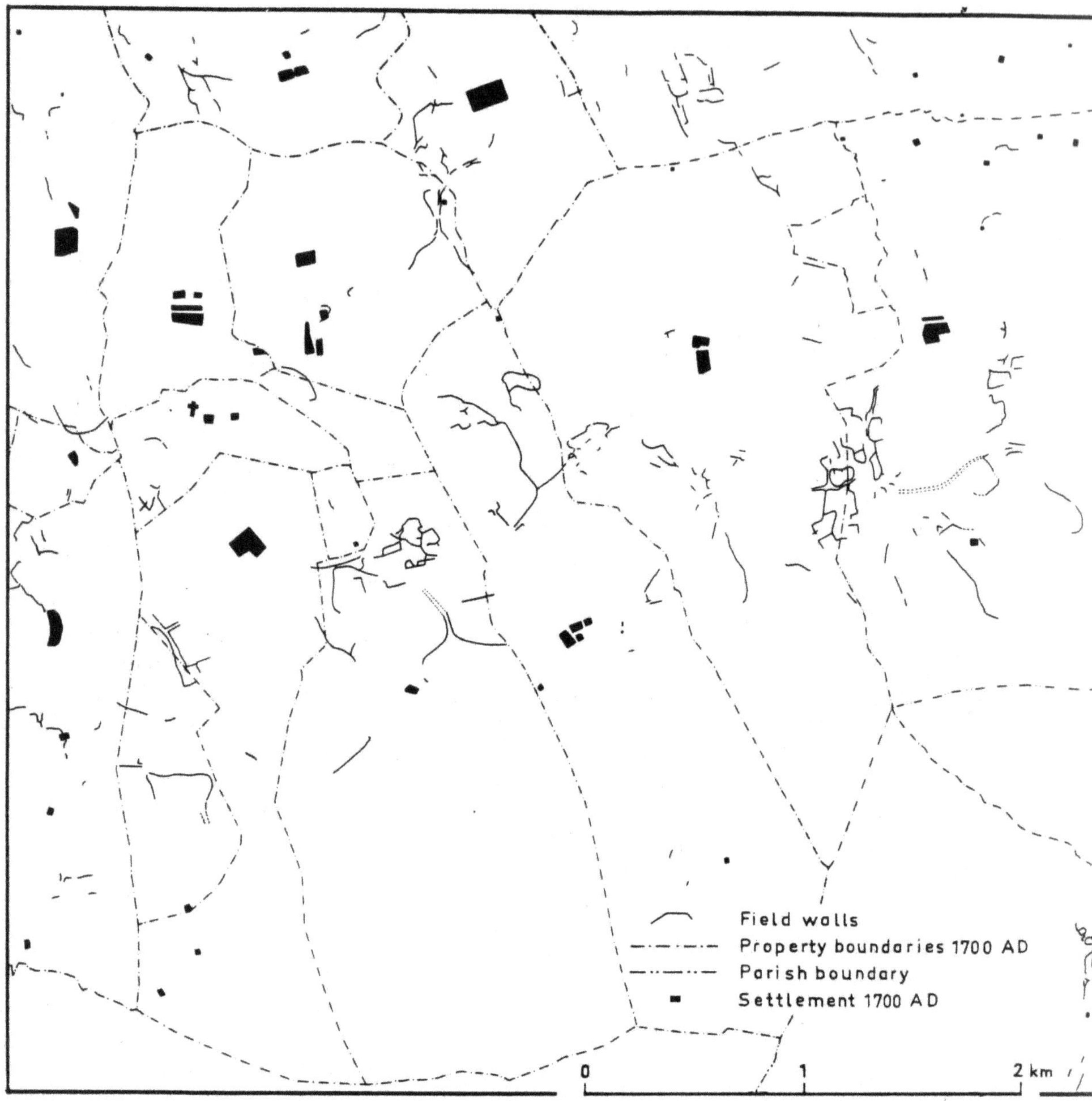

FIG.: 3 A comparison of field walls and the historic landscape in the Skärkind area.

sites are situated on or very close to later boundaries. Outside the investigated area there are also examples of parish boundaries of mediaeval or earlier origin which cut through prehistoric farm complexes. The restructuring of the agrarian landscape to which this is a witness evidently started as early as the middle of the Iron Age. Cattle paths and stone walls dating from the Roman Iron Age can be found overlain by graves dating from the Vendel and Viking periods.

Deserted farms now situated on land belonging to different vills had in the prehistoric landscape common cattle paths and were connected by the system of stone walls, suggesting a co-operation between single farmsteads in the uses of common pasture and in the maintenance of stone walls. This territorial organisation stretches over areas larger than the historical vills. The comparison of the eighteenth century landscape with the prehistoric thus shows two totally different, spatial systems superimposed on the same physical landscape. The basic differences of the two spatial systems can be traced back to the farming system practised during the different periods.

Fläret

The location and density of settlement on a stone-wall system have been investigated in the area west of the present farm Fläret (Fig.1). Due to its peripheral location, this area had been less altered by later activities than the Skärkind area. The stone-wall system stretches across several historical vills and in the south-west it is connected with further stone walls not documented here. A cattle path stretches in a north-westerly direction through the area and opens out to form a green at two places in the central part of the map (Fig.4). This part of the area had earlier been documented by Lindquist (1968) and he has also proved the existence of house terraces within the greens.

The settlement sites have been dated through small test excavations and the dated material is charcoal from fireplaces and settlement layers. Radiocarbon dates of material from settlement sites functionally connected with the stone-wall system are shown in Fig. 6. The diagram must be read with the investigation method in mind. A complete excavation of the five settlement sites would probably produce a more refined chronology. It is not probable that the radiocarbon dates cover the whole settlement period at each site.

With the possible exception of Fläret 3, which had produced datings earlier than the other sites and whose stone walls have no direct connection with the rest of the system, the datings suggest that the sites were occupied contemporaneously. The lack of datings in the fourth and fifth centuries may reflect the weakness of the investigation method. Undisturbed fireplaces and layers from lower levels have been preferred for the radiocarbon dating. In the upper layers of trenches at sites Fläret 1 and Fläret 2 potsherds from strainers used for cheese-making have been found. They are frequently found in fortified settlements of the fifth and sixth centuries and may indicate later datings than the radio-carbon samples.

In spite of a phosphate mapping covering the whole area of stone walls and test excavations at all the indicated sites, no settlement datings later than the sixth century have yet been obtained in the area. A dating of the stone walls to the end of the Iron Age or later seems to be out of the

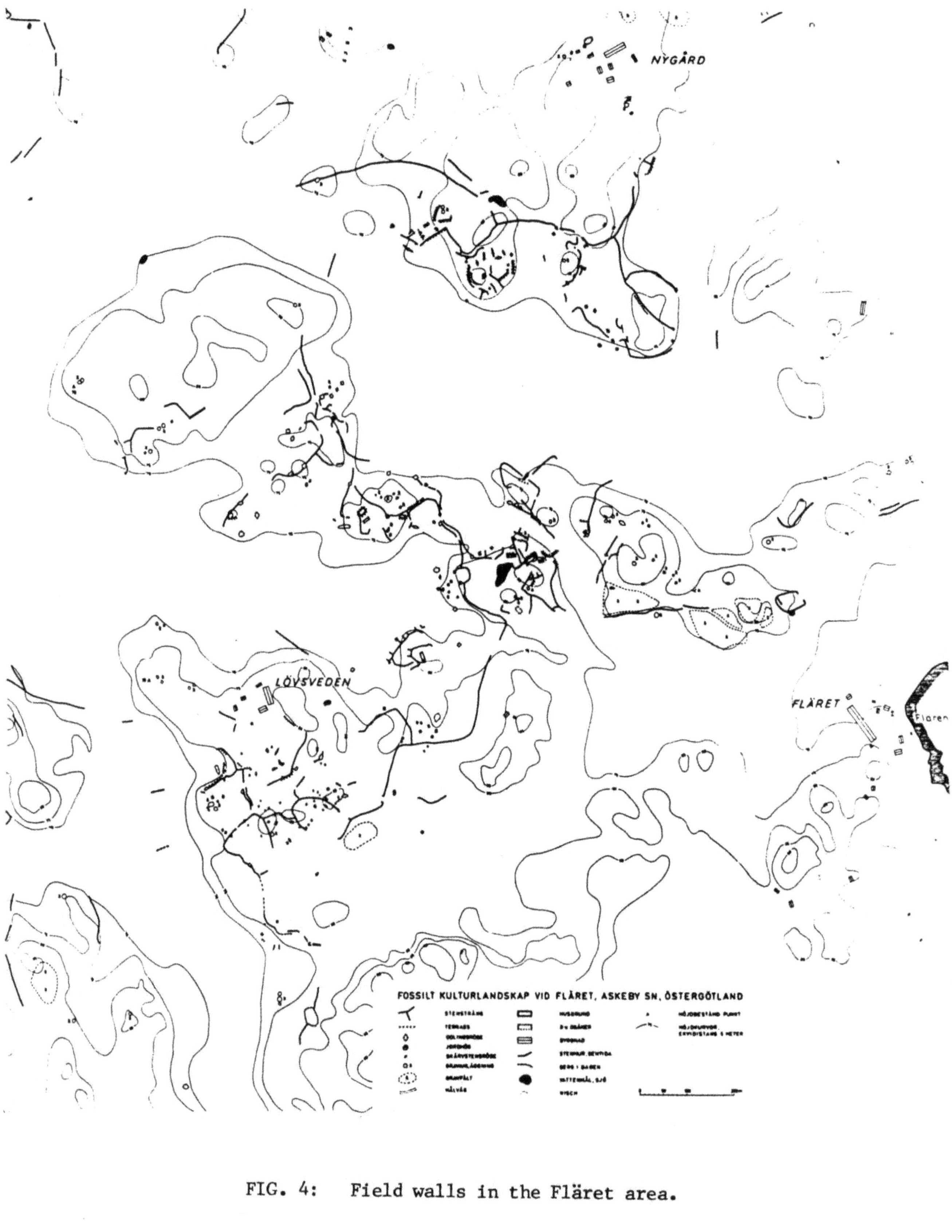

FIG. 4: Field walls in the Fläret area.

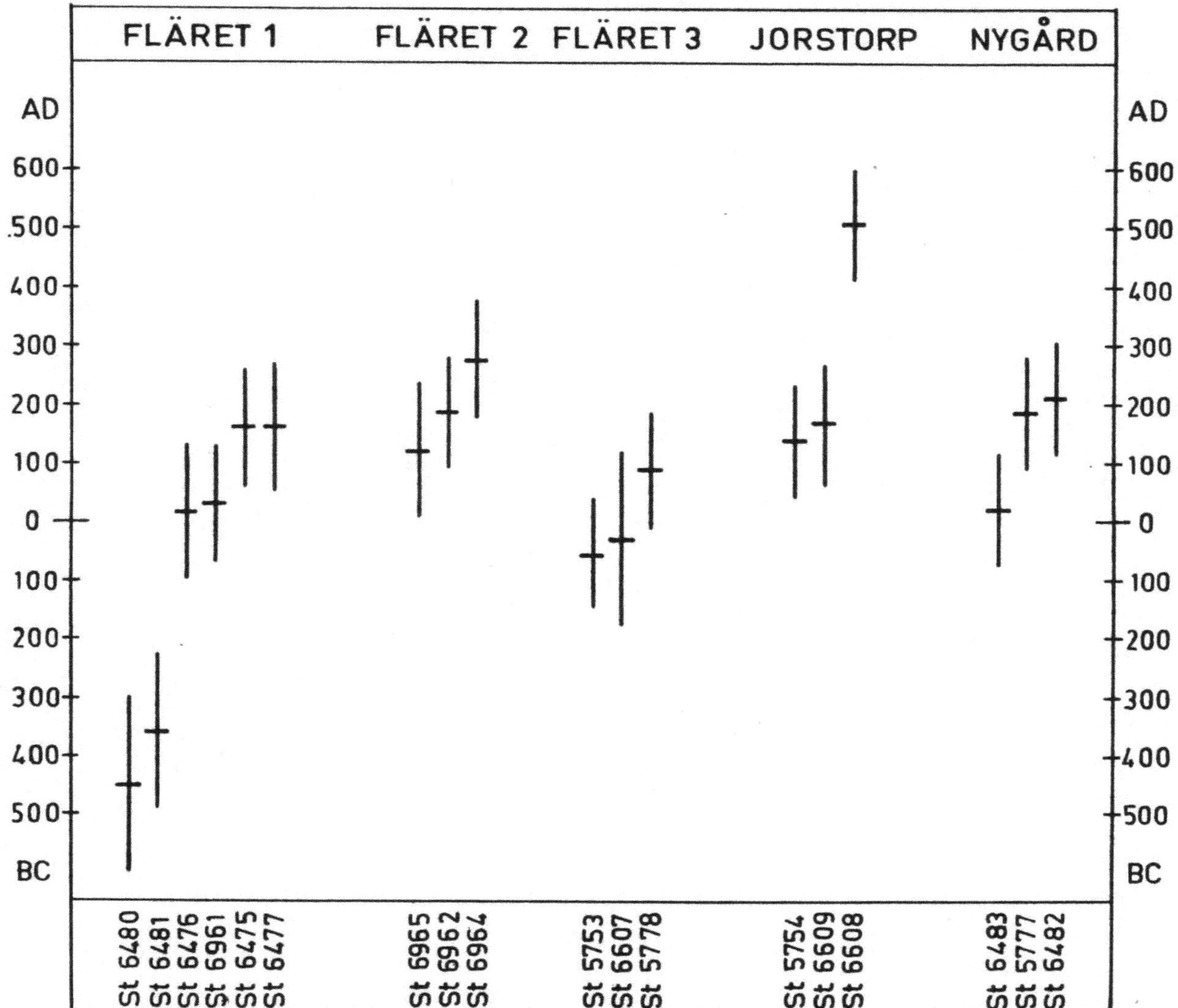

FIG. 5: Radiocarbon dates of charcoal from settlements in the Fläret area. The values are corrected according to Damon et al, 1974.

question, bearing in mind the functional connection between the settlement, cattle paths and stone walls enclosing the infield. Some direct datings of stone walls have also been made. A fireplace underlying a stone wall has been dated in the third and fourth centuries B.C., while a fireplace at the Nygård site overlying a stone wall was dated in the first and second centuries A.D. At the site designated Fläret 2, a cultural layer overlying a stone wall was dated in the second century A.D. Taken together, the datings of settlements and stone walls indicate that the stone-wall system was established during the first and second centuries A.D.

During the second and third centuries and maybe during the fourth and fifth centuries the number of farms in this area of 4 square kilometres was thus four or five. This corresponds to a density of one farm per square kilometre.

The agrarian landscape: A summary

The basic unit in the agrarian landscape was the single farm. In principle, the farms in Ostergötland had the same structure as the farms in south-western Norway of the simple type (Myhre 1973:21) or the single farms on Gotland during the same period (cf. Carlsson 1979:109). In Östergötland, the enclosed infield comprised both arable land and meadow. A cattle path connected the green around the settlement with the common pasture. However, this principal farm structure in the physical landscape of eastern Ostergötland, with its mixture of small hills and lowlying clay lands, developed into a more complex structure. The grouping of many farmsteads around a common infield can be compared with the Norwegian farms of the complex type (Myhre 1973). The association between the basic farm structure and the more complex structure found in Östergöland has been treated in another work (Widgren 1979). The layout of the stone walls and the locations of the settlements suggest that the vestiges represent an infield system with intensively tilled fields and enclosed meadows.

The central parts of eastern Ostergötland were fully colonised during the fourth and fifth centuries A.D. Pollen analyses and the distribution of ancient monuments also suggest that there was an expansion into marginal woodlands during the period (Göransson 1977:125, Nilsson 1976b). In the denser parts of the landscape each square kilometre might have harboured a farm. The areas covered by a group of farms with a common enclosure might have varied, but in many cases they exceeded the mediaeval villages.

FARMING SYSTEM

The spatial organisation of settlements and stone walls has many parallels in the infield-outfield systems that functioned in historical times in different parts of Europe (cf. Uhlig 1961, Dodgshon 1978 (Scotland), Smith 1967:270 (England), Brandt & Rasmussen 1976 (Faroe Islands), Lindgren 1939 (Sweden).

The term "infield-outfield" has been used in Scandinavian archaeological literature (Welinder 1975:84, Myhre 1979) in a very broad sense, meaning a farming system "utilizing its area at two different levels of intensity: an intensively farmed infield and an outfield exploited at a low intensity" (Christiansen 1978). In the English geographical terminology, the term has been restricted to systems of land-use "whereby the infield was manured and grew crops continuously, and the outfield was cultivated in temporary breaks" (Adams 1976:155; cf. Uhlig 1961:287). In such a system, one usually finds three levels of exploitation: infield (sown annually), outfield (shifting cultivation) and common grazing.

It is suggested that this kind of farming system had its roots in a simpler, infield system with "a single cultivated area or infield, surrounded by commonty" (Dodgshon 1973:18). The outfield, with its shifting cultivation, is, according to Dodgshon, to be regarded as a secondary element established at the commonty.

The infield systems established on Gotland, in Jaeren and in Östergötland during the Roman Iron Age were of this simple type. A diagrammatic representation of the movement of livestock and the use of their manure in such an infield system with common grazings is presented by Dodgshon (Fig. 6). The strength of such a system lies in its low establishing costs (Christiansen 1978); the length of the fences is small, compared with systems with regular fallow, and the tilled area is small. Infield systems are usually associated with low yield ratios. At the same time, the effects of an increase in manuring are very great, when operating with low yield ratios (Christiansen 1978, van Bath 1963).

The stability of the system is based on the flow of nutrients from the common pasture and the meadow to the arable land in the infield. The establishment of infield systems in Scandinavia during the Roman Iron Age thus represents the first integration between arable farming and cattle-breeding. The relation between the size of the arable land and the number of animals is crucial to the stability of the system. The winter fodder harvested on the meadows fed not only the animals but indirectly also the arable land. The saying that "the meadow is the mother of the arable" expresses this interdependence between the different land states. Although the arable land only covered small areas, the calorie content of the cereals might have played a major role in the food consumption.

The ecological balance in such a system is dependent on decisions made at three levels corresponding to different territorial levels. The spatial correspondence between farmstead and cultivated fields suggests that the individual farm formed the basic unit, with a private usufruct of the cultivated fields. But since the farms were knit together by a common system of stone walls, this "enclosure society" (sw. hägnadslag) must have played a central role in the agrarian system (cf. Erixon 1962). The Swedish mediaeval laws point to the essential function of the fences in the local community (Myrdal 1977).

In infield systems in which many farms had a share in the same infield, there were always regulations on the use of the infield. The private usufruct - if it existed - was restricted to the period between sowing and harvesting. The members of the "enclosure society" exercised a common right of pasture over the infield after harvest (Lindgren 1939:157; Brandt & Rasmussen 1976:50).

Changes of land-use within the infield, such as converting meadow to arable land, must also have been regulated within this community.

The rights of common grazing on the waste represent a third territorial level in an agrarian landscape in which an infield system with common grazing was practised. In the central part of eastern Oastergötland, the

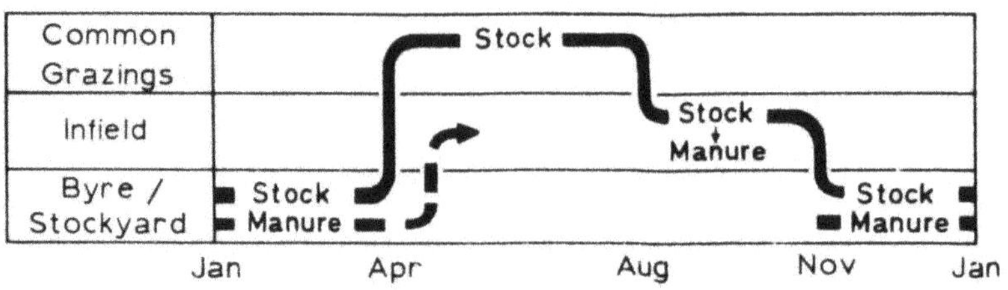

FIG. 6: Diagrammatic representation of the movement of livestock and the use of their manure in a system consisting only of infield and common grazings (from Dodgshon, 1973:18).

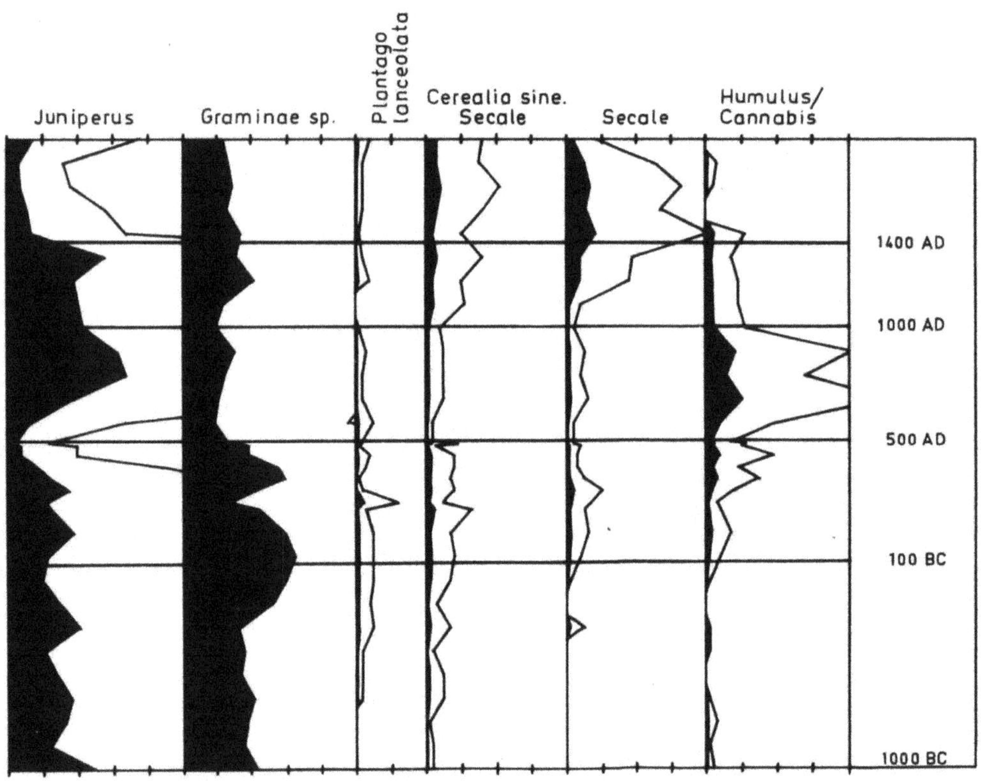

FIG. 7: Pollen diagram from lake Flären (detail). For the complete diagram see Widgren, 1977.

unenclosed areas were few and from the number of cattle paths running to some of them, one may conclude that many farms were dependent on the for grazing. Their use must have been regulated by an organisation at a higher level than the "enclosure societies". Regulations at this level can, for example, be found in the oldest written document on the Faroe Islands (Brandt & Rasmussen 1976:49). The regulations within the "enclosure society" and within the higher organisation exercising the right over the common pastures were of vital importance for the ecological stability of the farming system.

THE VEGETATIONAL DEVELOPMENT

The period between the establishment of the infield system and its final restructuring during the fifth and sixth centuries A.D. corresponds roughly to the period of agricultural expansion documented in many pollen-analytical works (summarized in Berglund (1969) and Welinder (1975)). During this period, the structure of the agrarian landscape was probably not constant. The archeological source material from the period represents the peak of the development (cf Welinder 1977:189). It allows only to some extent of conclusions about the changes during the expansion period. The pollen-analytical investigations of the vegetational development make possible independent, continuous description of changes in land-use.

A pollen diagram from Lake Fläran, which is situated in the close vicinity of the prehistoric settlement at Fläret, shows a clear expansion of the human influence in the landscape during the period 100 B.C. to A.D. 500 (zone B in Fig.8). The frequency of the herb pollen during this period is higher than in recent times. This - together with the high values for pine - witnesses to a very open landscape, characterized by large pastures. The establishment of the infield system coincides with the introduction of rye (Secale) and pollen of the hemp/hop type. The increase in agrarian production, evidenced especially by the curves for the cereals, reaches a peak at about A.D. 300.

The relation between arable farming and cattle-breeding can to some extent be analysed from the relation between the pollens of ribwort plantain (Plantago Lanceolata) and the cereals (Fig. 8 cf Lange 1971, 1975, Welinder 1975). The arithmetical mean of this ratio during the period studied is plotted as a straight line in the diagram. For longer periods, this ratio is lower than the mean only at the beginning of zone A (corresponding to the late Bronze Age) and in the period after A.D. 1000. In the Bronze Age, we may assume that the restoration of nutrition to the soil was achieved by shifting cultivation of some kind. In historical times, we know that the two-field system and, later, modern crop rotations and chemical fertilizers have partly replaced farmyard manure.

A change towards a greater role for arable farming is, however, also to be seen at a time corresponding to 300 A.D. in the diagram. During the last part of zone B, the expansion of the stock and the pasture lands evidently did not keep pace with the expansion of the cultivated lands. It may indicate exploitation very close to the limits of the farming system. From this date, a regression of the pasture lands and of the cereals can be seen, culminating at about A.D. 500, when the juniper, indicating pastured lands, has its lowest values for 3000 years. The simultaneous birch maximum is interpreted as an invasion of Betula verrucosa on drained soils earlier covered with juniper. Although there is a decline in the cereal frequency

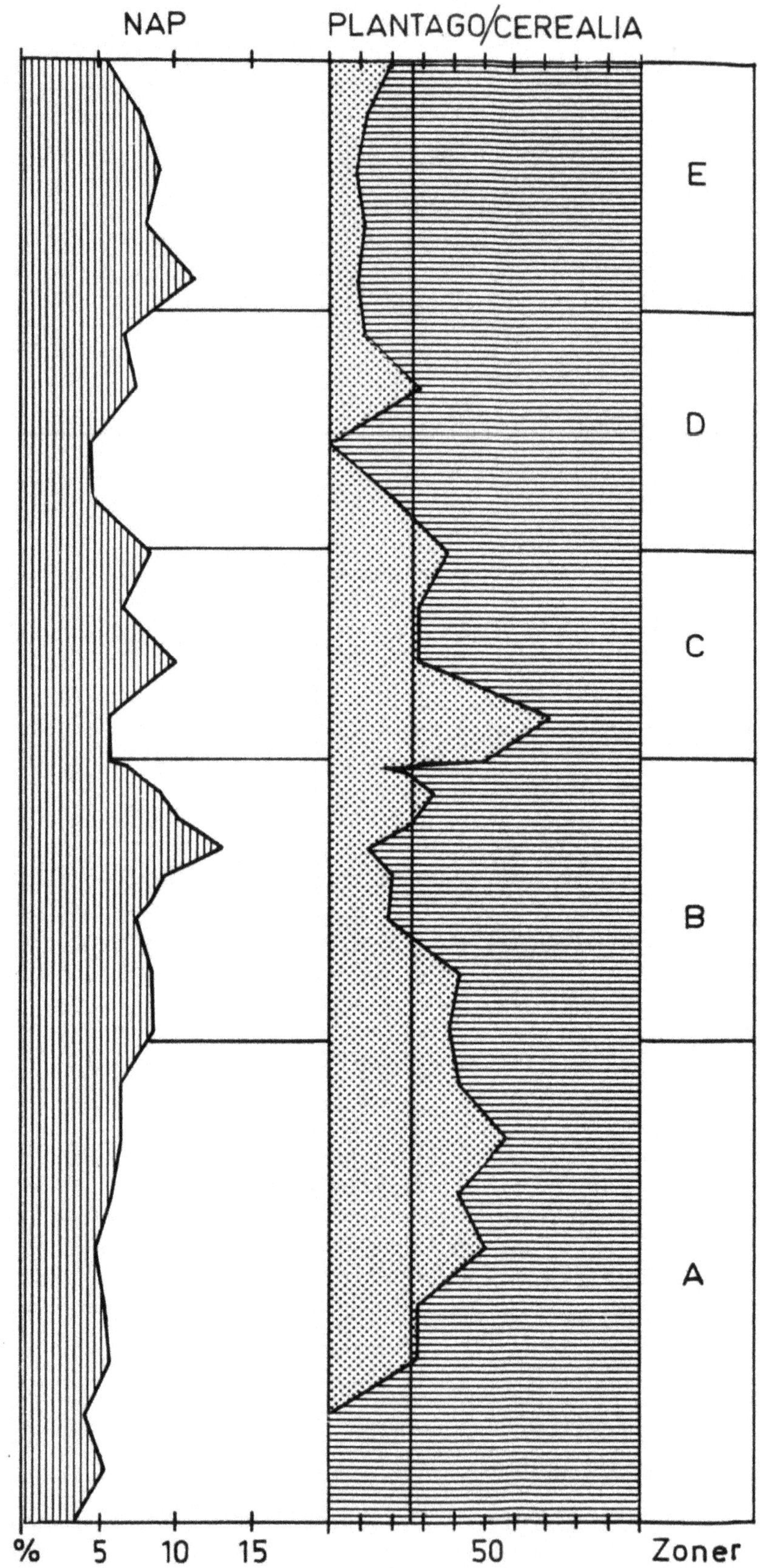

FIG. 8: Development of open land and of the pasture/arable index. The left column shows the ratio between pollen from herbs and pollen from arboreal species. The right column shows the ratio between the pollen from the ribwort plantain and the cereals (excl. *Secale*).

at this time, no break can be proved in the continuity of cultivation. The wild grasses, the juniper and the cereals all recover soon after the regression.

The vegetational development, however, shows that the restructuring of the agrarian landscape that took place around A.D. 500 was associated with an agrarian crisis, with decreasing food production in the area.

CONCLUSIONS

In considering the development possibilities of the farming system of the period, three points have to be considered:

1. The eastern central part of Ostergötland during the end of the expansion period was fully occupied and an expansion into marginal lands can be documented. A development of farming through the establishment of more farms in the central part was no longer possible.

2. A social and territorial organisation closely associated with the farming system must have existed. The ecological balance of agrarian production was dependent on the authority of this organisation, which was associated with other territories than those found in early mediaeval times.

3. Any change in the system of land-use and nutrient circulation would require a new spatial and social organisation. The system of closely related farmsteads knit together by a common system of stone walls might at one stage have hampered the further development of the farming system.

At the time of the agrarian crisis and the restructuring of the landscape which occurred in the fifth and sixth centuries, this system of farming practices and social organisation was evidently developed to a point beyond which no increase in production and population was any longer possible without drastic changes in social and/or spatial organisation. The subsequent agrarian landscape is very little known and at this stage it is not possible to depict the farming system of the late Iron Age.

ACKNOWLEDGEMENTS

Elisabeth Hedlund and Katarina Strömdahl-Lillteir drew the maps and diagrams. The text was linguistically revised by Neil Tomkinson, B.A.

The manuscript was completed in March 1980. A final publication of the research in Ostergötland has since then been printed: Mats Widgren, Settlement and farming systems in the early Iron Age. A study of fossil agrarian landscapes in Ostergötland, Sweden. Almquist & Wiksell International 1983. ISBN 91 - 22 - 00602 - 8. pp. 132.

BIBLIOGRAPHY

Adams, I.H. 1976, Agrarian Landscape Terms, London

Baker, A.R.H. & Butlin R.A. 1973, Conclusion: Problems and Perspectives, in Baker & Butlin (Ed): Studies of field systems in the British Isles, (Cambridge)

van Bath, S., 1963, The agrarian history of western Europe, (London)

Baudou, E., 1973, Arkeologiska undersökningar på Halleby. Del 1. (Stockholm).

Berglund, B., 1969, Vegetation and human influence in South Scandinavia during Prehistoric time, in OIKOS Suppl. 12, (Copenhagen).

Brandt, J. & Rasmussen, R.O., 1976, Historisk materialisme og Økologiske kriser, Fagligt Forum, Kulturgeografiska haefter, 1976 29-55, (København.).

Carlsson, D., 1979, Kulturlandskapets utveckling på Gotland, Visby.

Christiansen, S., 1978, Infield-Outfield systems - characteristics and development in different climatic environments, Geografisk Tidsskrift 77:1-5, (København).

Damon, P.E. Ferguson, C.W. Long A. Wallrek E.I. Dendro- chronologic calibration of the radiocarbon timescale, American antiquity Vol 39. 1974.

Dodgshon, R.A., 1973, The nature and development of Infield-Outfield in Scotland, Transactions of the Institute of British Geographers 59 (1973) 1-23.

Dodgshon, R.A., 1978, The origin of the two- and three-field system in Eengland: A new perspective, Geographia Polonica, 38, 49-63.

Edlund, N.D. 1926, Våra östgötska förfäders värn mot fienden, Norrköpings tidningar 20/2 - 13/3 1926, (Norrköping).

Erixon, S., 1962, Swedish Villages without Systematic Regulation, Geografiska Annaler, 1961:1-2, (Stockholm).

Göransson, H., 1977, The Flandrian Vegetational History of Southern Östergötland, (Lund).

Klang, L. & Widgren, M., 1973, Det fossila kulturlandskapet vid Skärkinds prästgård, Ostergötlands län, Kulturgeografiskt seminarium 1/73, (Stockholm).

Klindt-Jensen, O., 1955, Economic and daily life at Vallhagar, in Stenberger (ed): Vallhagar a migration period settlement on Gotland/Sweden, 832-862, (Copenhagen).

Lange, E. 1971, Botanische Beiträge zur mitteleuropäischen Siedlungsgeschichte, Schriften zur Ur- und Frügeschichte 27, (Berlin).

Lange, E., 1975, The development of agriculture during the first millenium A.D., Geologiska Föreningens Förhandlingar 97, 115-24, (Uppsala).

Lindgren, G., 1939, Falbygden och dess närmaste omgivning vid 1600-talets mitt. En kulturgeografisk studie. (Uppsala).

Lindquist, S.O., 1968, Det förhistoriska kulturlandskapet i östra Östergötland, (Stockholm).

Myhre, B., 1973, The Iron Age Farm in Southwest Norway, Norwegian Archaeological Review Vol 6 14-29, (Oslo).

Myhre, B., 1979, Agrarian development, settlement history, and social organisation in Southwest Norway in the Iron Age, in Kristiansen, K & Paludan-Müller C (eds): New Directions in Scandinavian Archaeology (224-271), (Odense).

Myrdal, J. 1977, Hägnaderna, arbetstiden och bygdelaget, RIG 60/3 66-75, (Stockholm).

Nilsson, C. 1976a, Fornlämning 4, del av gravfält, stensträng och boplatslämningar, ROBY, SLAKA SOCKEN, OSTERGOTLAND, Riksantikvarieämbetet, Rapport 1976 B 28, (Stockholm).

Nilsson, C. 1976b, Forntiden i Södra Kinda, En bok om Kisa socken, Band 2, pp 5-80, (Linköping).

Nordén, A. 1930, Stensträngarnas ålder och uppgift, Fornvännen

Nordén, A. 1942, Östergötlands järnålder 2, (Stockholm).

Smith, C.T., 1967, An Historical Geography of Western Europe before 1800, (London).

Stenberger, M., 1933, Öland under äldre järnåldern, (Stockholm).

Uhlig, H., 1961, Old hamlets with infield and outfield systems in western and central Europe, Geografiska Annaler XLII 1-2 285-312, (Stockholm).

Welinder, S., 1975, Prehistoric agriculture in Eastern Middle Sweden, (Lund).

Widgren, M., 1977, Pollenanalys från sjön Flären, Kulturgeografiskt seminarium 6/77, (Stockholm).

Widgren, M. 1979, A simulation model of farming systems and land use in Sweden during the Iron Age, Journal of Historical Geography Vol 5(1), 1979 21-32.

Widgren, M., 1982, Field evidence in Historical Geography - a negative sample, in Baker, A.R.H. & Billinge M. (eds), Period and Place, Research Methods in Historical Geography, (Cambridge University Press).

CHANGE AND CONTINUITY IN THE IRON AGE SETTLEMENT OF GOTLAND

Dan Carlsson

Background

The period A.D. 400-600 was a time of change in the greater part of northern Europe (Stenberger 1955 a, Lindquist 1968, Myhre 1972, 1973, Lange 1975, Wilson 1976, Schmid 1974 and others). As far as Sweden is concerned a number of pollen diagrams from different parts of the country show an apparently similar course of development, implying a period of regression of the cultural landscape during the Migration period, and another during the 14th century (Berglund 1969, Welinder 1974, Widgren 1977, Pålsson 1977). In certain areas with a specific kind of ancient remains, mainly represented by building remains visible above ground level (stone foundations), it is considered possible to trace this decline in the using of the cultural landscape in the field material (Stenberger 1933, 1955 a, Königsson 1968, Lindquist 1968, Myhre 1972 and others).

The interpretations put forward concerning the causes of the declining using of the cultural landscape on Gotland are probably so well known that they need not be repeated. For a summary of the different interpretations the reader is referred to Stenberger 1955, Nylén 1962, Gräslund 1973 and Beskow-Sjöberg 1977.

A basic hypothesis in the discussion of the Migration period devastation is that the building remains are all from deserted farms, a kind of abandoned impoverished settlement (Almgren 1957:243, Nylén 1962:180 and others). Certain farms of course continued to exist; the rich settlements and the stone foundations within these settlements 'must have been eroded by later settlements with their need of material' (Nylén 1973:31).

The stone foundations are evidently limited in time, and, as far as I know, is no other type of building from the period A.D. 200-600 known hitherto, with the possible exception of building No. 2 at Stånga (Carlsson 1979:78). It implies, of course, that other house constructions were also used, as for instance the house remains without stone walls found in the surroundings of Skedemosse on Oland (Beskow-Sjöberg 1977). Apart from the walls, interpreted as being built of peat, these buildings do not seem to diverge from the typical stone foundations on Oland as far as construction is concerned. The newly found building remains 'are situated in an area almost free from stone foundations (Königsson, E.-S. - Königsson, L.-K. 1976:54). It means, probably, that the local building material has been used. There are no such evident gaps in the distribution of stone foundations on Gotland except, possibly, the northernmost and southernmost parts of the island (see Figure 1). This fact indicates that no agrarian settlement of extensive proportions with divergent building construction, today no longer visible, existed.

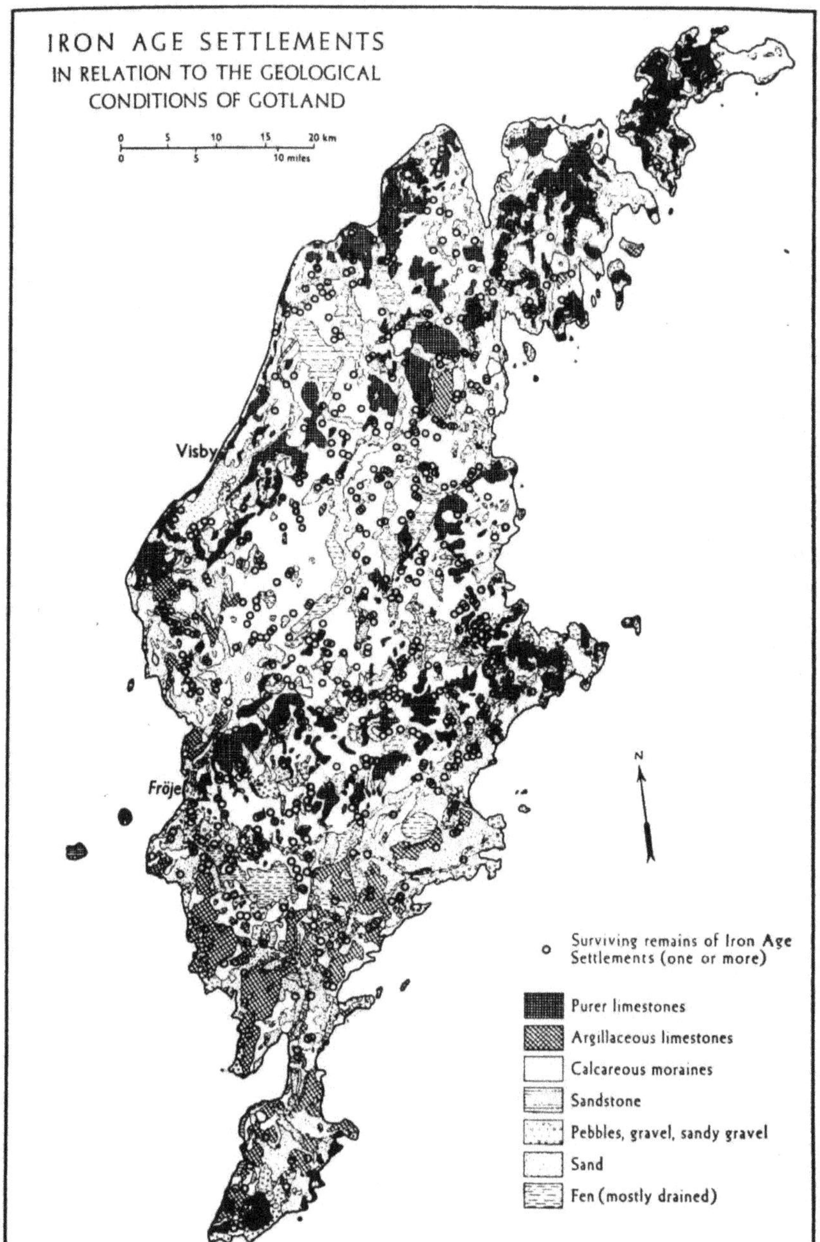

FIGURE 1: The distribution of the stone foundations on Gotland. Source, Pettersson, 1955.

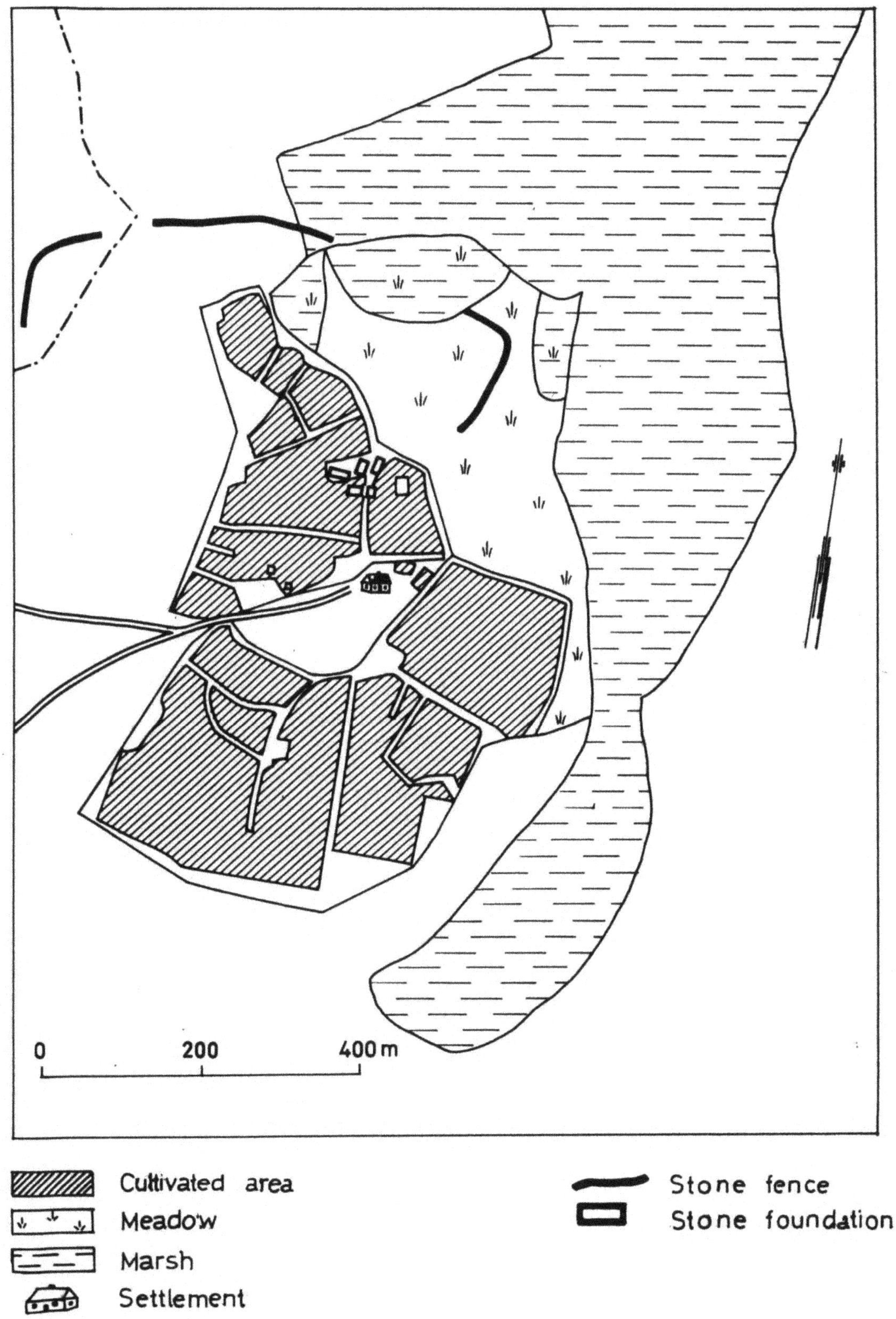

FIGURE 2: The farmstead Krasse in the parish of Guldrupe in the year 1702, together with the other prehistoric remains.

Infields, 17oo AD.

Settlement, 1700 AD.

Limit infields, 500 AD.

Settlements, 500 AD.

Single burials, 500 AD.

Cementeries

Parish border

Road

Moors

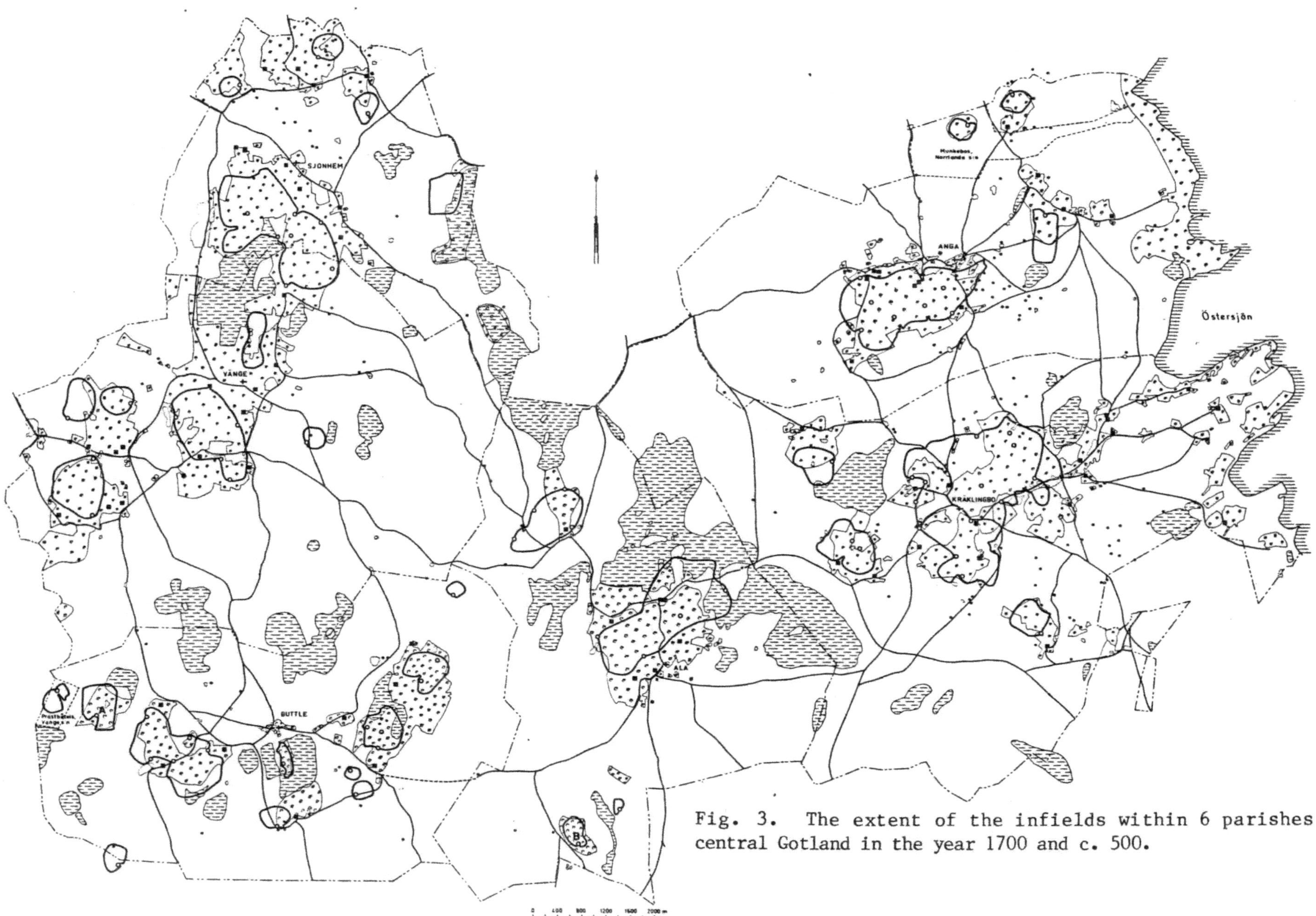

Fig. 3. The extent of the infields within 6 parishes in central Gotland in the year 1700 and c. 500.

The most far-reaching destruction of stone foundations has no doubt taken place in connection with the great breaking up of land for cultivation during the late 19th century and the beginning of the 20th century. The intensity of the destruction is likely to have varied greatly from one area to another. The parish of Buttle, which may be regarded as wooded district, seems to have an almost entirely intact collection of stone foundations, judging by the presence of the stone fences. The parish of När, on the other hand, which is today almost wholly brought under cultivation, shows only isolated house foundations. The presence of stone fences, among other things, indicates, however, that there were more farms with stone foundations in the parish. Let us presume that the average percentage of stone foundations destroyed by cultivation, or not registered, on the island is about 30, which figure may be an under-estimate.

It would imply that more than 2.400 house foundations once existed as the remains of a deserted impoverished settlement. The number of house foundations per farmstead in an area with well preserved prehistoric remains has been calculated to be 2.9 (Carlsson 1979:119), which means that 2.400 house foundations correspond to about 800 farms.

Then again, which part of the total settlement during the 6th century do these 800 farms represent? The general opinion is, as has been stated above, that the house foundations constitute the remains of abandoned and not re-occupied farms (Nylén 1962 and others). But is it reasonable to suggest that the preserved stone foundations, bearing in mind their number and their even distribution over the island, represent only the impoverished settlement? Some of the investigated house foundations have produced an unusually rich collection of finds. Rings in the parish of Hejnum and Stavgard in the parish of Burs can hardly be characterized as poor settlements (Biörnstad 1955). Furthermore, is it reasonable to suggest that <u>all</u> the stone foundations of the continuing settlement should have been eroded after a change in house construction? A comparison between the localization of the stone foundations and the cultivated fields about A.D. 1700 shows that not less than 20% of the house foundations are to be found within the cultivated field area (Carlsson 1977:36). The cultivated fields in the year 1700 are, to a large extent, still cultivated today, and, in spite of the long period of cultivation, a large number of house foundations remain as obstructions in the fields. Stone foundations have also been preserved in direct contact with the recent settlements (Figure 2).

However, there has been, so far as can be judged, a certain reduction in the number of farms during the end of the Migration period and the beginning of the Vendel period, which can be seen in the pollen diagrams (Pålsson 1977). It is, of course, very difficult to judge the extent of the abandonment. But let us, for the sake of simplicity, suggest that it has been of the same dimensions as the 14th century abandonment on Gotland which implies a reduction of the number of farms by about 10% (Ersson 1974:97). Following the prevailing interpretation of desertion, a tenth of the Migration Period settlements would thus include about 800 farms. The total amount of farms on Gotland about the year 500, would, according to these calculations, be about 8.000. It may be compared with the number of farms during the 13th century, which Ersson (1974:98) estimates at about 1.500. About the year 1700 there were 1.325 taxable farms on Gotland (Moberg 1939:23). It is worth remarking that the 13th century was probably the period during historical times that had the largest number of farms. Even if calculating upon a 50% desertion of farms during the Migration Period, which seems incredible in itself, the equation will be unsolvable. The numbers are of course uncertain, but still they point at the absurdity that the house foundations that can be observed in the open only represent the deserted 'poor settlements' of the period. It would seem to be clear that the surviving house foundations, including the estimated 30% that have been eroded by cultivation, or that have not been recorded, represent the total number of settlements from the period in question. This means that both deserted farmsteads and farms which continued to exist, are included in the recorded material on house foundations. In other words, a large number of the Early Iron Age farms observable in the open did survive the crisis during the Migration Period - early Vendel Period and continued to exist after that albeit in other forms. The fact that such a large number of the foundations have been preserved, also in close contact with the recent settlements, is certainly due to the construction of the stone foundations, which meant that the new buildings were seldom placed on the old foundations. In consequence, the succeeding houses were, as a rule, built at a greater or lesser distance from the earlier stone foundations.

The Cultural Landscape about 500 - the Cultural Landscape 1700. A Comparison.

When comparing the extension of the cultural landscape about A.D. 1700 with the 6th century landscape, as it shows itself by the surviving stone foundations and the stone fences, one may notice an apparent congruency in the extension of the agrarian cultural landscape at the two dates (Figure 3). The 6th century infields almost completely correspond to those of the year 1700. The same is true of the number of settlements at the two different dates. About the year 500 the number of settlements within the area of investigation may be estimated at 75. The corresponding number in the year 1700 is 72. As the number of settlements in the year 1700, probably corresponds to a great extent to the number of settlements during the Late Iron Age, one may suggest that about 80% of the stone foundation settlements within the area of investigation continue in the historical farms. This means that the Early Iron Age settlement and the historical settlement is one and the same cultivation unit. On the other hand, it is not necessarily true that the buildings from the 7th century and onwards have always been located on one and the same site (that of the historical farm). This has been shown by, for instance, the investigation at Burge in the parish of Lummelunda (Thunmark 1979).

Conclusive records of continuity between Early Iron Age farms and historical farms could be provided by excavations on the building sites of the historical farms with a view to finding their origin. This is of course a very awkward undertaking, bearing in mind the erosion and disturbance of older cultural layers that has certainly occurred in continuously used sites. It would be simpler to do the equivalent investigations on a deserted farm site, where it is possible, by means of cadastral material, to prove that the buildings have been moved, or that the settlement has been deserted at an early date. Within the area of investigation there are in the first place two possible objects of investigation. One is Ungelhem in the parish of Buttle (A) and the other is Fjäle in the parish of Ala (B) (see Figure 3). Adjoining the two stone foundation settlements are remains probably dating from the Late Iron Age and the Middle Ages, which fact very likely implies that the stone foundation farm existed, though in a changed form, into the Middle Ages. If this suggestion is correct, the settlements survived the critical period during the 6th century, but were deserted during the 14th century agrarian crisis.

Fig. 4 omitted.

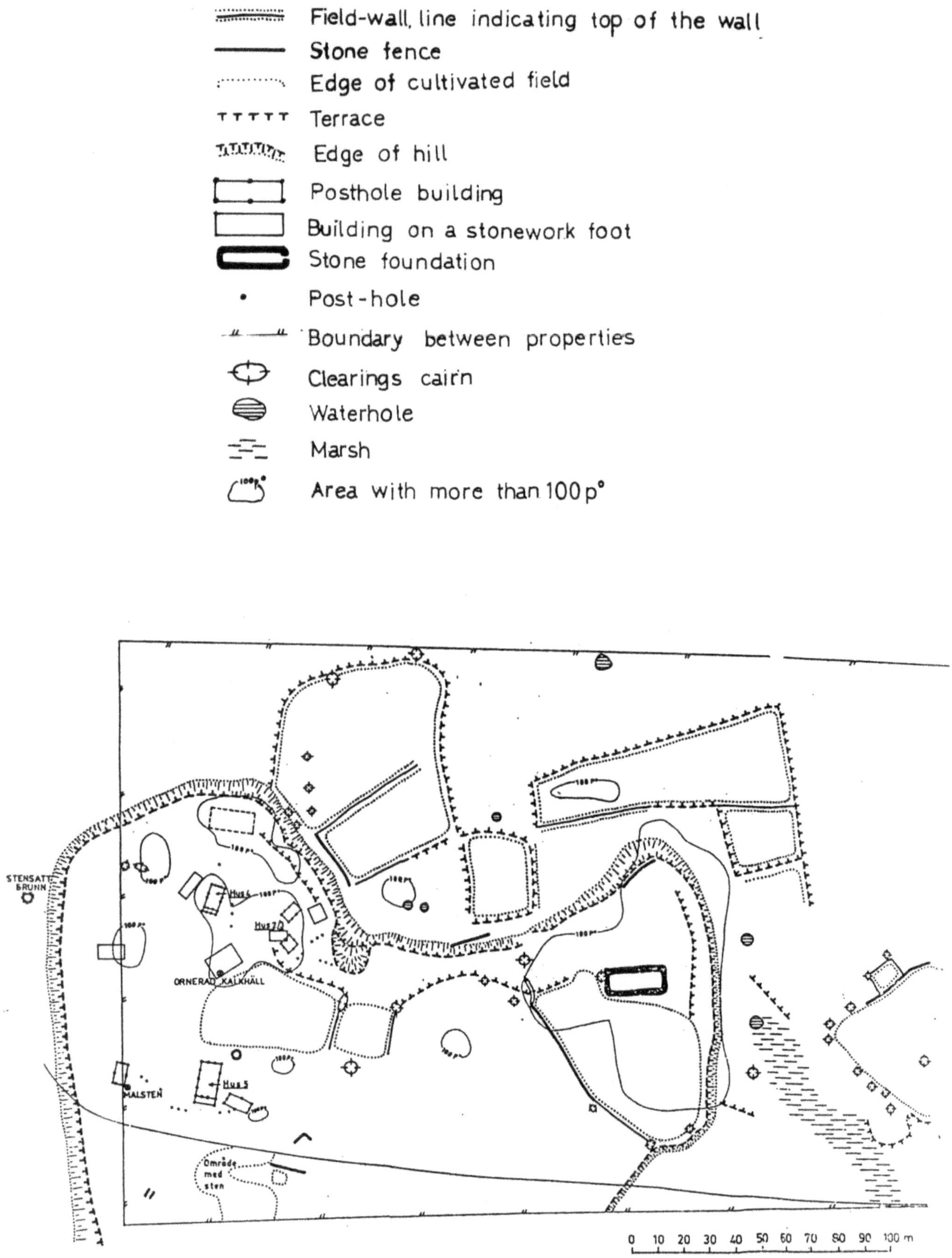

FIGURE 5: The fossilized cultural landscape connecting on to the settlement remains.

I chose to investigate Fjäle, for two specific reasons. In the first place the area has never, as far as can be judged, been cultivated after the desertion. Secondly, it was possible to distinguish the building remains of the Fjäle farmstead at an early date (Figure 5).

The deserted farm Fjäle

The investigations were intended to try to demonstrate continuity of settlement between the stone foundations on the eastern part of the plateau and the other building remains to the west (Figure 4, 5). On the basis of the general dating of the stone foundations to about A.D. 200-600, the suggestion was made that the western building remains had their origin in the early Vendel period. The excavations were limited to one summer season as a consequence of scanty resources of time and money.

The building remains within the western site were of two types - on the one hand there were low stone foundations of about 0.5 m limestone slabs just discernible on the surface, on the other there were rows of postholes where some of the supporting stones were visible. The first construction was interpreted as the foundations for 'bulhus' (see for instance Bohrn 1942). The posthole buildings were suggested to be older, bearing in mind that such houses are known from the Viking period (Thunmark 1976). Probably the last mentioned house construction is the form of building succeeding stone foundations. Considering this, three, on the surface clearly defined, posthole buildings were chosen for investigation. One of the posthole houses was overlapped by a 'bulhus' foundation, which fact was clear already before the excavation. In order to minimize the area of excavation the investigations were made in a separate coordinate system for each house construction. Finds and constructions were registered per square meter, and were levelled and registered on a plan on the scale of 1:20. Bones, charcoal (except concentrations of charcoal) and burnt clay were gathered per square meter and layer. Each layer was photographed from above and from the side in colour and black and white.

A total of about 1000 finds were registered. Only that part of the find material that may be used for dating will be considered here.

Buildings 2 and 3

Before the removal of the turf there were visible a number of postholes on the surface, which when connected, formed a 8 x 6 meter rectangle (building 2). In the northern corner the construction was overlapped by a stone foundation, just visible in the grass (building 3).

Directly under the turf lay a dark, 0.15 - 0.25 m thick, cultural layer, lying directly on the limestone bedrock. The cultural layer was excavated in two strata. Within the investigated area were found more than 800 finds. Furthermore there was plenty of bone and charcoal. Besides the two clearly distinguishable house foundations there were more postholes, probably older than the two houses (Figure 6). Below follows a description of the different constructions (Figure 7).

On top is building 3, about 7 x 5 meters, with its long axis orientated NNW-SSE. The foundations consisted of a stonework footing made up of 0.2-0.8 m long and 0.1 m thick limestone slabs. The NE long side of the house

FIGURE 6: Buildings 2 and 3. In the background building 4. Photo, author.

was completely missing, and no traces of it whatsoever were found. In the western corner there was a hearth about 2.5 x 2.2 m, which contained plenty of burnt clay and 0.2-0.3 m long stones. This building was probably used as a dwelling-house. In favour of this interpretation there is not only the hearth but also the many finds, including a rich deposit of bone material. Besides a large number of iron and pottery finds there were also found three very worn silver coins dating from the late 12th or the early 13th century. By means of the pottery the house can be dated to about 1200-1350. In close connection with the NW short side of the building a ground sill was found, lying parallel to the wall. The sill is therefore likely to belong to the building. A C14 sample gave the result A.D. 1055 ±90 (all the C14-samples are corrected according to Damon et al. 1974).

Building 2 measured about 8 x 6 meters. Its long axis is orientated in the NNE-SSW. On both long sides stood four posts and in each gable there was a central post, which probably carried the rooftree. Between the two western postholes in the northern gable were, for at least a meter length, limestone slabs placed in a row, which probably made up the bedding for a sill log. It is, of course, difficult to say why just this part of the wall was provided with a stone foundation, but it is possible that it indicates an entrance. Three C14 samples of wood from two different postholes gave the following dates: A.D. 1155 ±90, A.D. 1105 ±90 and A.D. 1190±90 respectively.

Unburnt wood was in all the postholes. These samples have been examined by Thomas Bartholin in Lund, and turned out to be exclusively pine. This is also true for buildings 4 and 5. As the posts were unburnt, there was no risk of confusion with the charcoal that was found scattered here and there in all the buildings. Thereby the C14 datings in all probability do refer to the posts.

The function of the building is uncertain, but the find material, including among other things pottery and plenty of bones, indicates that it was probably a dwellinghouse. There was no clearly defined hearth. On the other hand, parts of the building contained plenty of charcoal, and in the bedrock could be seen a 2.0x1.5 m wide and 0.1-0.2 m deep pit, which may be interpreted as a hearth. The cultural layer on the bottom of the pit had a similar composition to the rest. The pit is older than building 3, which is shown by the fact that the pit is overlapped by the eastern short side of that house.

A still older phase in the construction could be discerned. It consisted of isolated minor postholes together with a thin cultural layer, which could be seen for instance under the sill stones between two posts in the northern short side of building 2 (see Figure 7).

On the basis of the slight thickness of the cultural layer and its homogenous character, it is very difficult to separate the finds from the different buildings. Within the excavated area it is in building 3 that the largest number of finds, including bones, was found. But the distribution of the finds is rather uniform over the whole area, also outside the buildings, with the exception of the southwestern corner of the excavated area (Figure 8). The cultural layer was at its thickest in the southeastern part of the area, and here also were found two of the objects that may date from the Vendel period. The first is a 2.8 centimeter long miniature bronze sword. It has a striking resemblance to the miniature swords from Eketorp, which have been dated to the early Vendel period by Näsman (1973) (Figure 9). The second object is a yellow, half transparent, glass bead of the same type

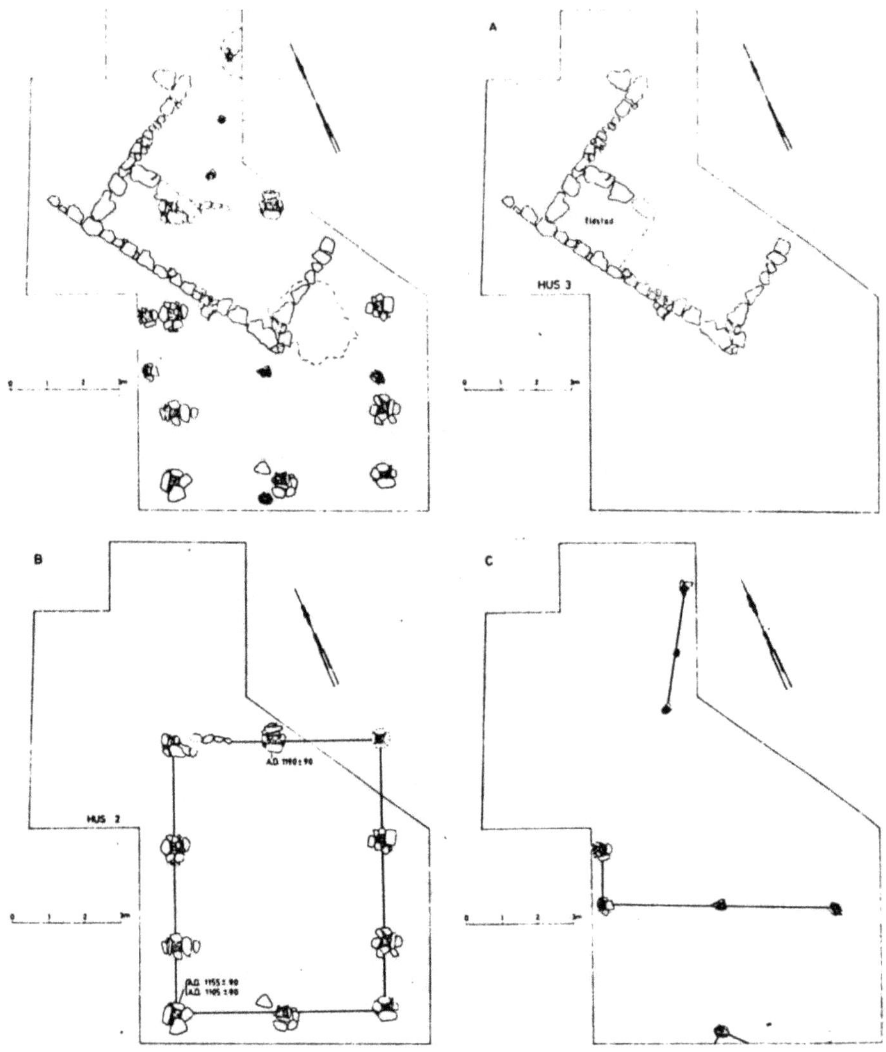

FIGURE 7: Buildings 2(B) and 3(A). Probably older than buildings 2 and 3 are a number of smaller postholes (C).

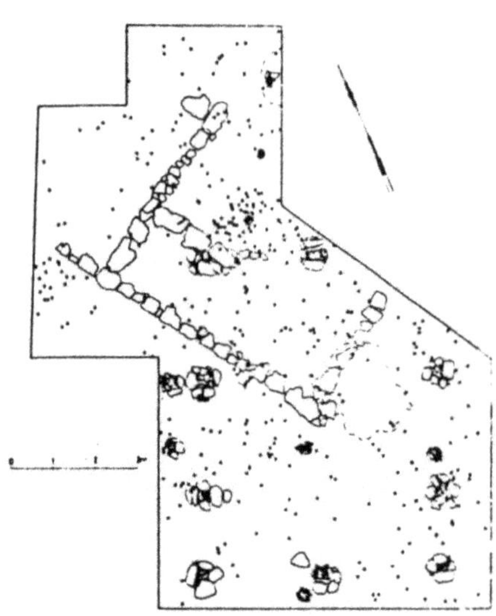

FIGURE 8: Buildings 2 and 3. The distribution of the finds in situ.

FIGURE 9: Buildings 2 and 3. A miniature bronze sword, en face and in profile. Length, 2.8 cm. Photo L. Lindqvist.

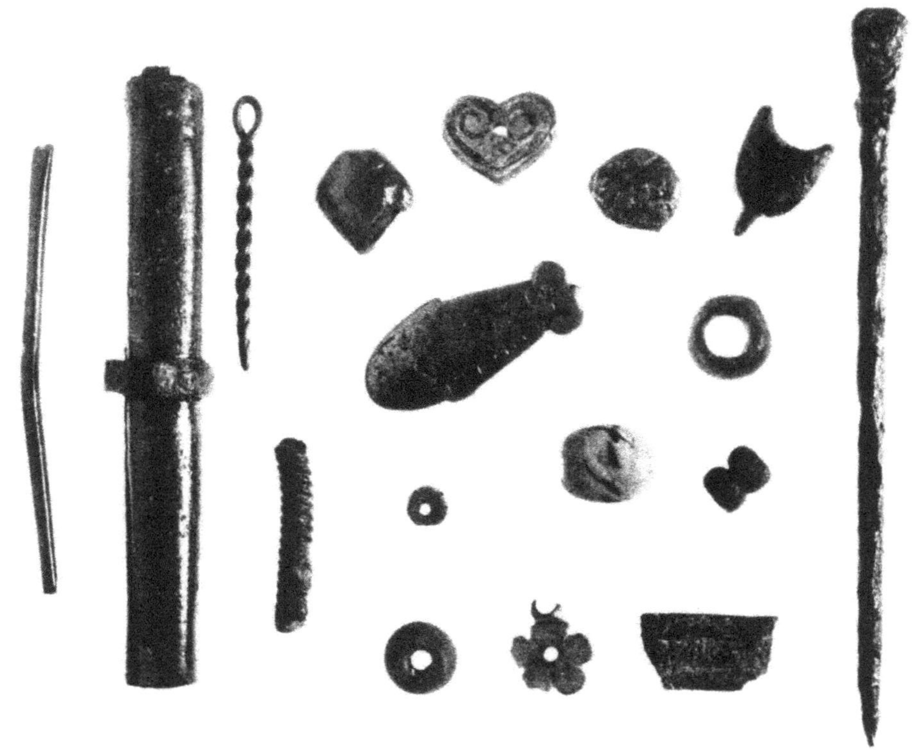

FIGURE 12: Building 4. Parts of the find material. The three artifacts below from building 5. Photo L. Lindqvist.

FIGURE 10: Buildings 2 and 3. Parts of the findmaterial. Photo L. Lindqvist.

as Nerman 1969, Figure II, Taf. III, which has been dated to the period VII:1, that is 550–600 (Figure 10). The third object that may date from the Vendel period is a fragment of a red, probably conical, glass paste bead.

Several objects probably date from the Viking period, probably its later part. Among these is a bronze ring brooch, a square bronze button with rune-stone style ornament (possibly from the transition to the Middle Ages) and a filigree-worked silver bead (Figure 10).

It can be pointed out that some of the finds are earlier than the C14 dating of the posthole building. This can probably be explained by the fact that the dating of the posts does not give the date of construction of the building. Posts dug down into the ground probably had a rather limited lifetime. This meant that they were occasionally replaced (Thunmark 1976:131). At Fjäle all the excavated postholes contained charcoal, bones, or stray iron objects like nails, rods and horseshoe-nails. These finds will have ended up in the postholes in connection with the repairing and exchange of posts.

It is obvious from the dating of the two buildings that the time gap between them was very short. That building 3 overlaps building 2 is also clear from the fact that the northwestern posthole of the second building was found below the hearth of the first building. Building 2 was probably constructed in the Viking period, provided the Viking period finds really are associated with the building.

Building 4

The building measures 10.5 x 5.5 meters, its long axis orientated NE-SW. A number of postholes could be discerned on the surface before the excavation. The cultural layer was apparently thin and was rarely more than 0.15 m thick. There were no inner constructions in the building except for a small heap of limestone overlapping the eastern part of the southern short side. The heap contained scattered bones. The dimensions of the postholes varied in different parts of the building (Figure 11). The heaviest posts, with a diameter of 0.2–0.3 m, stood at the corners and along the long sides. In the middle of the two long sides were two posts placed close together. The northern most two of each pair were made up of stones placed on edge. The other two were much simpler as far as construction is concerned. Besides these postholes there were on the southern long side two additional postholes, probably indicating an entrance. Close inside the entrance there was a layer of hard packed clay over an area of about 2 x 1 m.

Parallel to the northern long side, in direct connection with the two closely placed posts, unburnt wooden fragments were found over an area of about 0.2 x 1.5 m. These fragments were probably the remains of a sill log.

Wooden fragments from 6 posts in all have been C14 dated. The spread of dates is worth noticing (A.D. 695 ±120, A.D. 865 ±90, A.D. 940 ±90, A.D. 970 ±90, A.D. 1140 ±105 and A.D. 1360 ±155 respectively). The great spread in the C14 datings is probably a result of the replacement of rotten posts. The C14 dates indicate that the building was used into the early Middle Ages. A plausible starting-point for the building is represented by the C14 date of A.D. 695.

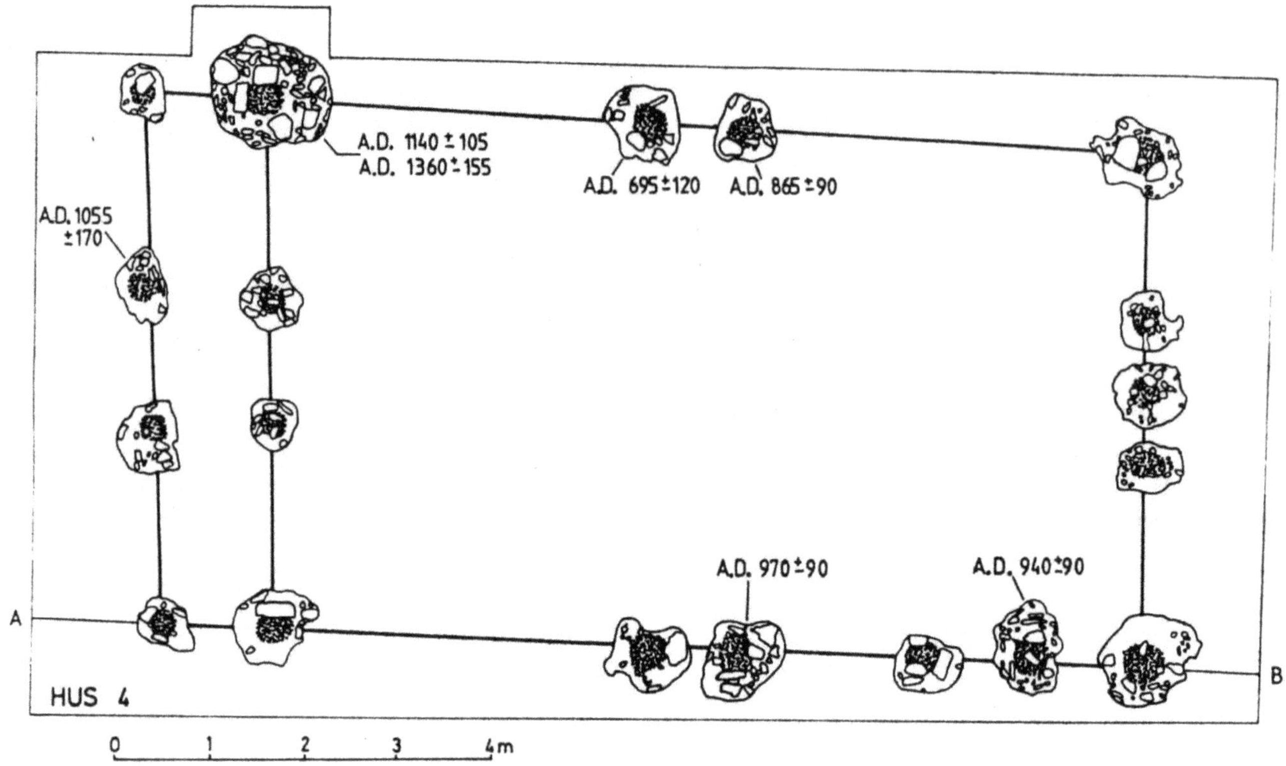

FIGURE 11: Building 4. Plan.

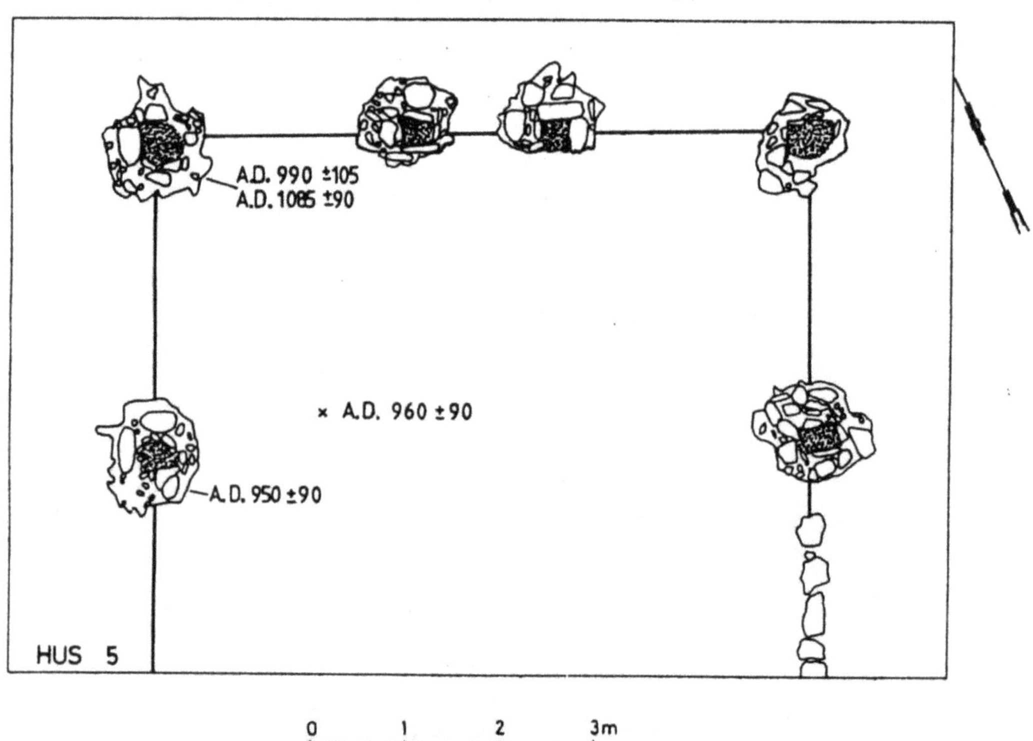

FIGURE 13: Building 5. Plan.

The find material in building 4 was quite uniform, and consisted mainly of various kinds of iron objects. Among other things were found a lot of iron arrow-heads. Pottery was completely absent except for one glazed potsherd dating from the 13th century. The larger part of the datable find material is from the Viking period. It includes among other things a bronze needle-case, a heart-shaped belt mounting of silver inlaid in niello technique, belt and strap-end mountings of bronze and silver, and a few beads (Figure 12).

Probably of older date is a fragment of a spiral ornamented bracelet of bronze. The object has been worn on one side, which indicates its use as a bracelet. It most resembles Figures 1533, 1535, in Nerman 1969, which, in time, means A.D. 650-700.

A probable date for the construction of the building is, on the basis of the C14 datings, the middle of the Vendel period. This dating is confirmed by the probably Vendel period bracelet. The evidence may seem weak, with only one find from the Vendel period. However, from a general point of view, it is the case that from the earliest phases of a settlement there are very few objects left to recover. I would call attention to the distribution of datable objects at Vallhagar, where 50 artifacts have been assigned to the Migration period and only 7 to the Roman Iron Age (Stenberger 1955 b: 1146). Also characteristic are Beskow-Sjöberg's (1977) house investigations on Oland. She sums up the results of the investigations of two houses at Sorby Tall as follows: 'The table shows that the C14-dates stretch from the 2nd to the 7th century A.D. Datable finds appear only in the second half of the period, so that the settlement would be dated to be Migration and Vendel periods on the evidence of the objects alone. The C14 dates imply, however, that it was occupied earlier' (Beskow-Sjöberg 1977: 123).

A continuous settlement means, for natural reasons, that older remains are all the more destroyed. The result of this is the almost complete absence of artifacts from the oldest phases of a settlement. When excavating settlements, therefore, C14-analyses are necessary for the dating of the beginning of the settlement.

Building 5

The building was clearly outlined before the removal of the turf by a number of postholes. The size of the building was estimated at about 15x7 meters. The house, excavated only in its northern third, has a certain resemblance to building 4, for instance in the construction of the postholes and in the gables having two posts rather close to each other (Figure 13). Between three postholes along the eastern long side (partly outside the excavated area) there was a row of limestone blocks, very probably the foundations of a sill log. As in building 4 the southern (un-excavated) gable had some kind of extension.

The find material was very poor, and consisted mainly of, besides bones, minor iron and bronze objects. Two of them may be given an approximate dating. One is a silver pendant in the shape of a flower, probably dating to the early Middle Ages. A similar pendant of bronze was found in building 2/3. The second object is a green glass-paste bead, common in the early Vendel period (Nerman 1969, Taf. III and IV).

FIGURE 14: Grave 17. Photo author.

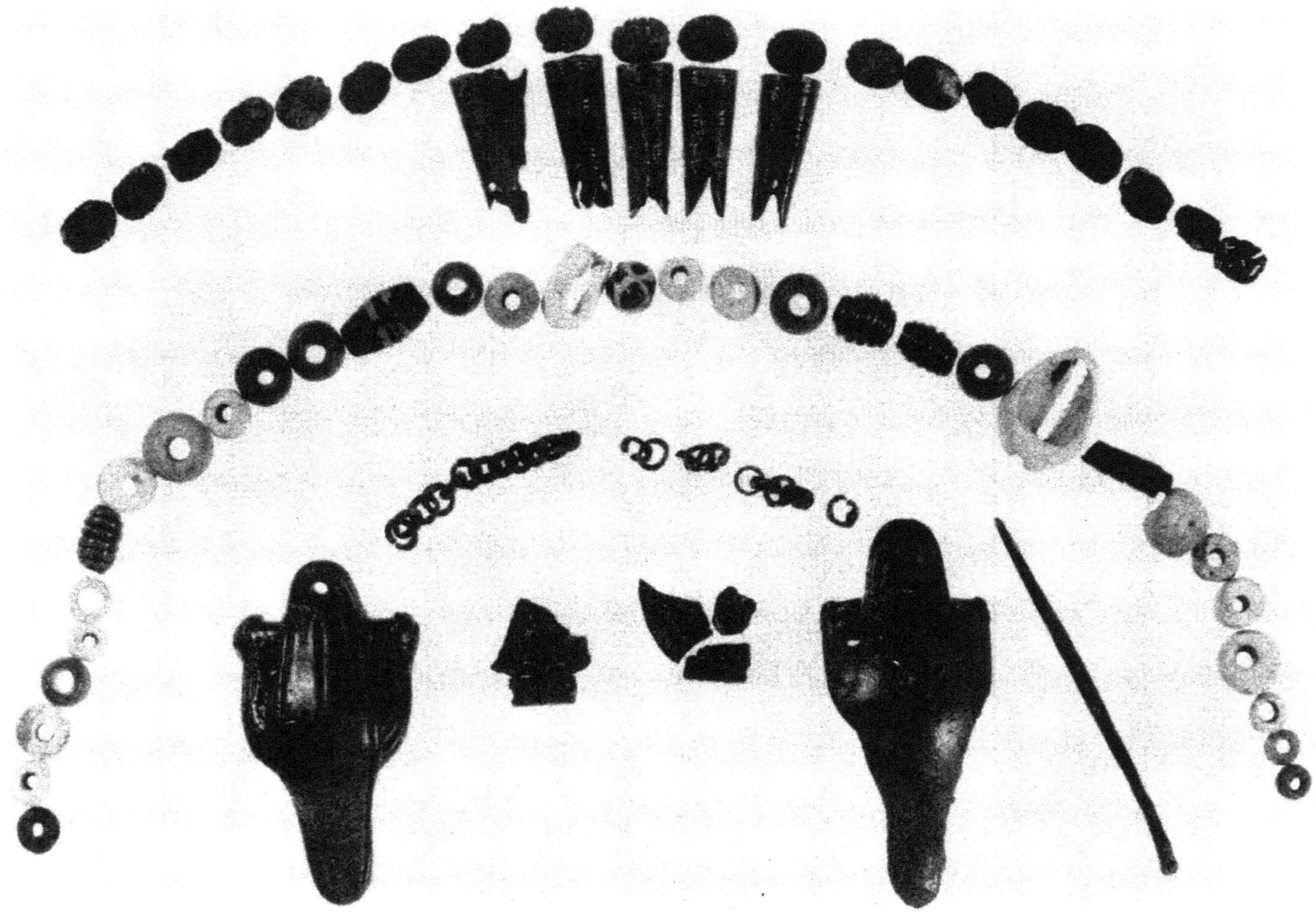

FIGURE 15: Grave 17. The artifacts. Photo L. Lindqvist.

In the north-eastern part of the building, over an area of 2 x 1 meters, was a great amount of charred grains of corn, almost exclusively barley. The building was probably used as a storehouse, and the presence of charred grain indicates that it was burnt down. This theory is confirmed by the fact that the upper part of the posts were charred, while the wood further down had not been touched by fire. Four C14 analyses have been made; two from the same post, A.D. 1085 ±90 and A.D. 990 ±105 respectively, one from another post, A.D. 950 ±90, and one from an unburnt concentration of wood in the north-western part of the building, A.D. 960 ±90. The life of the building is uncertain, but it probably existed during the second half of the Viking period and also a little into the Middle Ages.

Grave No. 17

About 300 meters south of the settlement, in connection with the parish boundary, there were three grave-fields of altogether about 40 graves. Besides the grave-fields there are 2 graves to the west of the settlement in close contact with the road connecting Fjäle with Visnar ängar in the south, Hexarve in the parish of Buttle in the west, and the settlement in the central part of the parish of Ala in the north. The grave-fields are situated directly on the bedrock. It stretches kilometers to the south, west and east. The grave-fields are therefore in all probability connected with the Fjäle settlement.

It is probable that the graves should not be assigned to the stone foundations, bearing in mind that graves, dating from the same period as the stone foundations are generally almost invisible above ground level (Nerman 1935:31, 102). There is a distinction between the grave-fields as regards the stone material. The grave-field situated furthest in the east contains a lot more stone-lined limestone than the other two. The stone lined graves were round, or nearly round, invisible except for a slight indication of a dry-stone wall. Some of the graves in the northernmost grave-fields are cairn-like. The absence of constructional details and the many limestone blocks indicate a date in the Late Iron Age, and it is probable that the inhabitants of the posthole houses were buried here.

If the suggestion that the settlement on the western part of the plateau dates back to the 7th century, and that the grave-fields are connected to Fjäle, is correct, it implies that we will find here graves from the 7th century and onwards. Trying to show that the 7th century actually was represented in the graves, one of those in the eastern grave-field was chosen for excavation. The choice was made bearing in mind that these graves, even if badly damaged are reminiscent of the dry-stone walled graves at the Trullhalsar grave-field in the parish of Anga, which date back to the early Vendel period (Nerman 1969).

The eastern grave-field contains about 20 graves, which represents half the number of graves. The excavated grave (No. 17), like other graves, had been robbed. The grave had a diameter of about 5 meters, and was 0.3 meters high (Fig. 14). The stones were mainly grey stones measured 0.2-0.4 meters. The grave was surrounded by a ruined dry-stone wall of limestone slabs measuring 0.2-0.6 meters. The central part was broken open and badly damaged.

Below a single-layer stone filling were found the remains of an unburnt skeleton, lying directly on the rock. Only parts of the legs and the feet were found in their original position. The remaining parts of the skeleton

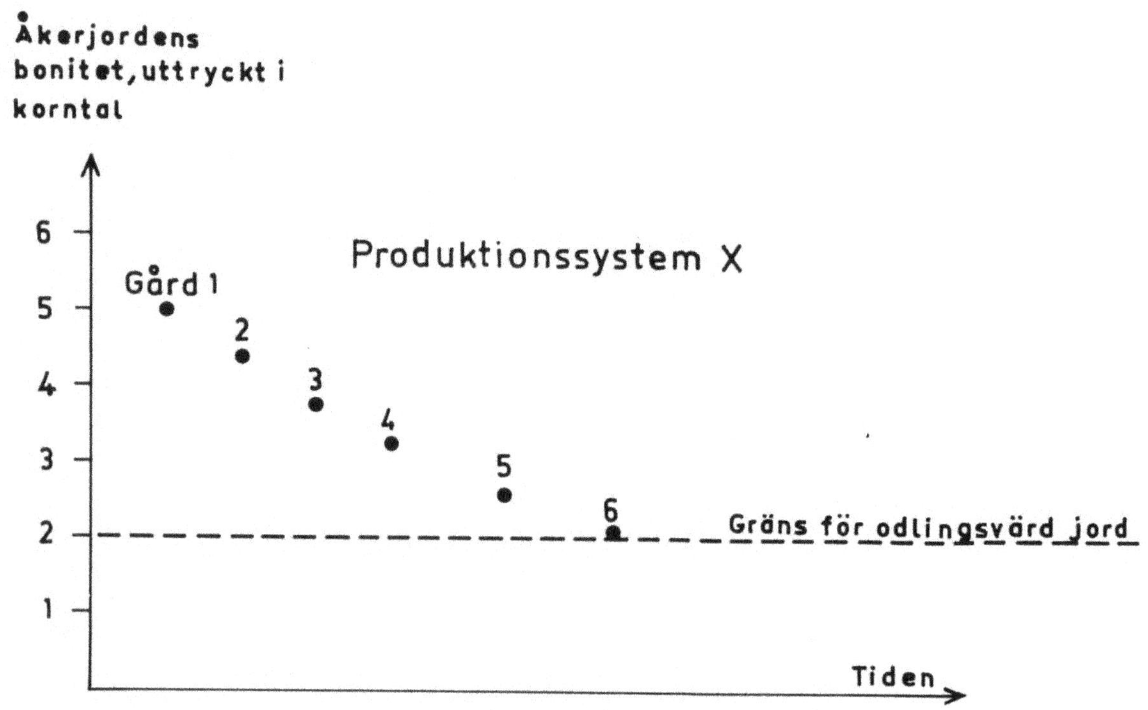

FIGURE 16: The diagram shows how the establishment of new settlements, within the existing system of cultivation in course of time takes place on the poorer land from an agricultural point of view.

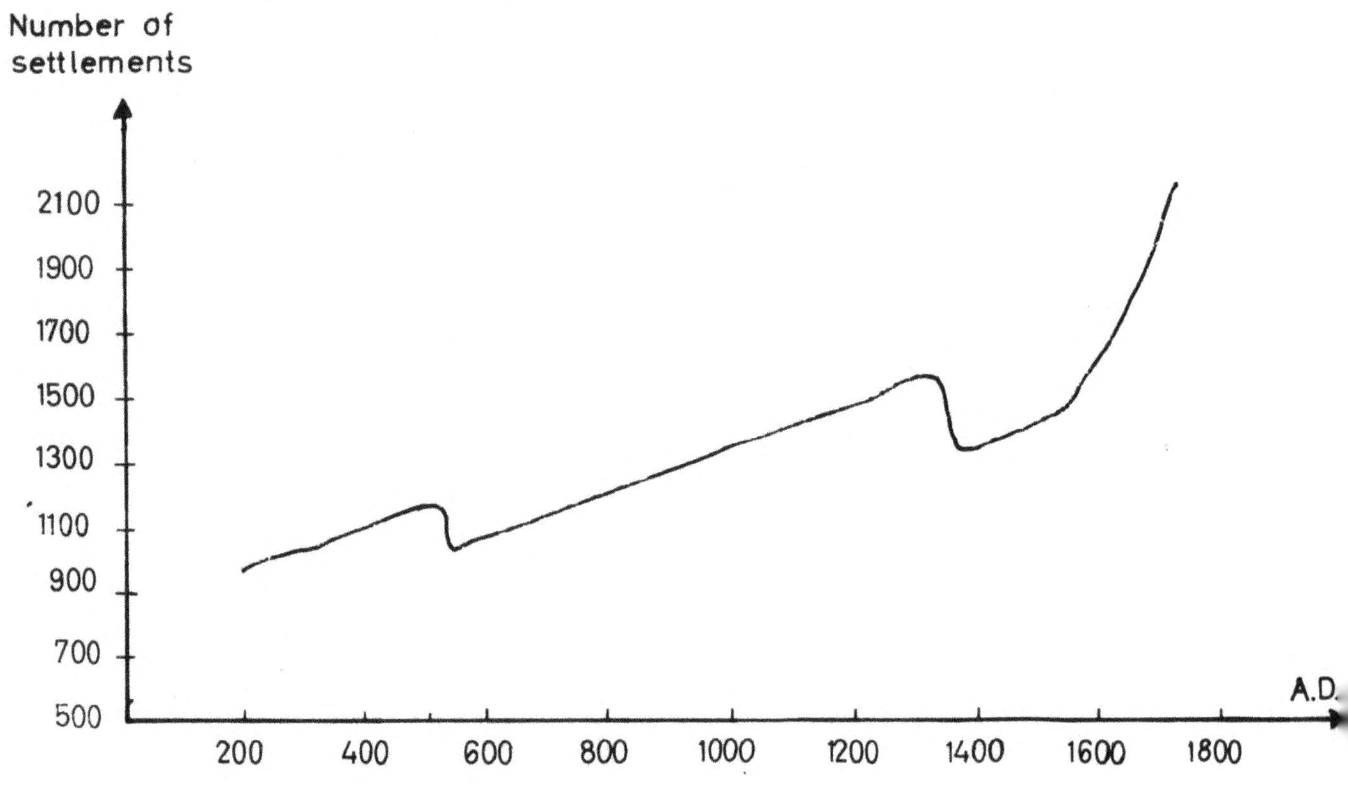

FIGURE 17: An interpretation of the development of settlement on Gotland in the period A.D. 200-1700.

lay scattered in the grave.

The position of the surviving bones and the finds shows that the corpse had been lying on her right side with the head to the north and with slightly flexed knees. In view of the fragmentary condition of the skeleton an osteological classification is very difficult, but it is probably that of a woman which is not contradicted by the finds.

The finds were, in spite of the robbing, quite numerous, and consisted of the following artifacts: two bronze brooches in the form of animal heads; parts of a necklace consisting of 13 glass paste beads, 13 limestone beads, 4 bronze beads, 2 shells, 5 fishhead-shaped pendants and 20 bottom plates of fishhead-shaped pendants (Fig. 15). Fragments of a bronze chain and fragments of two bronze bracteates were also found. The finds date the grave between A.D. 600 and 700.

Summary

The aim of the investigations was to try to prove continuity between the stone foundations and the other settlement remains. The stone foundations were suggested to have existed during the period that is the prevailing dating of house constructions of that kind - A.D. 200-600. The suggestion was that the settlement to the west was established about 600. The results of the investigations may be summed up as follows: The settlement in the western part of the plateau lasted up to the middle of the 14th century. We can trace the settlement back into the Viking period. The dating of building 4, together with the presence of a number of objects probably dating from the early Vendel period, indicates a settlement dating from the 7th century onwards. To this we may add a grave of the 7th century in one of the three grave-fields, which no doubt should be connected with the Fjäle settlement.

The dating of the oldest settlement is uncertain, and no definitely Vendel period buildings were found (with the possible exception of building 4), even though they probably existed. Why were no Vendel period buildings found? The main reasons are two. On the one hand, only a very small part of the settlement area has been excavated; and on the other, it is the clearest and best preserved and therefore the most recent post-hole buildings that have been investigated. A 600-year-long settlement naturally destroys its oldest features. I should instead have excavated constructions with very diffuse post-holes. The localization of these houses may be, in the first place, the area south-east of building 2/3 and the area between building 4 and building 2/3. The second area has a very high phosphate content (Fig. 5). In spite of choosing the wrong buildings to get an answer to the problem, a number of objects were found probably dating from the Vendel period.

Most facts speak in favour of the Medieval settlement having its origins at the beginning of the Vendel period, and constituting the continuation of the stone foundation farm. The Fjäle settlement is one of the peripheral single farmsteads, which, being well situated and long established in comparison with the central settlements, runs the greatest risk of desertion at critical phases in the agrarian development. If there is a connection between the stone foundation settlement and the historical farm at Fjäle, it is reasonable to suggest that the probability of continuity is greater in the central settlements.

BIBLIOGRAPHY

Almgren, B. 1957. Vallhagar. Byn och boken. Fornvännen. Stockholm.

Berglund, B. 1969. Vegetation and human influence in South Scandinavia during Prehistoric time. Oikos suppl 12:9-28. Köpenham.

Beskow-Sjöberg, M. 1977. The archaeology of Skedemosse. IV Kungl. Vitterhets Historie och Antikvitets Akademien. Stockholm.

Biörnstad, A. 1955. Previous Investigations of Iron Age Building Remains. In Vallhagar. A Migration Period Settlement on Gotland/Sweden. Köpenhamn-Stockholm.

Bohrn, E. 1942. En medeltida bondgår i Fole. Gotlandskt Arkiv. Visby.

Carlsson, D. 1977. Den folkvandringstida ödeläggelsen på Gotland. German summary. Gotländskt arkiv. Visby.

Carlsson, D. 1979. Kulturlandskapets utveckling på Gotland. En studie av jordbruks- och bebyggelseförändringar under järnåldern (The development of the Cultural Landscape on Gotland). A Study of Changes in Agriculture and Settlement during the Iron Age. English summary. Nyköping.

Damon, P.E., Ferguson, C.W., Long, A. & Wallick, E.I. 1974. Dendrochronologic calibration of the radiocarbon time scale. American Antiquity. Vol. 39, No. 2, 1974.

Ersson, P.-G. 1974. Kolonisation och ödeläggelse på Gotland. Studier av den agrara bebyggelseutvecklingen från tidig medeltid till 1600-talet. German summary. Meddelanden från Kulturgeografiska institutionen vid Stockholms universitet Nr B 27.

Gräslund, B. 1973. Aring, näring, pest och salt. Tor 1972-73. Uppsala.

Königsson, E.-S., Königsson, L.-K. 1976. Mark och bygd på Oland under äldre järnålder. Kalmar nations skriftserie, Vol. 51. 1976. Kalmar.

Königsson, L.-K. 1968. The Holocene History of the Great Alvar of Oland. Acta Phytogeographica Suecica 55. Uppsala.

Lange, E. 1975. The development of agriculture during the first millennium A.D. Geologiska Föreningens i Stockholm Förhandlingar, Vol. 97. Stockholm.

Lindquist, S-O. 1968. Det förhistoriska kulturlandskapet i östra Ostergötland. English summary. Acta universitatis stockholmiensis, Studies in North-European Archaeology 2. Stockholm.

Moberg. I. 1939. Gotland um das Jahr 1700. Eine Kulturgeographische Kartenanalyse. Geogr. Ann. 1938: 1-2.

Myhre, B. 1972. Funn, fornminner og ødegårder. Jernålderens boeteningsutvikling i Høyland Fjellbygd. Stav. Mus. Skrifter 7. Stavanger.

Myhre, B. 1973. The Iron Age Farm in south-west Norway. Norwegian Archaeological Review 6, No. 1, 14. Bergen.

Nerman, B. 1935. Die Völkerwanderungszeit Gotlands. Kungl. Vitterhets Historie och Antikvitets Akademien. Stockholm.

Nerman, B. 1969. Die Vendelzeit Gotlands. II. Tafeln. Kungl. Vitterhets Historie och Antikvitets Akademien. Stockholm.

Nylén, E. 1962. Bebyggelseproblem i Nordens förhistoria. Tor. Uppsala.

Nylén, E. 1973. Bygden, Skeppen och Havet. German summary. Antikvariskt Arkiv 49. Stockholm.

Pettersson, B. 1955. The Vallhagar Country: Some Natural Features relating to its History In Vallhagar. A Migration Period Settlement on Gotland/Sweden. København-Stockholm.

Pålsson, I. 1977. A Standard Pollen Diagram from the Lojsta Area of Central Gotland. Societas Upsaliensis pro Geologia Quaternaria. Uppsala.

Schmid, P. 1974. Was geschah im 5. Jh. - Siedlungs-archäologische Befunde aus der frühen Völkerwanderungszeit. Niederdeutsches Heimatblatt (Mitteilungsblatt der Männer vom Morgenstern). Bremerhaven Nr. 296.

Stenberger, M. 1955a. The Reasons for the Abandonment of Vallhagar. In Vallhagar. A Migration Period Settlement on Gotland/Sweden. København-Stockholm.

Stenberger, M. 1955b. The Finds and Dating of the Vallhagar Settlement. In Vallhagar. A Migration Period Settlement on Gotland/Sweden. København-Stockholm.

Thunmark, L. 1976. Burge i Lummelunda. Gotländskt arkiv. Visby.

Thunmark, L. 1979. Burget på Burge - en storgård på gränsen mellan heden och kristen tid. German summary. In Arkeologi på Gotland. Visby.

Welinder, S. 1974 Kulturlandskapet i Mälarområdet. Dep. of Quaternary Geology, Univ. of Lund. Report 5.

Widgren, M. 1977. Pollenanalys från sjön Flären, Ostergötland. Kulturlandskaputveckling från bronsålder till nutid. Kulturgeografiskt seminarium 6/77. Kulturgeografiska inst. Stockholms universitet. Stockholm.

Wilson, D.M. 1976. The Archaeology of Anglo-Saxon England. Editor. London.

SETTLEMENT AND EXPLOITATION OF NATURAL RESOURCES IN NORTHERN SUNNMORE A.D. 200–1050

Bergljot Solberg

The settlement pattern in a preindustrialized society will be influenced mainly by the natural resources within the area and the social organisation and technology of the people who exploit these resources. In the present study, the settlement pattern in Northern Sunnmore from A.D. 200 to 1050 is examined and the relationship to social organisation and natural resources evaluated.

Northern Sunnmöre represents a transection of Western Norway stretching from the coastal islands to the innermost projections of the fjords (Figure 1). The natural resources in this area show great variation from the outer to the inner portions, and based upon variations in topography, the area can be divided into two separate ecological zones demonstrating marked differences in the size of arable land, pasture and local climate. This division also coincides with that favoured by geographers (Sömme 1954).

Zone I (the outer area) consists of both islands and peninsulas covering a total area of 303.5 km^2 (Figure 2). The island of Giske is the only island without any mountainous terrain. In 1863[x)], arable land in zone 1 represented 6.3% of the whole area, or 19.1 km^2, while 8.3% or 25.2 km^2 was grassing area. In Norway, this is a fairly high percentage since even in modern times, the average of cultivated land is only 3.2% for the country as a whole.

The outer and the inner zones are separated by Storfjorden. Zone II (the inner area) covers 477 km^2 surrounding a branch of the fjord Hjörundfjord which is 35km long. The mountains around the fjord run up to 1600–1700 m and drop precipitously into the fjord (Figure 3). The land suited for cultivation is largely located to the bottom land of the valleys and to some peninsulas. In 1863, only 0.7% or 3.4 km^2 of the area was cultivated while 2.4% or 11.35^2 was grassing area.

---

x) The estimates of cultivated land are based upon "Forarbeid til matrikkel i henhold til Lov av 6. juni 1863" because by that time largely self draining land was used for cultivation, as artificial drainage had not yet come into use.

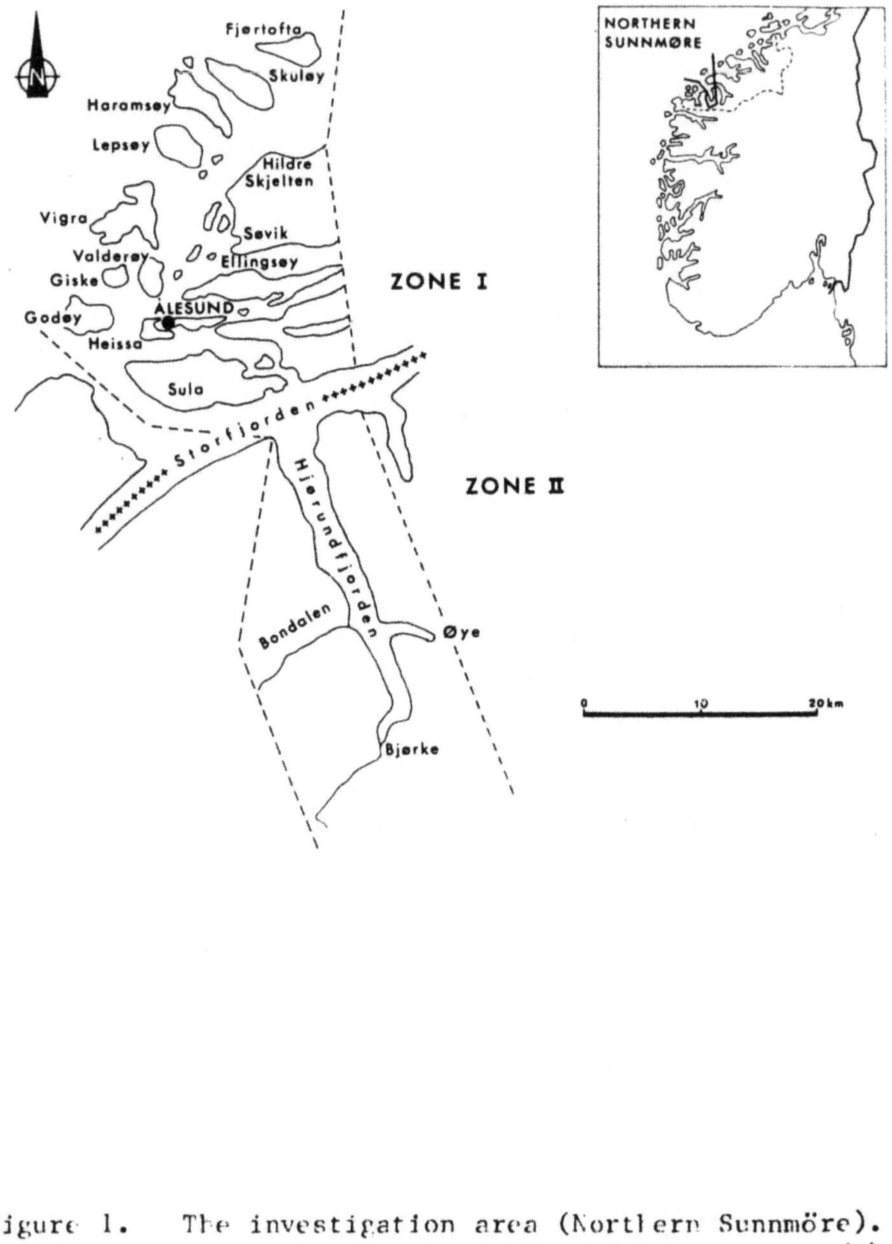

Figure 1. The investigation area (Northern Sunnmöre). Based upon variations in topography the area is divided into an outer (I) and inner (II) zone.

Figure 2. From the outer zone (I) of Northern Sunnmöre part of the island of Fjörtoft. Note the large area of strandflat.

Figure 3. From the inner zone (II) of Northern Sunnmöre - the farm Finnes in the Hjörundfjord. Typical for this zone is the location of the agricultural land to small peninsulas and the bottom land of the valley.

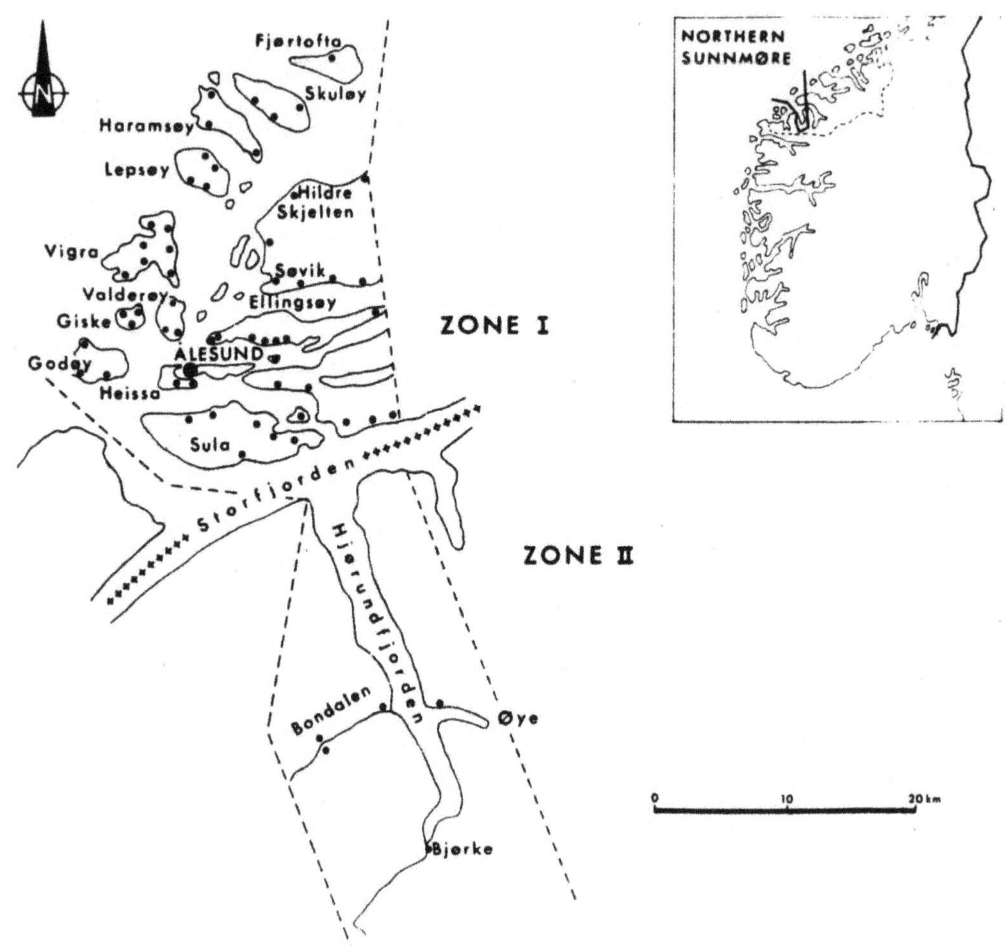

Figure 4. Farm settlements in Northern Sunnmöre by the end of the early iron age. Note the large number of farms in the outer zone (I) and the low number in the inner zone (II).

Settlement

The estimate of farm settlement is based upon archaeological material x) i.e. house grounds, grave finds and grave structures together with farm names.

In any given region with no systematic excavations finds will appear more or less by chance. Therefore, the exact number of finds should not be stressed too much, as there is every reason to believe that the numbers are too low - indicating not the real number of f.inst. prehistoric farms but only a fraction. However, if systematic variation in the occurrence of finds appears, one should pay more attention to these differences. If they cannot be explained as consequences of varying degrees of modern activities like farming activities or construction they should be regarded as a reflection of variation in prehistoric activities i.e. settlement.

Only two house grounds, each from zone I and from the early iron age, have been excavated. The localisation of farms, therefore, depends mainly upon grave remains, and in order to establish the farm settlement the following assumptions are made: 1. During the iron age the graves were located close to the farmsteads. This is strongly supported by the results of excavation of farm remains with such a solitary localisation that the burials can only belong to that farm (Hagen 1953, Bakka 1965, Bakka 1976). 2. Stone cists which may have contained inhumation burials and burial mounds with stone settings serve as indicators of settlement during the Roman and Migration periods. Similar stone cists and mounds with stone settings were also built in the early bronze age. In the areas where such burials are on fertile soil close to later farmsteads, it may, therefore, be difficult to separate remains from the bronze age and the Roman/Migration period. However, when bronze age burial structures are located on agricultural land, the land usually is the best in the area and often demonstrates evidence of continous habitation in the later prehistoric periods (Myhre 1979). Stone cists and stone settings, therefore, strongly indicate farm settlement in the Roman/Migration period. 3. Burial remains close to the farmsteads also indicate occupancy in the pre Christian period, and the late Viking period should be regarded as a terminus ante quem for such farms.

Stray finds may sometimes represent graves and may therefore point to settlement. In the present work the finds containing "strike-a-light", pottery, weapons and brooches are considered as possible remnants of graves.

Studies of Norwegian farm names (M. Olsen, O. Rygh, Sandnes & Stemshaug) reveal that the names with the endings: -bö, -vin, -heim, -stad, -land and -set belong to the prehistoric period. The names ending with -bö, -vin and -heim are considered to have originated during the period before A.D. 600. Names ending with -stad (Stenvik 1978) and -land (M. Olsen 1926) may also go back to the same period. In the present work, however, such names are ascribed to this period only in the presence of additional criteria (Table 1).

---

x) All visible prehistoric remains in the area are registered but there has been no systematic archaeological investigations. Accordingly, the finds are mainly the results of either agricultural activity or rescue archaeology.

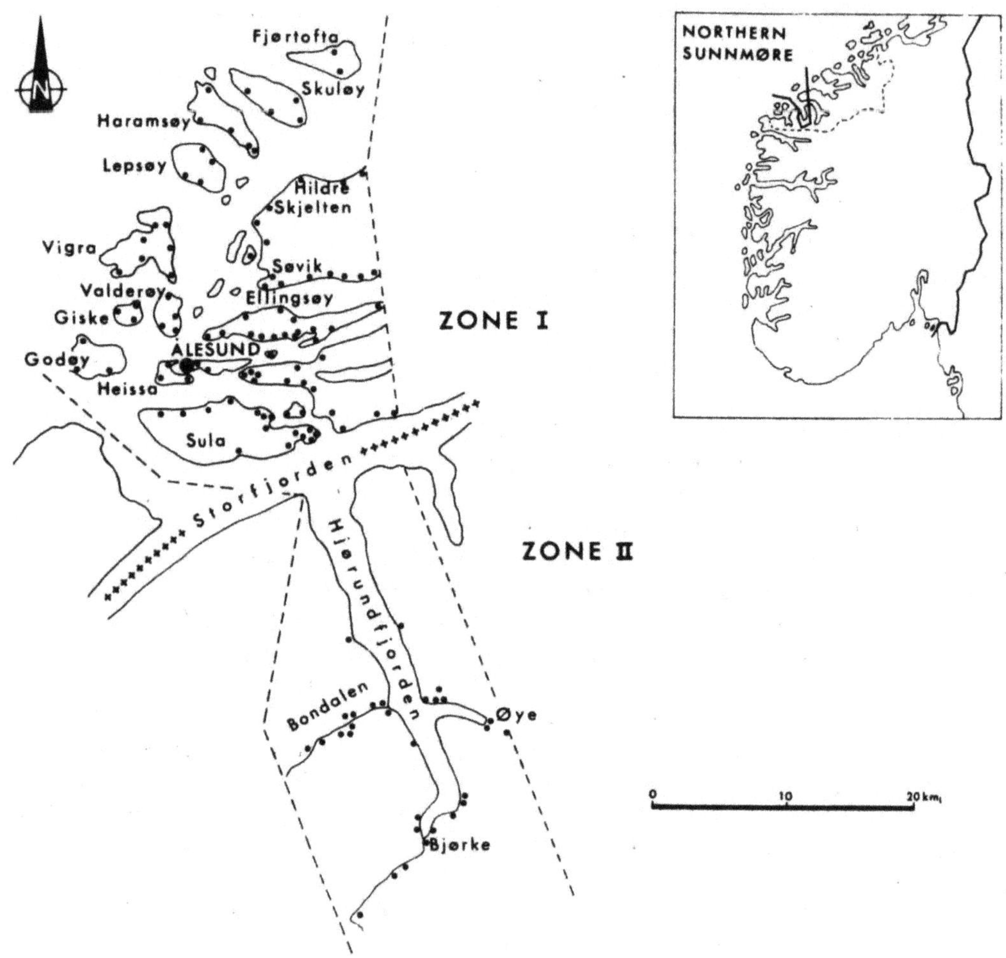

Figure 5. Farm settlements in Northern Sunnmöre by the end of the late iron age. When the number of farms is related to agricultural resources the settlement density is about even in the outer and inner zone.

Table 1 shows the number of farms established in Northern Sunnmöre from A.D. 200 to 600 when the following criteria were used: House grounds, grave finds, grave structures, stray finds, farm names and a combination of these criteria. The number of farms was several times higher in zone I than in zone II. Three and 32 farms in zone I fullfilled three or two criteria, respectively, and none and four farms in zone II. Based upon one criterium only, 56 farms were established in zone I and five in zone II (Figure 4).

During the period 600-1050 the number of farms increased in each zone (Table 2). Nine and 41 farms in zone I fullfilled three or two criteria, respectively, and five and 23 farms in zone II. Based upon one criterium only, 98 farms were established in zone I and 30 in zone II (Figure 5). Accordingly, by the end of the Viking period, the difference in farm settlement between the two zones was far less pronounced than by the end of the Migration period.

The number of visible prehistoric remains in the two zones also differ markedly. Visible grave structures total 2006 in the whole area and only 47 of these are from zone II. In zone I, the grave structures are located mainly to burial-grounds - altogether 1627 in 63 different burial-grounds. In zone II, however, only one burial-ground has been established.

The concentration of burial remains, the many burial-grounds and the number of grave and stray finds from the Roman/Migration period demonstrate a relatively stable and dense population in zone I compared to a sparsely populated zone II. By the end of the Viking period, however, the differences between the zones was far less pronounced (Figure 5) and when the number of farms in each zone is related to the size of arable land and pasture, the settlement density was about even in the two zones.

Caves and rock shelters

In addition to the farm settlements, traces of settlements have also been found in caves. Culture layers are reported from 5 caves/rock shelters which are located in zone I (Figure 6). Two of these, at Skjong and Rönstad, are big caves up to 140 m deep, while those at Havnsund and Skylehammar represent rock shelters. The rock shelter from the small island of Erkna has not been excavated.

The culture layers of the caves contained both archaeological and osteological material. Due to the heavy precipitation and the acid soil in Sunnmöre the conditions for preservation of bones are very poor. In the caves and rock shelters, however, the ground is dry with very little soil leakage, and the conditions for preservation of osteological material are favourable. Accordingly, in the present research area, osteological material has only been found in caves/rock shelters.

The osteological material from the Havnsund rock shelter and the Rönstad cave is, however, not preserved as the excavations took place already in the 19th century. Accordingly, only material from the Skjong cave and the Skylehammer rock shelter is used here.

The traces of habitation in the caves and rock shelters in the Roman and Migration periods may represent: 1. permanent settlements of groups of people who made their living from a combination of animal husbandry, fishing and hunting (Odner 1973, Hagen 1977) or 2. seasonal occupation during the year

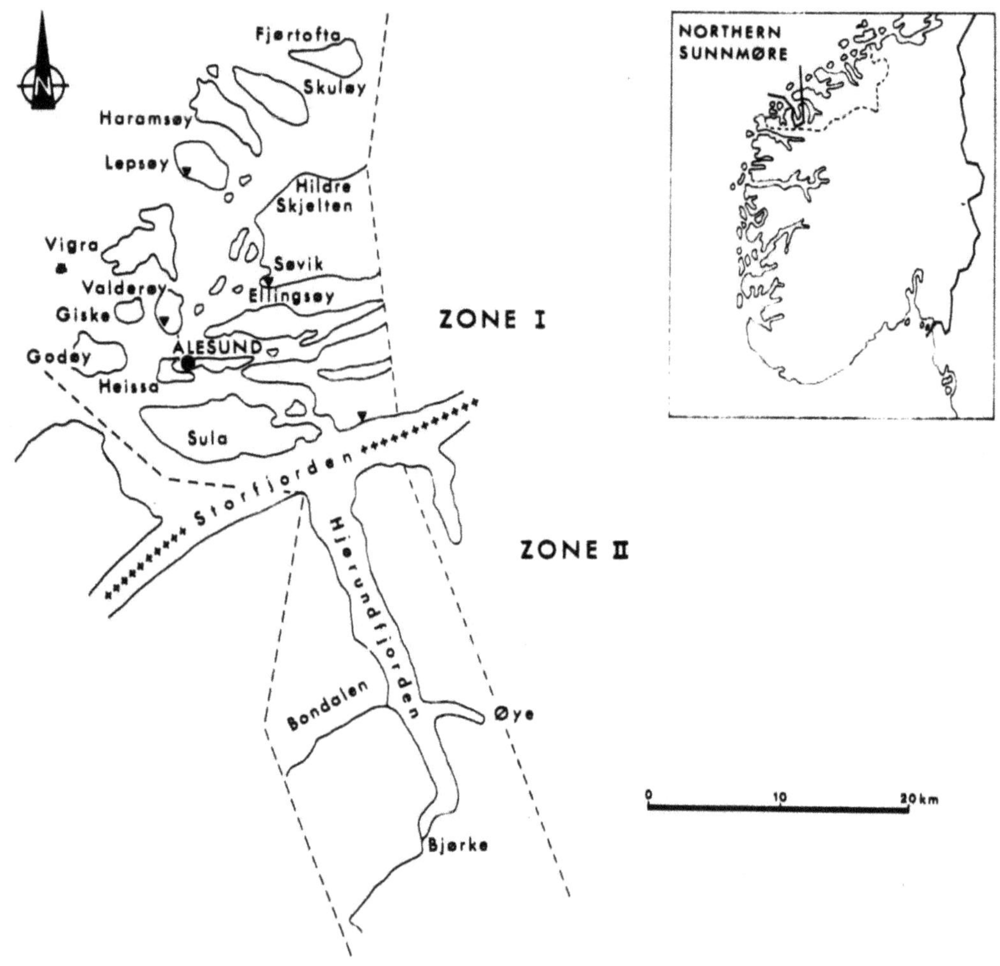

Figure 6. Localisation of the caves in Northern Sunnmöre inhabited during the early iron age.

when farmers from adjacent areas participated in seasonal fisheries and hunting expeditions (Bakka 1973).

Social organisation

The number of settlement units represent only one aspect of settlement. Another important factor is the social organisation which may have varied considerably during the iron age. If the farms along the Norwegian coast in the late Roman and Migration periods resembled the farms in southwestern and northern Norway (Hagen 1953, Myhre 1977), then it should follow that the farmsteads consisted of one or more long houses with separate sections for human and animal inhabitants. Most of the excavated houses are located on marginal soil, but in spite of this fact, they were up to 60-70 m long.

The size indicates that a large number of animals were kept and the settlement unit was fairly large and probably consisted of a composite family (Hagen 1953). Large farms probably had servants and even thralls.

Most likely, the farms varied considerably with regard to size and productivity. Variation in composition and quality of the grave contents seems to represent individuals with differnt social status, and the graves along the western coast of Norway indicate a stratified society from the late Roman period and throughout the Viking period.

In Northern Sunnmöre altogether 184 grave finds from the Roman throughout the Viking period are reported. Figure 7 shows the grouping of these graves on the basis of the number of artefacts. It appears that the great majority, altogether 131, contained from one to three artefacts. Only 53 graves contained four or more artefacts.

The graves in the area can also be grouped according to the quality of the grave contents. In the present work, the 70 grave finds which have been dated as close as within one century, are divided into three groups (Table 3) according to the presence of gold (group I), at least two artefacts of silver and/or bronze and/or at least three weapons (a full set) (group II) and the absence of these criteria (group III). Altogether 8 graves belong to group I, 37 to group II and 25 to group III. The additional 114 graves which are not dated within one century also belong to group III which then represents 139 grave finds.

The oldest find in group I dates from the turn of the 2nd and 3rd century A.D. Altogether 5 graves date from the 4th century and two from the 5th century. After that period, group I is no longer represented.

Another characteristic for group I is that all but one of the 4th century and 5th century graves are cremation burials. Bronze cauldrons mainly of the Vestland type were used as urns. Several of the graves also included drinking stoups of glass - in one case of silver. Two graves contained a medallion or a bracteate of gold. Three of the 4th century graves are exceptionally rich in gold, containing gold objects weighing 625.5, 311.16 and 156.46 g, respectively. These graves rank among the richest in Northern Europe in the 4th century (Hagen 1973).

In group I the graves have one more trait in common - 6 of the 8 graves are from large chairns with diameters of 30-40 m and two from chairns of 10-15 m in diameter. The size of the visible grave structures combined with

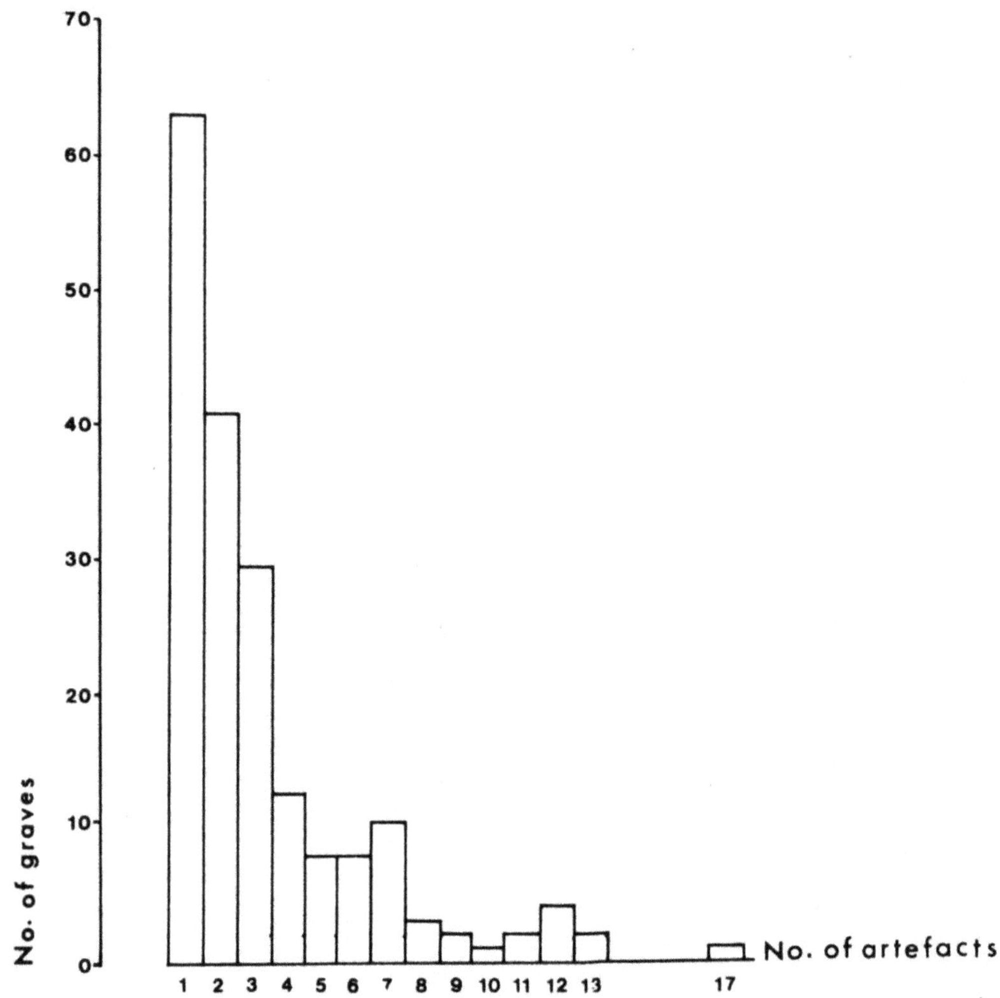

Figure 7. The relationship between the number of grave finds in Northern Sunnmöre during the iron age and the number of artefacts.

the superior quality of the grave goods indicate the presence of an aristocracy. Group I is represented only in zone I and only in the late Roman and first half of the Migration period.

Group II is first represented by the turn of the 2nd and 3rd century in zone I and is present throughout the Viking period. In zone II, the first manifestation of group II dates to the 6th century. Some of the graves are secondary burials in big chairns, but most of the finds are from grave structures varying from 3-4 m in diameter to approximately 23 m. Some graves seem, however, to have had no visible structure above the ground. Five boat graves - of a total of 6 in the whole area - belong to group II. Most likely, this group represents members of well-to-do farmers families. The boat graves indicate that some of their means may have come from seafaring activities. The presence of scales and weights in one of the boat graves may point to trade. Another indication of trade or may be raiding, is the presence of Anglo-Saxon and Irish objects. All such items found in the area belong to graves from group II. This group does not rank among the richest graves in the country and graves of similar wealth are found in most regions of Norway.

Group III with altogether 139 graves represents the average grave finds. In the early iron age the graves often contained pottery and, in the late iron age, a brooch, a weapon or a tool.

The graves in the area indicate a stronger degree of stratification in the late Roman period and first half of the Migration period than later. In the late Roman period a class of people in Northern Sunnmöre has been able to accumulate considerable wealth. They have also held such an esteem in society that by their passing away big sepulchral monuments were erected. These big grave monuments are located along the sailing route which was the "highway" in former days.

After the 5th century no exceptional rich grave has been found in the area. From now on the richest graves are represented by group II. This may indicate that the social conditions within the area became more even. The graves in group II represent the well-off farmers families.

The marked difference in social stratification before and after the 6th century A.D. may indicate that from the 6th century on : 1. the area did no longer produce surplus of any importance to be traded against foreign goods, 2. the social organisation changed and people became more equal and/or 3. the trade routes no longer passed through zone I.

EXPLOITATION OF NATURAL RESOURCES

In prehistoric time, settlement patterns usually have been closely related to the exploitation of the natural resources within the area. During the iron age in Northern Sunnmöre, the resources for agriculture- i.e. cereal-growing and animal husbandry - and fishing were the most prevalent but the resources for hunting were also important. In the following, the differences in these resources between zones I and II are presented and the relationship to settlement pattern is discussed.

Agriculture

The islands and peninsulas of zone I are characterized by large areas of strandflat i.e. morainic deposits running from the foot of the mountains to the shore. The strandflat is well suited for primitive agriculture (Highham 1969). In addition, the climate x) allows a longer growing season in zone I than in zone II. The mean temperatures for the warmest and coldest months - July and January, respectively, are 13.2°C and 2.4°C in zone I and 14.9°C and 0.1°C in zone II xx). The lower precipitation in zone I, 1000-1400 mm per year, compared to 1400-1600 mm in zone II, favours cereal growing. The mild climate in zone I also reduces the danger of frost damage to the crops.

Also the conditions for animal husbandry are more favourable in zone I than in zone II - especially with regard to the necessary amount of work per animal. Because of the lower mean temperture during winter time, zone II has a longer period with snow covering the ground - 92 days - compared to 54 in zone I. Accordingly, the animals must be fed in the barn for a longer period in zone II than in zone I. For the same reason the amount of fodder needed for winter supply is less in zone I than in zone II. In zone I, 10 cows could be fed with the same quantity of fodder as six in zone II (Ström 1762). It was also easier to gather the fodder in the outer area than in the fjords. Haying could be done in only three weeks in zone I but lasted for the whole summer in the fjords. The main reason for this difference was that the majority of the fodder in the fjords was collected up in the mountains far from the farmsteads (Ström 1762). In addition, the results of a pollen analysis from the island of Fjörtoft indicate that the resources for agriculture in zone I have been more favourable before the 5th century than later on.

In summary, therefore, particularly when using primitive technology, the natural resources for cereal-growing and animal husbandry are better in zone I than in zone II.

The archaeological material which directly points to agricultural activities consists of 4 iron celts, 4 scythe blades and 2 sickle blades - the oldest find is a celt dating from the 6th century. The paucity of agricultural tools from the early iron age can be explained by the burial customs. Not until the Merovingian/Viking periods were such implements buried with the deceased. Additional finds pointing to agricultural activities are tools for preparing products deriving from animal husbandry: spinning wheels and weaver's reeds from both the early and late iron age - evidence of the production of textiles of wool and may be linen.

While the archaeological material indirectly shows that domesticated animals have been kept, the osteological material from the Skjong cave and the Skylehammar roch shelter represents primary evidence. Over the centuries, however, the majority of the bones are gone and most likely, the present material represents only a small fraction of the original bones.

---

x) The estimates concerning temperature and precipitation are based on: Det norske metereologiske institutt 1958: "Lufttemperaturen i Norge 1861-1955" and "Nedbören i Norge 1895-1943" (1949).

xx) The observations are from Hellesylt in the neighbouring fjord as no observation regarding temperature and precipitation from Hjörundfjord exists.

Whether this fraction reflects the frequency distribution of the original amount of bones has been a matter of dispute. H. Olsen (1967), however, in his analysis of the osteological material from Varanger in Northern Norway, concluded that the percentage of bone fragments from each species may be taken as a valid measure of the original species frequency.

In the Skjong and Skylehammar caves, sheep and/or goat bones constituted the majority of the mammal bones - 63 and 42% respectively, indicating that these animals have played an important role in the food supply. Cattle was also relatively well represented totalling 13.2% at Skjong and 18.9% at Skylehammar. In the Skjong cave also bones of horses, pigs, dogs and cats were found.

Osteological material and tools are evidence of animal husbandry and agricultural production. Further knowledge about the agricultural production may be obtained by pollen analyses. One pollen diagram has been produced from the island of Fjörtoft (zone I) where culture layers with asbestos ceramics have been located (Kaland 1979, personal communication). The findings of asbestos pottery in Western Norway are correlated with a neolithic economy based upon combined cereal-growing (verified by plough marks on one locality - Aaotnes 1976) and animal husbandry. The pollen diagram demonstrates a phase of cereal-growing and grassing. This cultural phase is, however, covered by a 0.8 m moor deposit (Figure 8). The alteration of culture layer to moor deposit has been dated by radiocarbon to 1490 ± 110 B.P. (T. 1836 - Gulliksen, Nydal & Skogseth 1978). Thus, the pollen analysis demonstrates that cereal-growing and animal husbandry were practiced in this part of zone I at a period preceding the 6th century A.D. After that time moor began to develop. If this has been a general trend in zone I it may seriously have reduced the natural resources for agriculture.

The building up of moors is largely a product of disturbance of the water balance of the soil - mainly as a consequence of deforestation (Kaland 1974). Deforestation leads to deterioration of the quality of the soil - creating podsol in the upper layers - because important chemicals leak away. In a few years grassland is turned into heath and moors. The heath can be used as fodder for the animals. But to serve that purpose it must be burned regularly. This is an obstacle against the growing of bushes and trees, and a cycle is created which allows nothing but heather to grow. The heath landscape on the coast of Norway may, therefore, be regarded as a consequence of human activities. This artificial landscape has a reduced production capacity compared both to a wooden grassland, to deciduous forest, and to meadow. Figure 9 demonstrates the differences between the yearly harvest of forage (hay and pasturage) for domestic animals. The yearly yield is considerably lower for the heath than for meadow (N. Malmer 1969). The change of the landscape from wooden grassland to heath and moors is, therefore, nothing less than a catastrophy from a productional point of view (A. Simonsen 1979).

The results of pollen analysis indicate that such a transformation of the soil occurred on the island of Fjörtoft during the Migration period. On the island of Vigra the find of a grave chairn with asbestos ceramics covered by moor indicates that similar changes took place on this island (Solberg 1976, Aaotnes 1976). In zone I the findings of tree roots in the moors on the islands and peninsulas further support this theory (Balvoll 1964). These phenomena indicate that in zone I the pressure on the land resources caused changes in the ecosystem. If similar changes have occurred all over zone I a marked deterioration of the resources for agriculture would follow.

Figure 8. Heath and farm landscape of the island of Fjörtoft. The transformation of moors to farmland did not start until the 19th century when artificial drainage was introduced.

The archaeological material indicates that during the early iron age people favoured zone I. This is in accordance with the superior resources for agriculture in this zone during that period. In the Migration period, however, signs of over exploitation of zone I occur. At the same time the earliest graves appear in zone II. This seems more than a mere coincidence. Most likely, during this period some people have moved from zone I to zone II which now represented a valuable alternative to the outer area.

Fishing

The archaeological material pointing to fishing consists of net sinkers of stone. One sinker has been found in the Skjong cave and three finds are from Viking period graves.

Fortunately this sparse archaeological material can be supplemented by osteological material from the Skjong cave and the Skylehammar rock shelter. Bones of fish are represented with 244 defined fragments at Skjong and 224 at Skylehammar. At Skjong, cod bones constitute the majority of the material - altogether 72.1% compared to 38% at Skylehammar. The other well represented species are Molva molva which at Skylehammar constitute 54% and at Skjong 18%. The representation of coal fish, however, is very sparse being only 4% at Skong and 5.8% at Skylehammar.

The composition of the fish bones indicates seasonal habitation of the caves. The large percentage of cod bones and the small percentage of bones from coal fish at Skjong compare closely to the results from the Varanger finds where cod constituted approximately 80% and coal fish 10% (H. Olsen 1967). The large percentage of cod bones indicates seasonal fisheries. In Finnmark, seasonal fisheries of cod take place during the winter. The small number of coal fish bones, however, indicates that the dwellings were abandoned during the summer. If they had been inhabited throughout the year the representation of fish bones should have been about 50% cod and 35% coal fish (Olsen 1967). The percentage representation of fish bones at Skjong favours a similar conclusion: the people inhabiting the cave seem to have taken part in a seasonal fishery of cod and there has been little or no fishing during summer time.

In zone I, such a seasonal fishery of cod has indeed taken place in historical times. It is named the Borgundfjord fishery and it used to take place during 3 weeks in February-March (Ström 1762). Zone I, therefore, is one of the best places for fishing along the Norwegian coast. From 1766 we are told: "The greatest riches in this Parish are the fishery which excells that of all other parishes not only in Sunnmöre but in whole Norway". That year the inhabitants in the parish produced approximately 648 tons dried cod and more than 500 boats from the area and surrounding districts participated in the fishery.

In each zone the opportunities for fishing were good - in zone II not for fishing in a large scale, but in zone I they have been especially favourable, partly due to the seasonal appearance of cod. The osteological material from the caves indicates that people during the early iron age took advantage of this opportunity. The lack of traces of habitation of the caves after A.D. 600 may be caused by the fact that people during this period have built houses close to the seashore to stay in during seasonal fisheries (Magnus 1974).

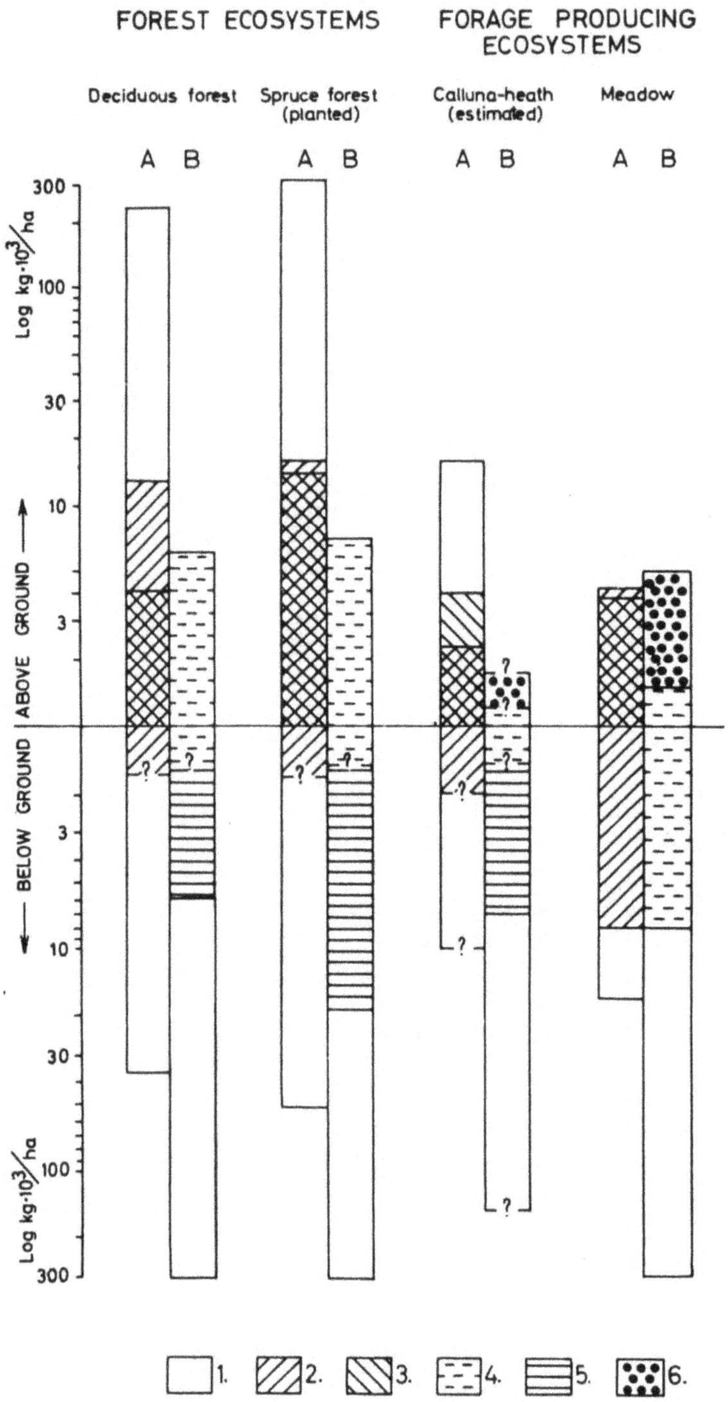

Figure 9. Generalized figures illustrating the distribution of the organic matter and its components in four South Swedish ecosystem types. - Explanations. Column A (to the left): Plant biomass. Column B (to the right): Dead organic matter and harvest. 1 = total amount of plant biomass above and below ground (column A), respectively, total amount of organic matter below ground (column B). 2 = increase in plant biomass during the growing season. 3 = photosynthesizing organs. 4 = yearly loss of organic matter from the plant biomass through litter formation above and below ground. 5 = detached litter on the ground. 6 = yearly harvest of forage (hay and pasturage) for domestic animals. The figures give the dry weight. The storage figures represent late summer conditions. (N. Malmer 1969).

Hunting

The archaeological material directly pointing to hunting mainly consists of arrowheads and spearheads of bone (Brögger 1910).

Arrowheads have been found in four graves, but the most important find consists of approximately 60 well preserved arrowheads from the Skjong cave. The finds from the caves show occupancy in the Roman and Migration periods (Brögger 1910).

Osteological material supplements the archaeological findings and indicates which species were hunted. Bird catching seems to have been of importance in the Skjong cave where bones from altogether 43 species have been found - mostly seabirds. The most common bird was the little auk (Plotus alle) which constituted 48% of the defined bird bones. These bones indicate that the cave has been inhabited during winter time because this bird stays at the Norwegian coast only at this time of the year. The bones of birds in the Skjong cave may be explained from its close localisation to the bird mountain at Skjongholmen (Øvrelid 1964). Also eggs and down were most probably collected. Bird mountains are found only in zone I.

Mammals were probably among the important game. In the Skjong cave sea mammals like seals, porpoise and otter have been favoured. Sea mammals have been plentiful in the area up to the 18th century. On the island of Vigra hunting was performed in a rather primitive way. After closing a bay with a net the seals were clubbed (Ström 1766). Also the name of the island of Erkna which means a special kind of big seal (O. Rygh 1918), indicates the presence of these mammals in the area. Sea mammals appear regularly only in zone I.

Deer was also frequently hunted. At Skylehammar, deer bones constituted 26.7% of the mammal bones. Also at Skjong the deer has been hunted. Most likely, the conditions for hunting land animals were far better in the iron age in both zones than in the historical period.

The people who inhabited the caves have also collected shells. Particularly shells of Patella vulgata and Littorina littorea were plentiful in the Skjong and Havnsund caves.

In zone I, during the period 200-600 the osteological material represents evidence of use of the whole range of resources: animal husbandry, fishing, hunting and gathering. The presence of bones of the little auk strongly indicates that the Skjong cave was occupied during winter time. The percentage representation of bones from cod and coal fish likewise indicates habitation during the winter and participation in a seasonal fishery of cod. Little or no fishing seems to have taken place during the summer.

Accordingly, this cave has been inhabited during seasonal hunting and fishing. Probably the occupants came from adjacent areas. Such participation in seasonal hunting and fishing probably represents a continuation of a practice already established in the bronze age (Aagotnes 1976). This assumption is supported by results of radio-carbon measurements of bone material from the Skjong cave. The dates are 1940± 60 B.P. and 2420 ± 60 B.P., respectively (T 3442-43). These dates contradict the hypothesis that caves and rock shelters in Norway were the permanent dwelling places of specialized hunters and fishermen in the late Roman and Migration periods

(Odner 1973 and Hagen 1977). The discontinuation of their habitation after A.D. 600 may indicate that fishing, hunting and gathering ceased to be of importance in the economy. A far more reasonable explanation, however, is that people who participated in such activities no longer stayed in caves, but in houses built close to the seashore. Remains of such houses have been excavated in Hordaland (B. Magnus 1974).

GENERAL DISCUSSION AND SUMMARY

The ample and varied natural resources in zone I seem to have favoured a mixed economy based upon cereal-growing, animal husbandry, fishing, hunting and gathering. This economy, favouring zone I, seems to have determined the settlement pattern in Northern Sunnmöre until the Migration period. The concentration of burial remains, the many burial-grounds and the number of grave and stray finds from the period 200-600 demonstrate a relatively stable and dense population in zone I. In zone II, the presence of farms cannot be demonstrated until the 5th century. This does not mean, however, that this zone has not been inhabited. But the marked difference between the many finds in zone I and the lack of iron age finds in zone II up to A.D. 400 strongly indicate that zone I has been far more densely populated than zone II. This settlement pattern from Northern Sunnmöre strongly resembles that of Northern Norway during the same period (Sjovöld 1962). In each area, the coastal zone represented the best conditions for agriculture. In addition, sea mammals, birds and fish were abundant.

In the 4th and 5th centuries the population in zone I seems to have been strongly stratified and the leading social group has been wealthy. This group depended upon a surplus produced by people employed in agriculture, fishing and hunting. Parts of this surplus have probably served as exchange goods in trade. After the 5th century, however, graves of the leading social class are no longer represented in the area.

The results of pollen analyses from the island of Fjörtoft may at least partly explain why graves from this wealthy group are no longer to be found. The pollen diagram demonstrated that in the 5th century this locality which had previously been farming area now had changed into heath, probably as a result of over exploitation of the land. If the results of this analysis are valid for larger portions of the outer islands, a reduction in the agricultural output has occurred, reducing the surplus needed by the leading social group to maintain its position. Therefore, in the period around 500 the ecosystem in zone I may have been strained while zone II still contained unoccupied land suitable for farming. This may explain the growing number of grave finds in this area from the 5th century onwards.

However, the growth was not continuous. Along the Norwegian coast - including the area of investigation - a marked decline in the number of grave finds occurred by the end of the 6th century coinciding with the disappearance of rich grave finds in many areas. In the eastern part of Norway a similar phenomenon occurred in the early Merovingian period (Gudesen 1980). Various causes for this decline have been suggested: over exploitation of the land (Berglund 1969, Iversen 1967, Königsson 1968), plague (Helgen 1982, Myhre 1979 and Vinsrygg 1979) and deterioration of the climate (Bröndsted 1966, Königsson 1968). If the decline was diacronous the first explanation might be favoured. If, however, the decline was simultaneous all over the country, the two latter explanations seem more probable. Lately, evidence of a syncronous recession both in Western and

Eastern Norway has been presented (Solberg 1981), favouring plague as the cause of the recession. And indeed, in 542-43 an epidemic plague in the Byzantian empire followed by a series of epidemics has been reported. In France, there was an epidemic as late as 588 (Russell 1975). The Norwegian archaeological material demonstrates regular trade connections between Norway and the Rhine area during the Migration period. Therefore, there is a strong possibility that plague may also have reached Norway.

In Norway, plague caused a reduction of the population by 50-70% from the mid 14th century and onwards having a disastrous effect upon the aristocracy of the country because of the strong reductions in their incomes (Sandnes and Salvesen 1978). If something similar happened in Norway around 600, this may well explain the deserted farms in southwestern Norway, the strong reduction in the number of grave finds and the disappearance of graves of the social upper class.

In Sunnmöre, the most prominent indication of a reduction of the population is the lack of grave finds. From the whole region only one find clearly belongs to the 7th century. This does not mean that the area was depopulated, but it strongly indicates a levelling out between the social groups.

In both zones, there is an increasing number of finds from the 8th century continuing into the Viking period. This represents a marked difference compared to the previous period (before A.D. 600).

Not only is there an increase in the number of farms in both areas, but the increase was far stronger in zone II than in zone I. By the end of the Viking period, in zone I, the number of farms almost doubled while in zone II, the number of farms increased 7-8 times. When the number of farms is related to agricultural resources, i.e. area of arable land and pasture, the settlement density was about even in the two zones.

BIBLIOGRAPHY

Aagotnes, A. 1976. Problemer omkring en boplass med asbestkeramikk på Flatebakken, Ristesund, Kvamsöy. Thesis. Bergen University Library.

Bakka, E. 1965. Ytre Moa. Eit gardsanlegg frå vikingtida i Aardal i Sogn. (Summary). Viking XXIX.

Bakka, E. 1973. Omkring problemet om kulturdualisme i Sör-Noreg. In Bonde - veidemann, bofast - ikke bofast i Nordisk forhistorie. Tromsö Museums Skrifter XIV. (Tromsö).

Bakka, E. 1976. Modvo og Ytre Moa. To garsdsanlegg frå jarnalderen i Sogn. Nordiska arkeologmötet. XII. Berättelse. Iskos 1. (Helsingfors).

Berglund, B. 1969. Scandinavian landscape during the Late Post-Glacial. Oikos Suppl. 12. (Copenhagen).

Balvoll, G. 1964. Jord og naeringstilstand i jorda på Vigra. Stensiltrykk nr. 15 1964. Institutt for grönsakdyrking. Norges Landbrukshögskole. (Vollebekk).

Bröndsted, J. 1966. Danmarks Oldtid I-III. (Copenhagen).

Brögger, A.W. 1910. Vestnorske hulefund fra aeldre jernalder. Bergens Museums Aarbok nr. 12. (Bergen).

Det Norske Meteorologiske Institutt 1943. Nedbören i Norge 1895-1943. (Oslo).

Det Norske Meteorologiske Institutt 1958. Lufttemperaturen i Norge 1861-1955. (Oslo).

Forarbeid 1863. Til matrikkel i henhold til Lov av 6. juni. Riksarkivet. (Oslo).

Gimingham, C.H. 1972. Ecology of Heathlands. (London).

Gudesen, H.G. 1980. Merovingertiden i Øst-Norge. Kronologi, kulturmönstre og tradisjonsforlöp. Universitetet i Oslo. Oldsaksamlingen. Varia: 2. (Oslo).

Gulliksen, S., Nydal, R. & Skogseth, F. 1978. Trondheim Natural Radiocarbon Measurements VIII. Radiocarbon Vol. 20. no. 1. (New Haven, Connecticut).

Hagen, A. 1953. Studier i jernalderens gaardssamfunn. (Summary). Universitetets Oldsaksamling Skrifter 4. (Oslo).

Hagen, A. 1973. Fra Sunnmörsledens jernalder. Kommentar til et forso "k. Honos Ella Kivikoski. Finska fornminnesföreningens tidsskrift 75. (Helsinki).

Hagen, A. 1977. Norges Oldtid. (Oslo).

Helgen, G. 1982. Odd og egg. Merovingertidsfunn fra Hordaland, Sogn og Fjordane. Arkeologiske avhandlinger. Historisk Museum, Universitetet i Bergen. No. 3 - 1982. (Bergen).

Highham, C.F.W. 1969. The economic Basis of the Danish Funnel-Necked Beaker (TRB) Culture. Acta Archaeologica. Vol. XL.

Iversen, J. 1967. Naturens udvikling siden sidste istid. Danmarks Natur 1. (Copenhagen).

Kaland, P.E. 1974. Ble lyngheiene skapt av fimbulvinter eller ved menneskeverk? Forskningsnytt 1974 nr. 4. (Oslo).

Kaland, P.E. 1979. Personal communication.

Königsson, L.-K. 1968. The Holocene History of the Great Alvar of Øland. Acta Phytogeogr. Suec. 55. (Uppsala).

Magnus, B. 1974. Fisker eller bonde? Undersökelser av hustufter på ytterkysten. (Summary). Viking XXXVIII. (Oslo).

Malmer, N. 1969. Organic matter and cycling of minerals in virgin and present ecosystems. Oikos Suppl. 12. (Copenhagen).

Myhre, B. 1977. Jernaldergården på Ullandhaug. 1. Huset i jernalder i Sör-Norge. Arkeologisk museum i Stavanger. Skrifter. (Stavanger).

Myhre, B. 1979. Agrarian Development, Settlement History and Social Organization in Southwest Norwary in the Iron Age. Studies in Scandinavian Prehistory and early History. Vol. 1. (Copenhagen).

Odner, K. 1973. Økonomiske strukturer på Vestlandet i eldre jernalder. (Summary). Univ. i Bergen. Historisk Museum. (Bergen).

Olsen, H. 1967. Varangerfunnene IV Osteologisk materiale. Innledning - fisk - fugl. (Summary). Tromsö Museums Skrifter Vol. VII. Hefte IV. (Tromsö/Oslo/Bergen).

Olsen, M. 1926. Aettegård og helligdom. Norske stedsnavn sosialt og religionshistorisk belyst. Inst. for sammenl. kulturforskning. Serie A, IXA. (Oslo).

Øvrelid, R. 1964. Borgund og Giske. Band III. Gardssoge. (Bergen).

Russell, J.C. 1975. Den tedligere pestboelgen. Europeisk middelalder, Ed. K. Lunden (Gjoevik).

Rygh, O. 1908. Gaardnavne i Romsdals Amt. Opplysninger til brug ved matrikelens revision. (Kristiania).

Sandnes, J. & Salvesen, H. 1978. Ødegårdstid i Norge.

Sandnes, J. & Stemshaug, O. 1976. Norsk stadnamnleksikon. (Oslo).

Simonsen, A. 1972. Breiavatnet og Stavangers eldste historie. Stavanger Museum Arbok 1971. nr. 81. (Stavanger).

Simonsen, A. 1979. Då Jaeren vart lynghei. Fra haug ok heidni. Nr. 2. Bind 7. (Stavanger).

Sjörs, H. 1971. Ekologisk botanikk. (Uppsala).

Sjövold, T. 1962. The Iron Age Settlement of Arctic Norway. Early Iron Age. (Tromso/Oslo).

Slomann, W. 1948. Medelpad og Jämtland i eldre jernalder. (Summary). Universitetet i Bergen Arbok 1948. (Bergen).

Solberg, B. 1976. Jernalder på Nordre Sunnmöre. Bosetning, ressursutnyttelse og sosial struktur. Thesis. Bergen University Library.

Solberg, B. 1981. Spearheads in the transition period between the early and the late Iron Age in Norway. Acta Archaeologica. Vol. 51-1980. (Kobenhavn).

Stenvik, L. 1978. Stadgårder. Et. forsök på arkeologisk datering av en navneklasse. Thesis. (Bergen University Library).

Ström, H. 1762. Physisk og Oeconomisk Beskrivelse over Fogderiet Søndmør, beliggende i Bergens Stift, i Norge. 1. Sorøe.

Ström, H. 1766. Physisk og Oeconomisk Beskrivelse Over Fogeriet Söndmör, beliggende i Bergens Stift, i Norge. II. (Sorøe).

Sömme, A. 1954. Jordbrukets geografi i Norge. A. Tekstbind. Skrifter fra Norges Handelshöyskole i rekken geografiske avh. 3A. (Bergen).

Vinsrygg, S. 1979. Merovingartid i Nord-Noreg. Arkeologiske avhandlingar. Historisk Museum, Universitetet i Bergen. No. 2-1979.

Vorren, K.D. 1976. På spor etter det eldste jordbruket i Nord-Norge. Hva kan botanisk forskning fortelle? Ottar nr. 89. (Tromsö).

TABLE: 1. NUMBER OF FARMS IN NORTHERN SUNNMORE FROM 200-600 A.D. ESTABLISHED BY ARCHAEOLOGICAL FINDINGS & FARM NAMES.

NUMBER OF CRITERIA*	House Grounds		Grave finds		Grave structures		Stray finds		Farm names		SUM	
	ZONE		ZONE		ZONE		ZONE		ZONE		ZONE	
	I	II	I	II	I	II	I	II	I	II	I	II
3			2		2				2		2	
	1		1		1						1	
2			14	2	14	2					14	2
			5						5		5	-
					2		2				2	-
					5				5		5	-
							2	2	2	2	2	2
	1								1		1	-
1			8		11		3		2	1	24	1
SUM	2	-	30	2	35	2	7	2	17	3	56	5

* Farm settlement is based upon the following criteria (see text): House grounds, grave finds, grave structures, stray finds and/or farm names.

TABLE 2: NUMBER OF FARMS IN NORTHERN SUNNMORE FROM 600-1050 A.D. ESTABLISHED BY ARCHAEOLOGICAL FINDINGS & FARM NAMES.

NUMBER OF CRITERIA*	Grave finds		Grave structures		Stray finds		Farm names		SUM	
	ZONE		ZONE		ZONE		ZONE		ZONE	
	1	11	1	11	1	11	1	11	1	11
3	9	5	9	5			9	5	9	5
2	8	15 3	8 24	15			 24	 3	8 24	15 3
1			54	2	1	1	2	4	57	7
SUM	17	23	95	22	1	1	35	12	98	30

* Farm settlement is based upon the following criteria (see text): Grave finds, grave structures, stray finds and/or farm names.

TABLE 3: Number of grave finds in northern Sunnmöre in relation to quality [1], area [2] and century.

CENTURY	QUALITY GROUP[1]						SUM
	I		II		III		
	ZONE[2]		ZONE[2]		ZONE[2]		
	I	II	I	II	I	II	
2nd and/or 3rd	1	-	1	-	-	-	2
4	5	-	6	-	2	-	13
5	2	-	7	-	5	1	15
6	-	-	5	1	-	1	7
7	-	-	-	1	-	-	1
8	-	-	1	-	1	-	2
9	-	-	5	4	6	6	21
10	-	-	5	1	2	1	9
Sum	8	0	30	7	16	9	70

1) Based upon quality the grave finds have been divided into three groups with the following contents:

I Objects of gold.

II Two objects of silver/bronze and/or a set of weapons.

III Absence of the criteria above.

2) Based upon variation in topography Northern Sunnmöre has been divided into an outer (I) and inner (II) zone - see text.

CHANGES IN LANDSCAPE & SOCIETY IN TORSTUNA PARISH, UPPLAND DURING PRE-HISTORIC TIME.

Ulla Göranson

INTRODUCTION

The landscape is a product of influences by man for hundreds of years. It is therefore not uniform but consists of elements from several previous evolutionary levels where some elements have disappeared, while others have been preserved thereby giving the area its special character. Land reforms, changes in settlement pattern, regularization of built up areas, changes in livelihood are examples of ways for man to change and "develop" his society. A "highly developed" landscape contains survivals from many changes. The more "developed" a landscape is, the larger will be the number of characteristic elements, the more intricate and complex the organizational linkages and the stronger the ties between the varied components.

My purpose in this investigation has been to show the stages through which the landscape in the investigated area has developed and to try to find the main causal factors within this process.[1)]

Area of Investigation

The investigated area, Torstuna parish in the landscape of Uppland, is located about 80 km W of Stockholm. It is a little more than 72 km^2 in area and consists today of 34 hamlets (Figure 1). Geologically it is comprised of a peneplan of primary rock split up by valleys, running in a NW-SE direction. Junctions between two or more valleys give rise to the larger plains that have made this area one of the best in Sweden for cultivation. The dominant soil types are till and rather heavy clay. The till which is most frequent in the northern part of the parish is lime-rich and therefore not too bad for cultivation but in fact the cultivated areas are mainly located in the two valleys running through the parish and the flat southern part where the clay layer is 1-2 m thick.

Today the parish is a highly mechanized and intensively cultivated agricultural district with the stress on corn-production. Seventeenth century maps show that the area was at that time cultivated to almost the same extent as today (Figure 2). Tilled land predominated and some hamlets had a total lack of meadow lands. At that time the two-field-system was practised in every hamlet and normally with two fields of equal size. Almost every hamlet was involved in a system of cooperation with its neighbour in that two fields bordering each other were used for the same crop, what in the southern part of Sweden is called vångalag. The hamlet buildings were normally located upon the transition zone between clay and till, i.e. they lay along the valleys. In some hamlets, however, the

Figure 1. The area investigated.

buildings were situated on pure clay soil. The maps also show that the buildings in most hamlets in the parish were concentrated to a regular toft in conformity to the principles of solskifte. As a whole, Torstuna parish is an area that already by the middle of the 17th century had highly developed agriculture but careful study reveals differences in land-use and settlement location which imply various stages in a process of change. For example, a concentration of all buildings within a hamlet to one single toft instead of separated farm-steads and a two-field-system with only two fields of equal size instead of a lot of small fields implies a higher level in this process. This investigation aims to describe the making of the landscape and discuss when and why such differences have arisen.

The Source Material

The focus of this investigation is the landscape created by continuously increasing cultivation. This provides certain difficulties when it comes to sources. Most investigations concerning prehistoric (which in Sweden is the time before A.D. 1050) landscapes have dealt with areas where the cultivation has decreased giving good opportunities for field-studies. The fossil remains have decided the area for investigation and research and studies have been limited to those parts of Sweden where such remains occur.

In an area where the cultivated areas has been under continuous usage one cannot expect to find too many fossil remains, but the process of change to an agriculturally developed landscape cannot be studied in a marginal area which is rich in remains. Thus field-studies can play only a small role in such investigation and in this case field-work was used to test hypothesis about changes which have been derived from other sources. The main sources are cadastral maps and other large-scale maps from the 17th to the 20th centuries, assessment lists from 16th and 17th centuries and the National Survey of Antiquities.

Maps

Torstuna parish is very well documented with older maps. From the earliest mapping of villages in Sweden, which was started in the 1630's, a complete collection of maps survives but in addition there are maps created during the land reforms of the end of the 18th and the beginning of the 19th centuries, as the following table shows:

Table 1: Number of surviving village maps from different periods of survey.

Geometriska jordeboken 1652	34
Geometrisk avmätning 1696-1757	9
Storskifte 1759-86	32
Laga skifte 1843-92	32

The most important of these maps series is the one from 1652 from which I have been able to create a complete picture of the land-use-pattern in the

Figure 2. Reconstruction of the landscape in 1652.

parish at that time. These maps were drawn before the revolutionary changes during the 18th and 19th centuries took place. I have assumed that these maps show conditions that were existing from around A.D. 1200 and onwards. This hypothesis is vital for the further analysis but it is also very difficult to confirm because of our limited knowledge of this period.

The general picture of this period concerning agriculture is a time of decreasing cultivation. An agricultural crisis is going on during the 14th and 15th centuries which is demonstrated in records by the occurrence of devastations of farms and decreasing payments due to poverty. Studies about this crisis have so far mostly dealt with agriculturally marginal areas but it might have had an effect also in the central parts at least to the extent that an increase in cultivated land is not taking place. Another fact that can be used to support my assumption is the taxation of the villages in so called markland that was introduced in this region around A.D. 1200. This taxation was based upon the cultivated area where 1 örtugland (= 1/24 of a markland) was the value of 1 tunnland of cultivated land. Comparing the taxation in örtugland with the amount of land under plough in 1650 one finds a correspondence that to me seems to show that these figures are the same. The similarities are even more striking when the area of land is converted into the medieval sizes of the tunnland. This accordance cannot be statistically proved since there are two medieval tunnland of different sizes and one is used in some hamlets while the other is used in other hamlets in the parish. In addition, these figures have been affected by changes that have taken place in some of the hamlets. (These two groups of hamlets with different sizes of the tunnland and these deviations are more thoroughly discussed in my dissertation).

I have used the village maps of 1652 as a fixed point at which I can describe the landscape in terms of the amount of land under plough and the amount of meadow-land per hamlet and farm-stead, the total amount of land under plough and the size and number of fields.

The proportion of land under plough was already very high in 1652. 28% of the total area of the parish was cultivated and on an average each farm-stead had 29 tunnland (about 35 acres) of cultivated land. Some hamlets, however, have no meadow land at all. The individual farms in hamlets with only 1-2 farm-steads have more land under plough than farms in larger hamlets. The average figure for these farm-steads is 38 tunnland (about 46 acres). During the 18th and 19th centuries, when there was a considerable expansion in cultivation in most areas in Sweden, no great changes in that respect took place in Torstuna parish, since the expansion up to a level when all possible land was cultivated had occurred earlier.

Assessment Lists

Peasants owning their land and tenants on land owned by the state are the two tax-paying categories of farmers which are always registered in the assessment lists. Other categories of farmers sometimes occur in the lists. Most peasants in Torstuna belong, however, to one of the two first mentioned categories so information about the rating of the farms is good.

Two different series of assessment lists have been used here. One of the series, started about 1540, gives the taxation rating of each farm-stead while the other list is a register of a special taxation which was taken between 1620 and 1641. This tax was based upon the amount of seed for sowing and the number of animals, and uses figures which have been shown to be a relict from medieval conditions and can therefore be used as information about the area of cultivated land at that earlier time (Hannerberg 1970:77).

When it comes to taxation, the farm-steads in Torstuna are about the same size as farm-steads in other investigated areas but the hamlets are a bit larger since the number of farm-steads per hamlet is above the normal size.

Archaeological Remains

The National Survey of Antiquities was carried through in Torstuna parish between 1951 and 1952. Later checks have shown that the register is fairly complete when it comes to the number of places with archaeological remains but rather less complete considering the number of graves or other remains at each place. In this kind of area with a very high degree of land under plough one can assume that a lot of remains have disappeared. There is a greater tendency for certain kinds of remains to disappear, for example, grave-fields from the latest part of the pre-historic period which were situated on clay soils by the rivers. As mentioned above, remains from cultivation and settlement can hardly be expected to be found in this kind of intensively cultivated area and indeed a very few traces of earlier fencing-systems are the only remains of this kind in Torstuna parish.

The archaeological remains show that the area was already colonized during the Stone Age (about 3500-1500 BC). A settlement dating from that time has been found on the ridge running through the area and scattered artifacts have been found in different parts of the parish, as have also remains from the Bronze Age (1500-500 BC).

From the Early Iron Age (500 BC-AD 500) there are eight grave-fields and a number of single graves. No traces of settlement have been found, but based on the grave-fields one can assume that the whole area was colonized at this time forming a sparse pattern of settlement.

Twenty-three grave-fields are dated to the Late Iron Age (AD 500-1050). As a rule grave-fields from this period are located next to the 17th century settlements implying a continuity during the whole period. In Torstuna the distance between grave-fields and each settlement is further than in other investigated areas, notably in those hamlets where the buildings are situated on clay soil by the river, which might indicate some kind of discontinuity in these hamlets. The place-names, however, support an assumption that the hamlets were already established during pre-historic times.

The Investigation

During the last 15-20 years research in historical geography in Sweden has to a great deal dealt with remains of pre-historic field-systems in different parts of the country. Though datings are few they point in the same direction and can therefore be used for the following chronology for the development of field-systems.

During the Late Bronze Age and Early Iron Age (around 500 BC-AD 200) large fields, so called celtic fields, were used. These were probably cultivated by a group of people larger than an extended family (Lindquist 1974:30-31). A system with only one small field was used during the period AD 200-1000 (Lindquist 1974:31). The introduction of a two-field-system has been dated to around AD 1000 in Västergötland (Lindquist 1975:157) and Närke (Sporrong 1971:197) and to around AD 1100 in Uppland (Sporrong 1971:71) but it seems as if in some areas the system was introduced already by AD 500-600 though datings are still lacking. The introduction of a three-field-system in Skåne is supposed to have taken place around AD 1200.

Very little is known about Swedish pre-historic society as a whole concerning status of ownership, technique of cultivation, etc., but assuming that there is a connection between different aspects of society, then a special type of cultivation will, for example, give rise to a special form of settlement, which in turn will suggest something about the organisation within the society. I think it is possible to use what is known to construct the following hypothetical scheme:

A hypothetical model of evolution

Time (level)	Field system	settlement	society	assessment
Before AD 400 (level A)	large, common fields, extensively cultivated	simple and ambulating	units larger than extended families	based on units, not referring to size
Around AD 500 (level B)	small, privately and intensively cultivated fields	steady and solitary	based on single families	
Around AD 600 (level C)	consolidating field-systems	agglomerating	families with some co-operation	
Around AD 800 (level D)	planned one-field-system		village community	based on the amount of cultivated land
Around AD 900	planned two-field system	agglomerated into villages		
Around AD 1000		regulated village tofts		

I will use this model as a back-bone for the analysing parts of the investigation.

Changes from Level A to Level B

In Torstuna parish and the region surrounding it no fossil landscapes with remains of settlement or field-systems of the kind that hypothetically existed on level A have been found. Based on datings of fossil remains

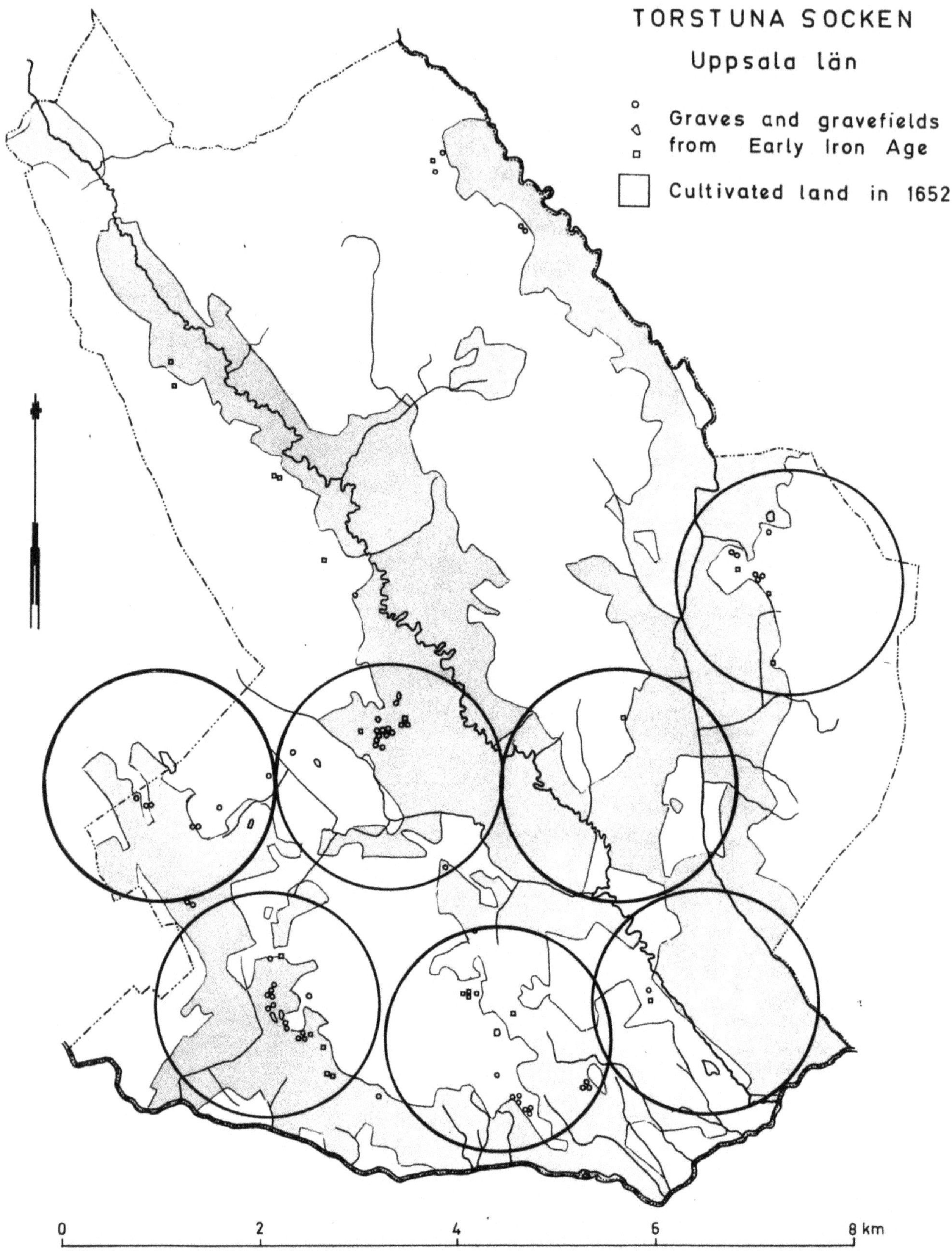

Figure 3. Units during the Early Iron Age.

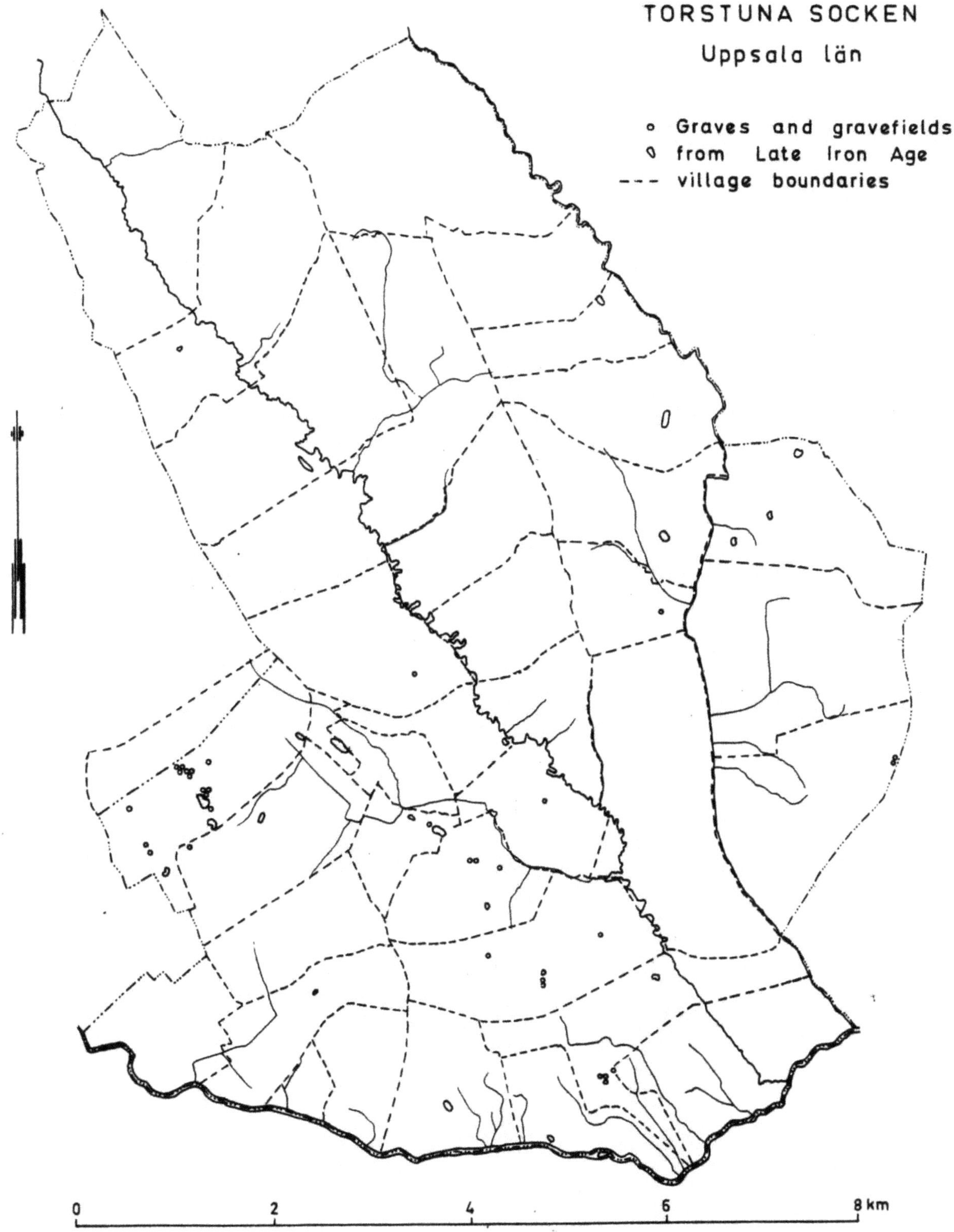

Figure 4. Units during the Late Iron Age.

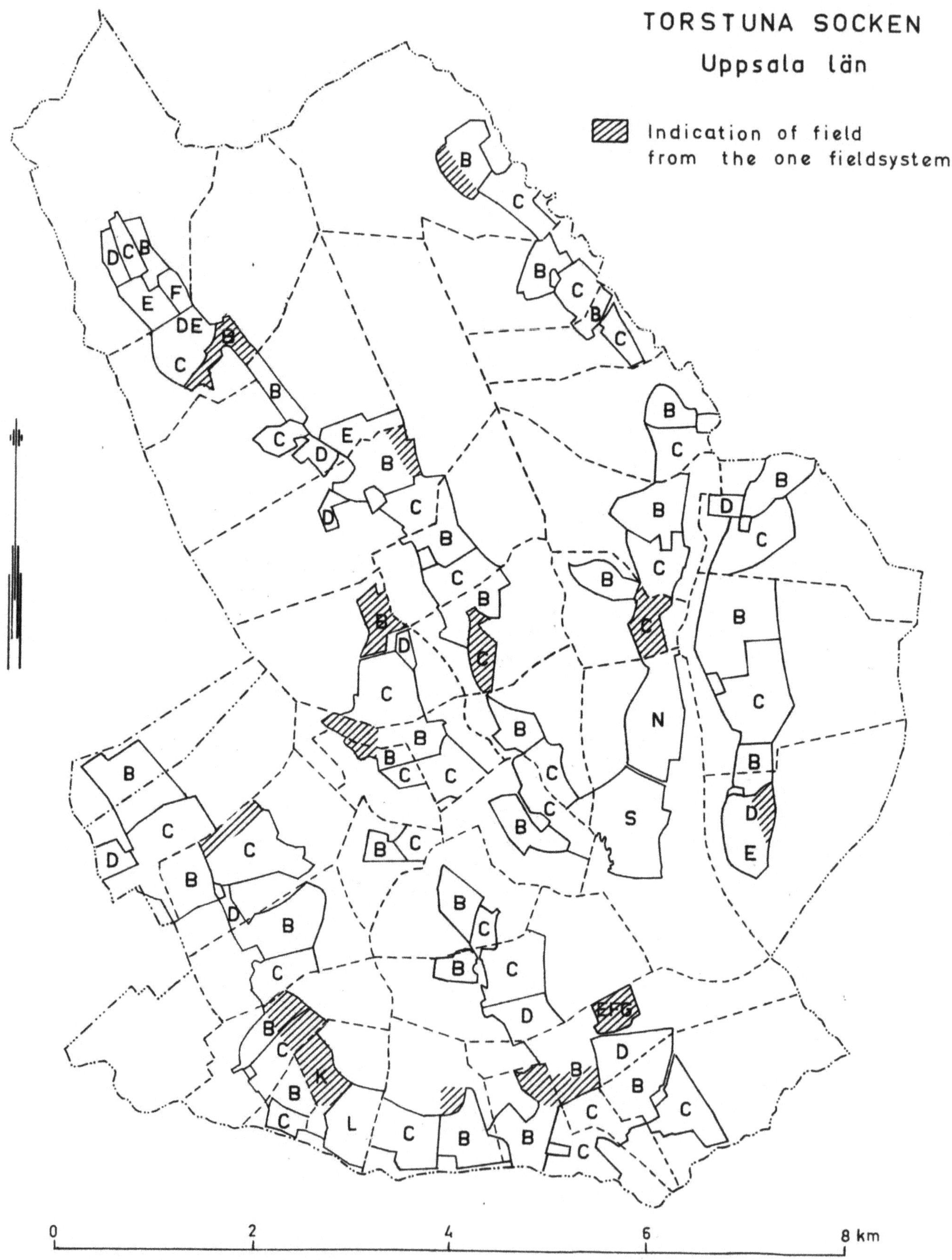

Figure 5. Enclosed fields in 1652.

from other parts of Sweden I assume that level A existed in Torstuna during the Early Iron Age. On possible way to check this hypothesis is to look at the spatial distribution of grave-fields dating from this time.

I have assumed that a fairly big group of people cultivated the field-systems remaining from this time. Calculations have shown that one family needs 3 ha. (7.5 acres) of cultivated land (Hannerberg 1971:64). A system of fields covering an area of about 150 ha (375 acres) where a 10 year fallow system is used would then be enough for at least 3-5 familes or 20-30 people. Such a large group of people should produce a lot of graves (about 150 graves per 300 years).

As a common feature, grave-fields dated to the Early Iron Age are rather large and have a rich variety of forms. In Torstuna parish there is only one grave-field of this kind, the remaining seven all being very small. These are, however, surrounded with single graves thereby creating an agglomerated spatial pattern of graves. Altogether there are six such agglomerations of graves in Torstuna. The number of graves in each of these agglomeration, however, does not reach the figure of 150 graves per 300 years. One reason for this might be the fact that a lot of graves have disappeared due to the intensive cultivation.

Another general feature of grave-fields dating from the Early Iron Age is their large distances from the present day settlements, and this is also the case in Torstuna. This might indicate that settlements were localised in a different way during the Early Iron Age than they were later.

Some assumptions can also be made concerning the "scale of the landscape" at this time. An extensive land use-system needs large areas. If an area of 150 ha had to be located on soils suitable for primitive cultivation in the presently discussed kind of landscape it would be easiest done with a block of land sited within the transition zone between till and clay soil. This rectangle would perhaps be of the order of 200-300 m in width and 2-3 km long. If the settlements are located in the centre, this arrangment would result in a pattern of rather large settlement agglomerations at a distance of about 2-3 km from each other.

In Figure 3 I have used the six agglomerations of graves as settlement centres. The mean distance between these centres is a bit more than 2 km. When I enclose an area with a diameter of 2 km around these centres these circles cover the main part of the infield land at 1652 in the southern part of the parish, though one unit seems to be missing in the very centre of the region. This is the "heart-land" of the parish where both the pagan and the christian centres are situated. I have therefore added one unit and assume that the map then shows the seven Early Iron Age units in the parish. The unit centres are all situated on the border between cultivated and uncultivated land. The most plausible place-names of these units also give support to the assumption that these units existed in the Early Iron Age.

In the model, the change from level A to level B means the creation of a society based on families. For a change in the cultivation it seems more plausible that it was intensified in the best parts of the former commonly cultivated fields than that the old fields were deserted and new land cleared at another place. This will give rise to a new, more scattered settlement pattern.

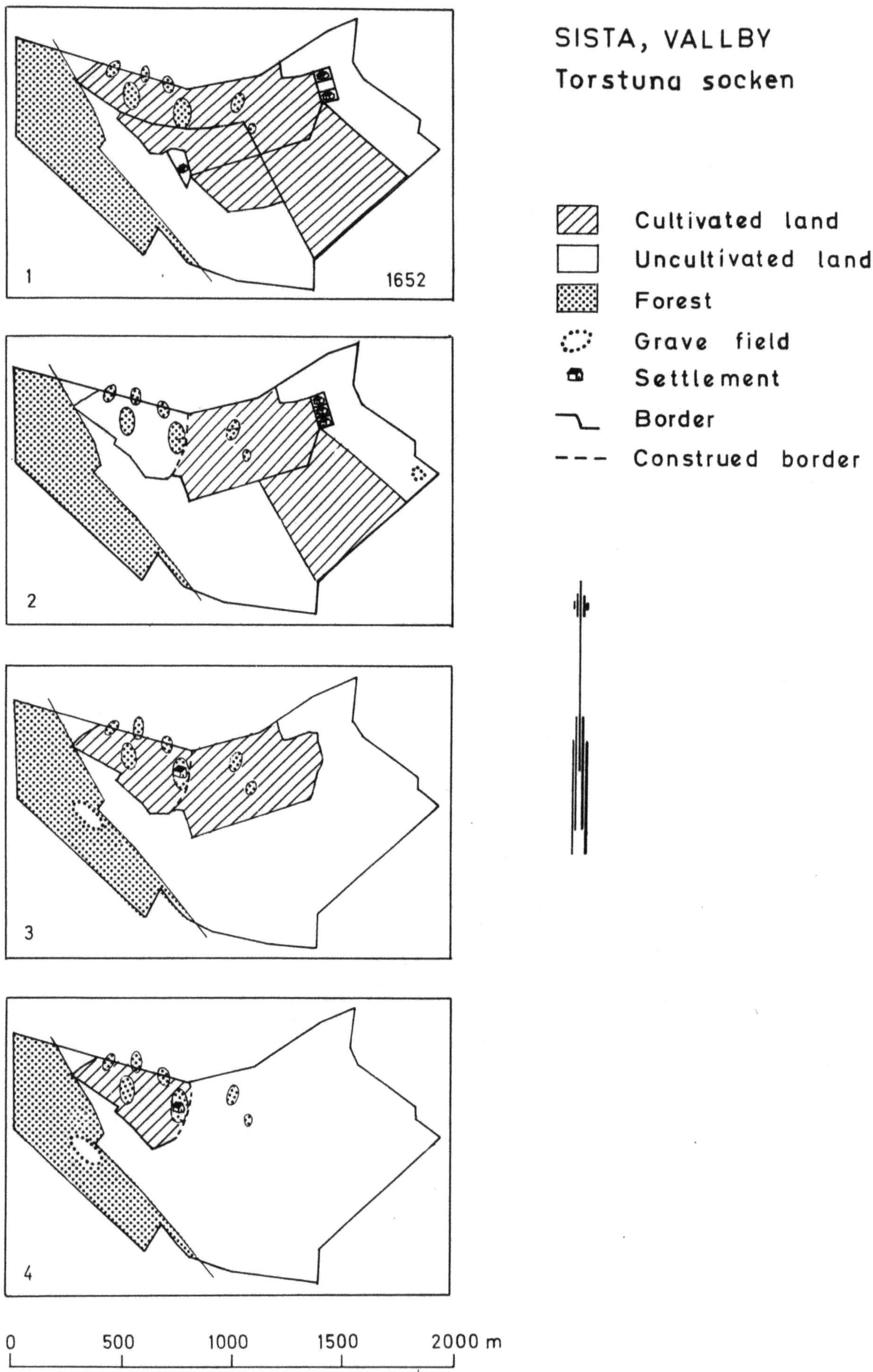

Figure 6. Reconstruction of changes in two villages.

Grave-fields dating from the Late Iron Age normally consists of fewer graves than those of this Early Iron Age but are of a more homogenous form. This is also true for the grave-fields in Torstuna dated to the Late Iron Age. As a rule these grave-fields are in close contact with the present village toft but this cannot be said to be the case in Torstuna, where the mean distance between the grave-fields and the present village tofts is more than 500 m.

The spatial distribution of grave-fields of the Late Iron Age is more uniform than that of earlier ones. The former units cover areas that are parts of more than one hamlet (Figure 4). Since most of these hamlets have one Late Iron Age grave-field of normal size, this seems to imply that the former units are split up and the present hamlets are established at this time though this splitting up is a process that still is going on in the 17th century.

The Introduction of a Two-field System

From the first two levels in the model there is no evidence from the investigated area concerning the field-systems. Only because other sources have shown a change in society have I assumed that there has been a change in cultivation from more extensive forms to an intensive cultivation on a family basis. The change was probably a very slow process that after a long time led to the development of a one-field system. The transition from this system to a two-field system is a very important step that can be elucidated with the help of maps of Torstuna parish.

Hannerberg has argued that the fields in the one-field system as well as in the two-field system possess carefully planned areas. He then develops other evidence using comparisons between material from Uppland and Wales (Hannerberg 1976). To simplify greatly, one can say that the fields for one <u>bol</u> which is a unit with a fixed size, in the one-field system has an area of about 14 ha (35 acres) and that the total area in the two-field system should be about 38 ha (95 acres). The new fields planned for the introduction of the two-field system subsequently had an area of about 24 ha (60 acres).

I have measured all the fields on the maps of Torstuna from 1652 and summed the figures to get the total amount of planned fields per village. Since the <u>bol</u> consists of two <u>hemman</u>, a field-size of about 19 ha should be found in this material if the fields in Torstuna were planned the same way as the fields in the area where Hannerberg made his study. A chi^2-test shows that the probability for that assumption was as high as 99%. I therefore assume that the two mentioned field-sizes can be found in Torstuna as well. But there are two ways to get this desirable size for the two-field system of 38 ha. Either one can keep the fields from the one-field system in its original size, i.e. 14 ha, and clear a new field of 24 ha, or one can enlarge the old field to 19 ha and clear one more field of the same size. This will give the advantage of two fields of the same size giving about the same harvest every year.

Based on these assumptions, I made a hypothetical separation of fields that were planned for the one-field system and fields that were planned for the introduction of a two-field system (Figure 5). It then became clear that there were some differences in the location between the two types of field. The fields from the one-field system are situated higher up the

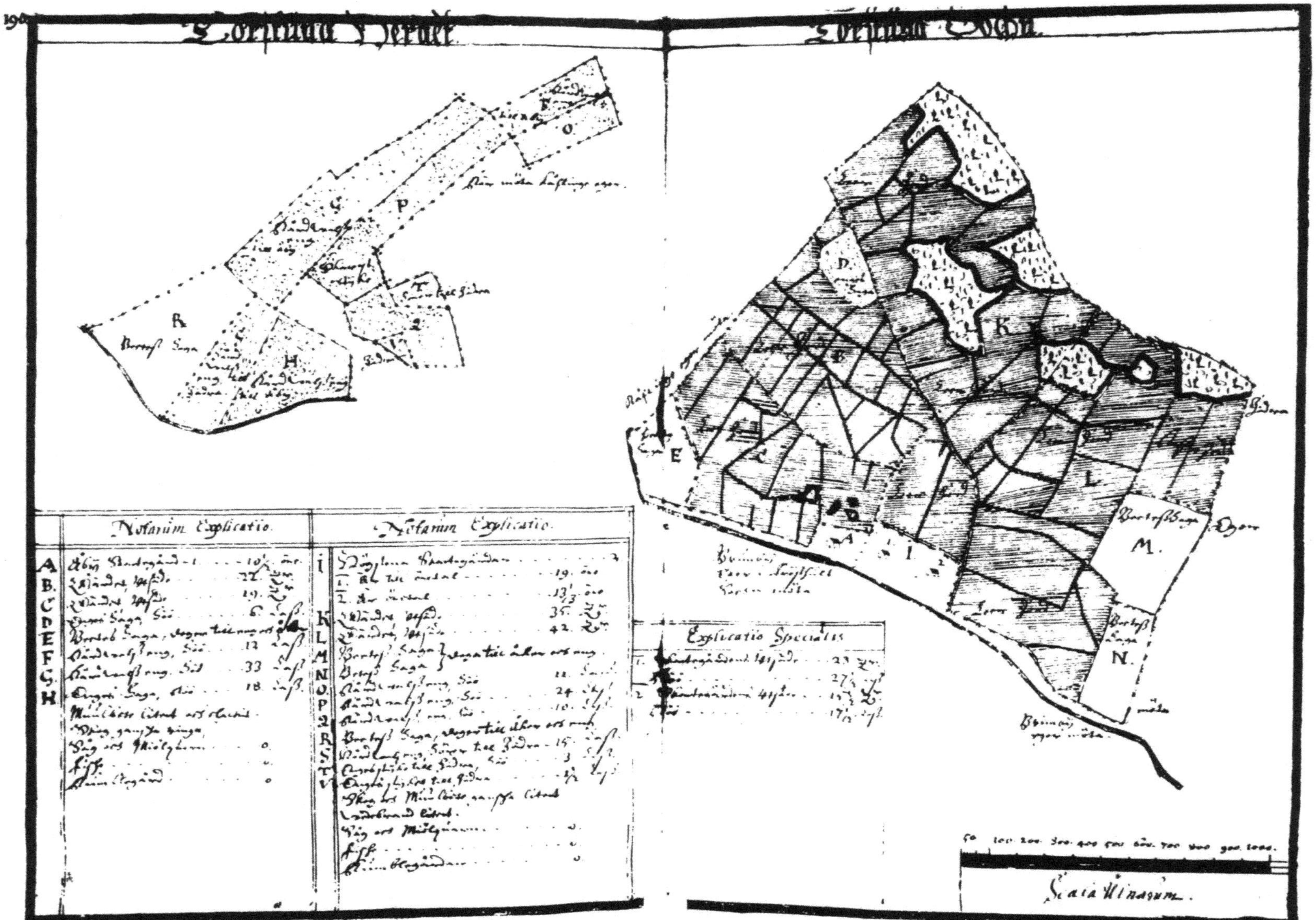

Figure 7. Högstena village in 1652.

slopes on lighter clay soils interspersed with till. Mostly these fields lie above the settlement while the later fields were cleared on the slopes below the settlement and on heavier clay soil.

What effect does the planning of a new field have on the introduction of the two-field system in the land-use pattern as a whole? When the one-field system is used the settlement is located on the transitional zone between clay and till. The field is situated close to and above the settlement. Within the enclosed field there is room for cultivated land as well as for meadow land. The need for another field will not arise until every inch of this first field is cultivated. At this stage the most important meadow must have been moved to heavier soils outside the enclosed field but still close to the settlement. When a new field is planned it is most probable that it will be located close to the meadow to get it as close to the settlement and the old field as possible. This new field is planned for cultivated land and meadow in equal shares but its peak use to its full extent was often not reached until the Middle Ages (Hannerberg 1975:37 f.). In some areas like Torstuna the information about the amount of cultivated land from the Middle Ages shows that cultivation of the meadow land had started at that time. The meadow will be moved again further away from the settlement. I assume that this is the situation when the localisation of settlements on clay ground in the middle of the fields will emerge. Some fields from the one-field system that now lie far away from the settlement will be deserted. These changes can be demonstrated with a reconstruction of conditions in a group of hamlets in Torstuna (Figure 6). If I have made the right interpretation of these changes there should be deserted settlement sites in the transitional zone in those hamlets where the settlement is located away from the unproductive areas.

Location of Settlement at Stage D

In order to verify my assumptions about a previous settlement location I made a field-survey. Areas with small islands of unproductive land surrounded by lighter clay soils and where a field of the size for the one-field system had been identified were searched. Thereby I found some remains I thought were house-foundations. They were localized as expected in the transitional zone between clay and till. The settlement in the hamlet today as well as in 1652 is situated by the river (Figure 7). A map from 1765 gave the information that this place was the former site of the village toft.

I carried out an excavation to be sure that the remains were house-foundations and to get a dating of the time when they were deserted. This would date as well the change in settlement location and give an idea as to the time of the introduction of the two-field system since that must have preceeded the change. Both radiocarbon dating of charcoal from the floor and from posts and artefacts were used for dating and everything indicated the period AD 700-800 for the abandonment of the houses. This is probably one of the earliest changes of settlement location in this parish. The process is most of all taking place during early medieval times (AD 1000-1200).

The regulation in settlement and field and the change in settlement location will give Toratuna parish its final landscape character but the reasons for these last changes are not exactly the same. There are hamlets with regulated tofts that remain in the old location but there are no cases where the location of settlement is changed without a regulation of the toft. The regulation seems to be caused most of all by a need to rearrange conditions after an accelerated process of land clearing. In hamlets with a regulated toft a large share of the area is brought under cultivation. This intensification in agriculture is in turn dependent on the fact that borders between the hamlets were fixed before the growth had started. This becomes most evident in the taxations, but also in other assessments of the hamlets. The more farm-steads a hamlet consists of the smaller is each farm-stead. The hamlets seem to have a fixed assessment that cannot be changed. The village tofts show the final assessment picture. Judging from metrological analysis of some of the village tofts one can assume that the fixing must have taken place during early medieval times at the latest.

The change in settlement location, however, seems to depend more on the amount of land under cultivation. In large hamlets the transport route from fields to settlement became too long and enforced a change in location. As a result conditions for cultivation got better at the same time as conditions for cattle-breeding got worse. Therefore one can say that the change in cultivation will have a cumulative effect where every step is in favour of available farming cultivation and also the cattle-breeding will be adapted to a niveau which is advantageous for this type of agriculture. The cattle-breeding will in this situation not give any surplus and you will therefore have to grow corn enough to meet the requirements for what you cannot produce yourself. A situation of a developing exchange and markets will arise. At the same time a lot of people must have been placed outside the system because of the fixation of present conditions that the assessment valuations and regulations of the hamlets will imply. I think that these conditions together with some others are the underlying features for the emergence of towns. In the areas around Torstuna parish where one finds the same kind of landscape, towns emerge in the 11th and 12th centuries, which fits very well with the dating of the regulation of the village tofts and the changes in settlement location in the Torstuna parish.

1. This article is a summary of my PhD thesis 'Kulturlandskapsförändring och Samhällsutveckling. En undersökning av rumsliga förändringar av kulturlandskapet i Torstuna socken i Uppland från 0 till 1650' ('Changes of the Landscape and Development of the Society. A Survey of Spatial Changes in the Landscape of Torstuna Parish, Uppland from AD to AD 1650'). Meddelande från Kulturgeografiska Institutionen, Stockholms Universitet B36. Stockholm, 1977.

REFERENCES.

Hannerberg, D. 1970. Det svenska agrarsamhällets historiska geografi. I. Akerareal, produktion, konsumtionsramar (The Historical Geography of the Swedish Agrarian Society. I. Cultivated area, Production, Frames of Consumption).

Hannerberg, D. 1971. Svenskt agrarsamhälle under 1200 år. Gård och åker. Skörd och boskap (Swedish Agrarian Society during 1200 years. Farm-stead and Cultivated Area. Crops and Cattle). (Stockholm).

Hannerberg, D. 1975. Den uppländska tolften som kameralt system och territoriell planering (The Tolft in Uppland as Cameralistic System and Planning of Territories). Meddelande från Forskningsprojektet Administrativa Runsliga System nr 29.

A MODEL OF MEDIEVAL RURAL SOCIETY BASED ON FIELD EVIDENCE FROM CENTRAL SWEDEN

Ulf Sporrong

1. Introduction

According to the written sources, Swedish early medieval rural society had relatively stringent rules governing the ownership, taxation, cultivation of land and settlement forms, but only a weak central administration. (Fritz 1972, Hafström 1964, Hannerberg 1976). The typical form of settlement in eastern central Sweden - the so-called Mälar region (Fig. 1) - was a small "irregular" hamlet consisting of a couple of farms which collaborated in many ways but which were always separated by privately owned strips in two different fields. This situation was very stable and existed for hundreds of years. The written sources also describe the dominant social structure of medieval society, which included a system of landowners, tenants and landless people 1) - almost the same situation as existed shortly before the industrial revolution in the 19th century. So, from our traditional sources, we know a great deal about the situation in the Middle Ages. We also know that the society of the early Iron Age probably was quite different from this with collective forms for living and land-use 2). When, then, did the situation change from the collective forms of the early Iron Age to the medieval pattern of privately owned strips of land in combination with new settlement within the structure of small hamlets?

My own research is focused upon this question and among other sources I have used different kinds of field-material in order to discover whether there were any new social and economic ideas which may have led to the change-over from a collective to a private land-use system. It is also my aim to date different kinds of traces still visible in the terrain of today. (Sporrong 1976).

An examination of the settlement structure of the Mälar area reveals many similarities, as well as to the remarkable differences. There is a fair correspondence between the physical resources of the landscape and the shape of the settlement units because, in many ways, the fullfillment of needs of an agrarian society depends on the available physical resources of the landscape. For this reason we often find more developed forms of settlement in the central districts of agrarian production than in the peripherial areas. To begin with, I would like to briefly describe the characteristics of the landscape of eastern middle Sweden.

2. The area of investigation

The Mälar area is made up of the provinces of Uppland, Södermanland, Västmanland and Närke. It is primarily a homogeneous physical landscape and, as mentioned, the provinces also have many similarities in terms of cultural influences through time. Along with Ostergötland, and parts of other bordering provinces, they make up the cultural area of eastern Middle Sweden. The region is one of the most interesting in Sweden in the sense

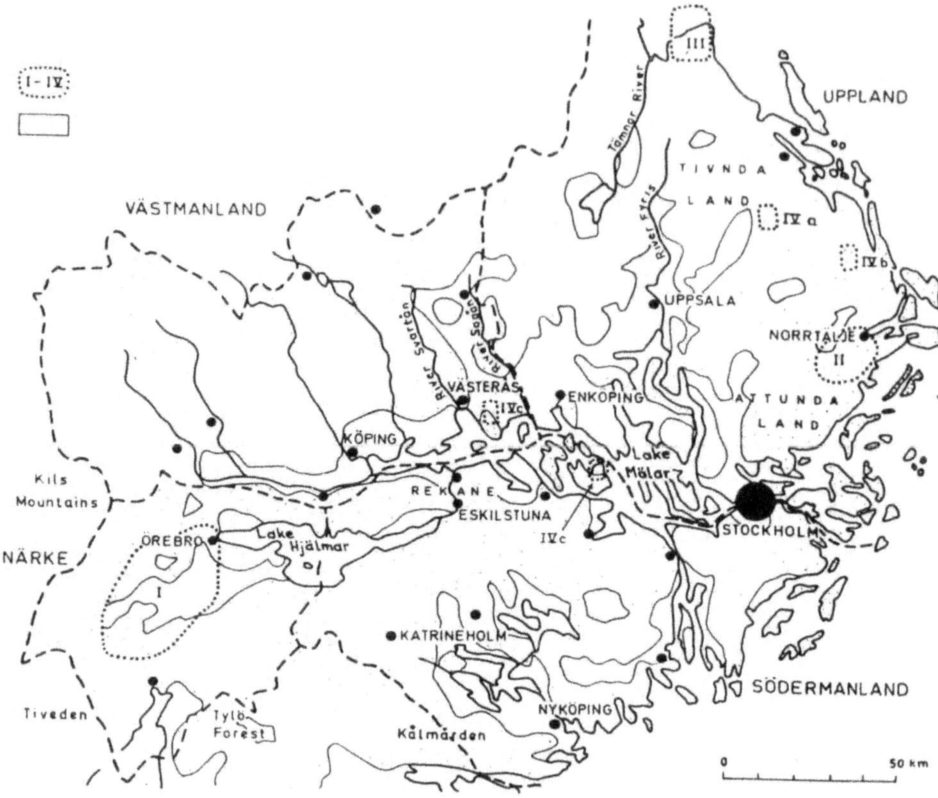

Fig. 1: "Mälardalen" in central Sweden. - The area around lake Mälar.
I-IV = Area of special investigation.
= Mainly forest.

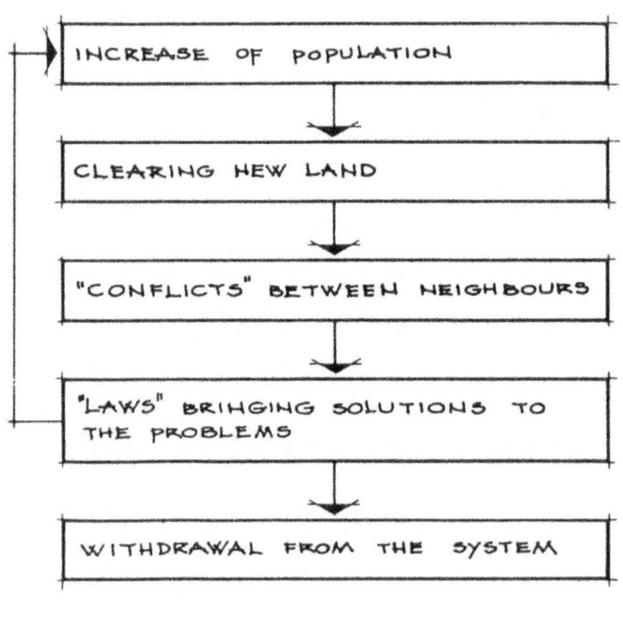

Fig. 2: The evolution and the agrarian landscape - a model.

that several of the country's most important historical places are located within its boundaries. In addition, many historical sources seem to be well-suited to a regional analysis, although there are very few works which examine settlement history from an interdisciplinary perspective (Welinder 1975).

The area's geological make-up is a peneplane which is rich in cracks and faults. Differences in levels (altitudes) seldom reach 50 meters within the central parts. The cracks follow strike directions in the underlying rock but two main directions can be noticed - one north-south and one east-west. The faults often run in an east-westerly direction. Lying centrally within the region are the Mälar and Hjälmar Lakes, which are both surrounded by level country. Around that mainly low-lying landscape lies a series of forest areas which illustrate the fault topography well: Kolmården, Tylö Forest, Triveden and Kils Mountain. In the north, the plains give way to the so-called Norrland terrain and it is actually only the north-eastern part of the area which lacks a natural termination of the Mälar Basin. The following largescale fundamental geomorphological features serve as a basis for dividing the region into 3 different areas: a) the lake area of Södermanland with gently undulating terrain but strongly influenced by a crack and fault topography, b) the Närke Flat Lands and bordering cambrosilurian bedrock and c) Uppland and Västmanland Flat Lands including bordering districts making up a very level landscape which, nevertheless, has a characteristic topography because of the crack valleys with rich clay sediment which divide the peneplane. For all intents and purposes, the whole area of investigation falls within the framework of what may be called the "fissure valley landscape". Exceptions to this are the Närke Flat Lands and the northern Flat Lands of Uppland, which form, geologically speaking, one of Sweden's flatter landscape types with altitude differences seldom over 10 meters (National Atlas of Sweden, sheet 5-8, 15-16).

The geological prerequisites for agrarian operations are not so exceptional apart from the conditions in Närke. All the more important is the part played by post-glacial soil types in forming the agrarian landscape. Above all, in Södermanland, Västmanland and in western Uppland, we find large clayey areas where the stiffest clays lie along the northern shores of Lake Mälar. The conclusion is that, disregarding north-eastern Uppland and south-western Södermanland, the area of investigation has the ideal prerequisites for agrarian operation based on agriculture.

This is also evident in the fact that this area of the country is rich in ancient monuments. The most densely populated areas are the Närke Flat Lands, the Mälar coasts, south-eastern and central Södermanland and the area around Uppsala, along with Attundaland in south-eastern Uppland. That impression is supported if one studies the distribution of Middle Age farms manors and towns 3). In other words, the preconditions suggest an established agricultural population reaching far back in time. This fact led to the central authorities and people of high status taking advantage of the area, as it provided an ideal environment for large property ownership and the exercise of power. This large area offers good but very changeable conditions for agrarian activity during different periods. Large, settled flat lands are found near Uppsala, Enköping, Västerås-Köping and Eskilstuna. Around those areas we find a shifting landscape, where the fissure-valley topography emerges strongly but where open countryside still occurs. A good example of the latter is seen in south-eastern Uppland and parts of Södermanland's lake plateau (north-west Nyköping and the area around Katrineholm). Otherwise there are few places within the latter area where

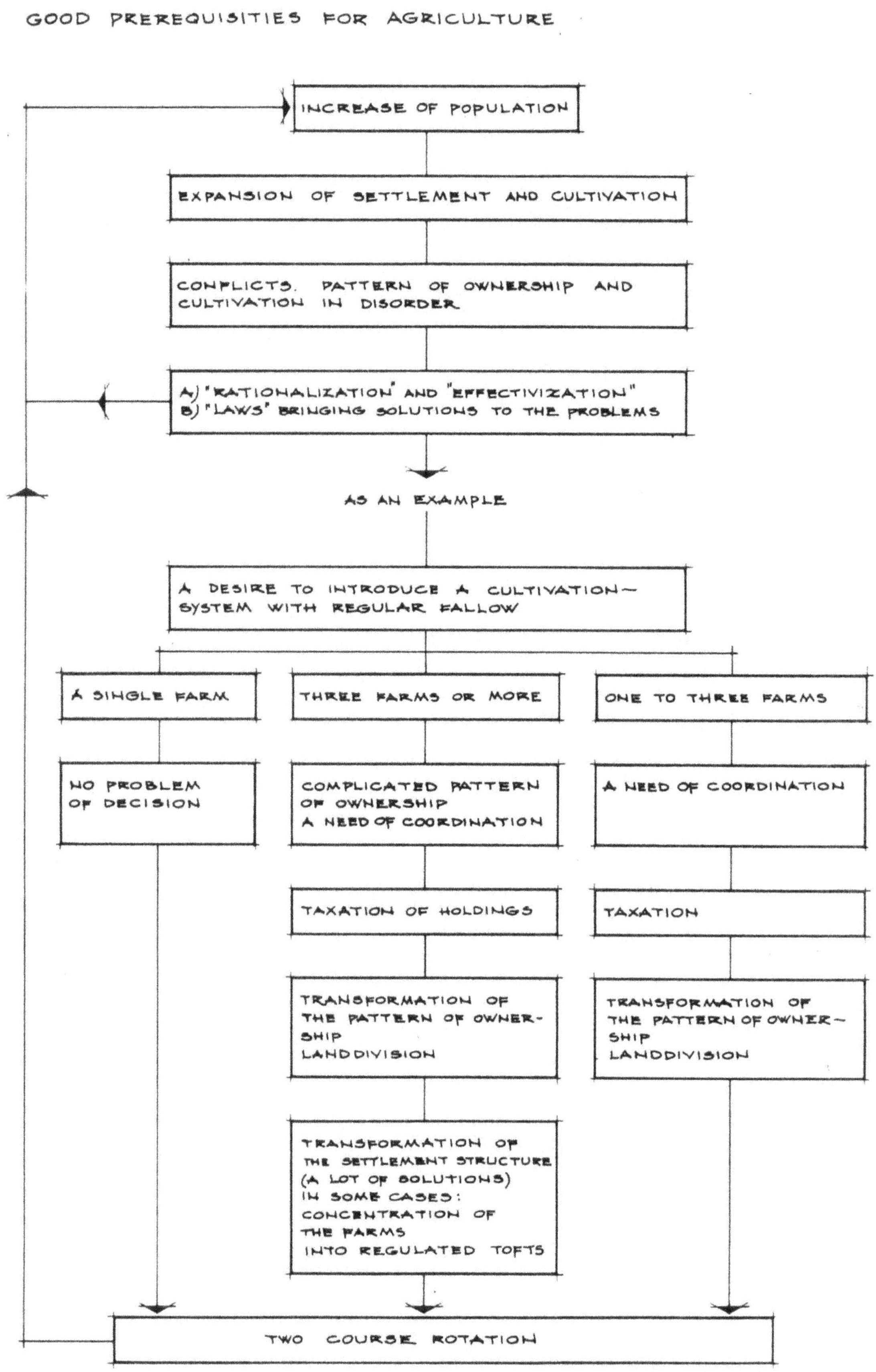

Fig. 3: The introduction of two course rotation in different types of settlement - a model.

the landscape is broken up and there is open cultivated countryside. Further, we find promising cultivation conditions in the forest districts which surround the valleys north of Lake Mälar and along the Tämnar River.

If, for a moment, we ignore the age of the settlement forms within the above geographical areas, we can see large differences in their shape. Forest districts and the characteristic fissure-valley landscape have small settlement units. These however, become larger and rather complex as we approach the open agricultural landscape. In the most central areas we find highly developed forms of settlement arrangement and land use: There are many examples of the so-called regulated villages and also examples of complicated field systems (Göransson 1978). These "morphological" traits say nothing about the age of the settlement - small units can be old while large ones may not. With the help of traces remaining in the field we shall describe some of the main steps in the evolution of agrarian medieval settlements in the following sections.

3. Formulation of a model. A description of the relationship between needs, resources and techniques in rural society.

The model wich we have developed to analyse the evolution of the rural landscape is a time/space model. It describes a specific sequence of events over time - an historical explanation of the agrarian settlement structure and it has a strong empirical basis.

We must first, however, define the dependent and independent variables. The terms population, work, and settlement are going to occupy a central place. Together they make up the rural landscape which we are studying. Population is the independent variable - it increases with more or less intensity during the whole period of study. The same goes for cultivatiable soils. I do not take a position as to how the influence between population, landscape and technique takes place in this case, although it ought to be pointed out that it is not necessarily only on those occasions when the agrarian population increases that the agrarian cultural landscape is influenced. One can also easily imagine that growth of a central place within a region also brings with it similar changes. Among other things, competition within the labor force can arise. Further, one can imagine agrarian products for sale around the central places which would intensify the cultivation pattern. Recessions, changes in property ownership and administrative factors are, naturally, also important factors in this respect, although the population variable is seen as the most important.

3.1 The Model

The model which we shall use to help develop a theory of rural evolution for the Mälar area is illustrated in fig. 2. It can be related to different types of physical environments, and it can take into account the time/space aspect in a long-term perspective. As certain of the investigation variables later are divided up into administrative and non-administrative sectors, the model will also take into consideration outer organizational influences. The innovations in cultivation techniques, however, are in the center of the model's construction. On the other hand, it takes less account of economic and social relationships because it is set in a definite context of spatial development - the transformation of rural landscapes.

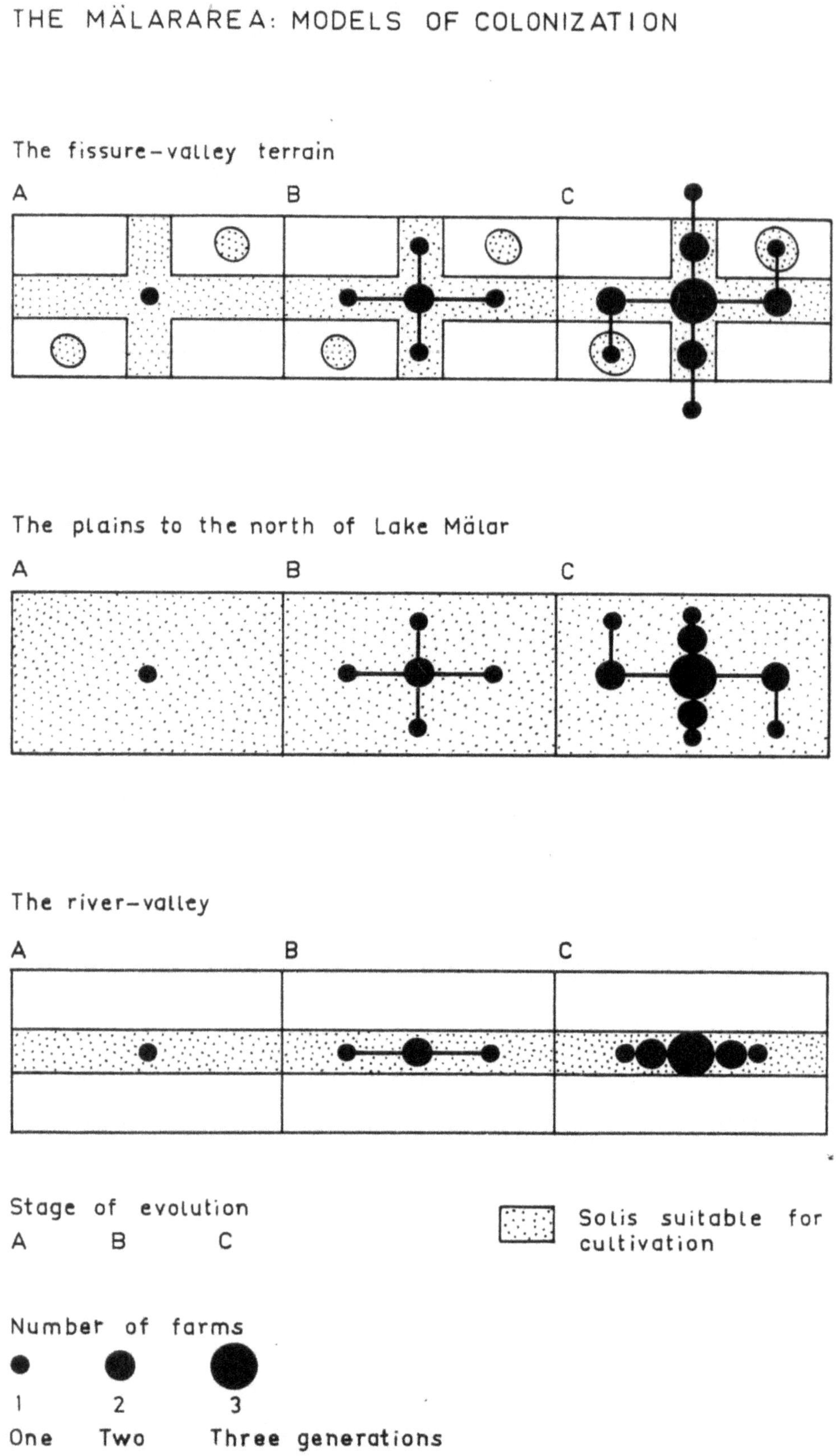

Fig. 4: The colonisation of the Mälar-area. A model of the physical landscape and its prerequisities for agriculture and settlement.

The model describes one specific segment of the long-range evolution of the agrarian landscape. It mirrors, in fact, a comparatively old stage with agriculture resting on private land ownership. (Most likely Late Iron Age and onwards). Further, the relationship mentioned previously between population and technique can be accepted as operational, so that population increase largely is influenced by technological development. That means that if a population increase is eliminated, for one reason or another, then many of the agrarian technical innovations which were important for changes in the development sequence will also be eliminated 4).

The figure (fig. 2) may require further comment. If cultivation possibilities exist and the population increases more or less continuously within the region, then exploitation of soils will successively increase. The reason for this is, of course, to support the growing population. Individual and free activities of new cultivation are possible within a productive agrarian landscape which has a low level of exploitation. But, as cultivation takes place, this gradually leads to contact and conflicts of interest with other people. The result can be a disorganized ownership and cultivation pattern. We ought to imagine that intensification in cultivation, parallel with a real expansion aims toward an increase of total production. In order to reach that goal, the farmer tries to, expressed in modern terms, rationalize and increase effectiveness in cultivation. One of the important older technical agricultural innovations, in this respect, is the adaption of a cultivation system with ordered fallow - in this case, two-course rotation. Rationalization leads, on the one hand, to increased productivity and the ability to support a growing population (not only within the agrarian sector), but, on the other hand, it can also lead to withdrawal from the system.

In Fig. 3 it can be seen that a specific process of rationalizations within agriculture can form a chain as follows: a new cultivation system with ordered fallow - the need for "surveying" and taxation ("jordrevning") - a new land distribution. It is the effects of this process which will now be examined. According to the model, the desire to introduce two course rotation implies that all property ownership which is affected by the reorganization must be evaluated before a change in the ownership of land can take place. I have divided the material into three groups based on settlements size: a) a single farm, b) two to three farms and c) three or more farms. If one wants to introduce the "two-field system" into a single farm, that should not bring about any problems. One draws a suitable boundary between the small enclosures and makes eventual allowances for losses in the form of fallow through new cultivation. The settlement is not affected. The result is usually a non-regulated settlement in combination with an undeveloped distribution pattern with irregularities in field divisions and with barren land between the field areas.

This kind of settlement can be old, as in cases where they lack further room for expansion, but in most cases we find them in peripheral areas, outside the true flat country. The environment can be made up of the more extreme fissure valley-terrain, as in the province of Södermanland, which is rich in lakes. The result is often small villages with irregular patterns of cultivation (Fig. 4).

The next group is made up of settlement units with two or three farms. We presume that the cultivated soils belonging to the different farms have come to be more or less interwoven with each other, so it is not so easy to construct a fence system which creates two "open-fields". For this reason,

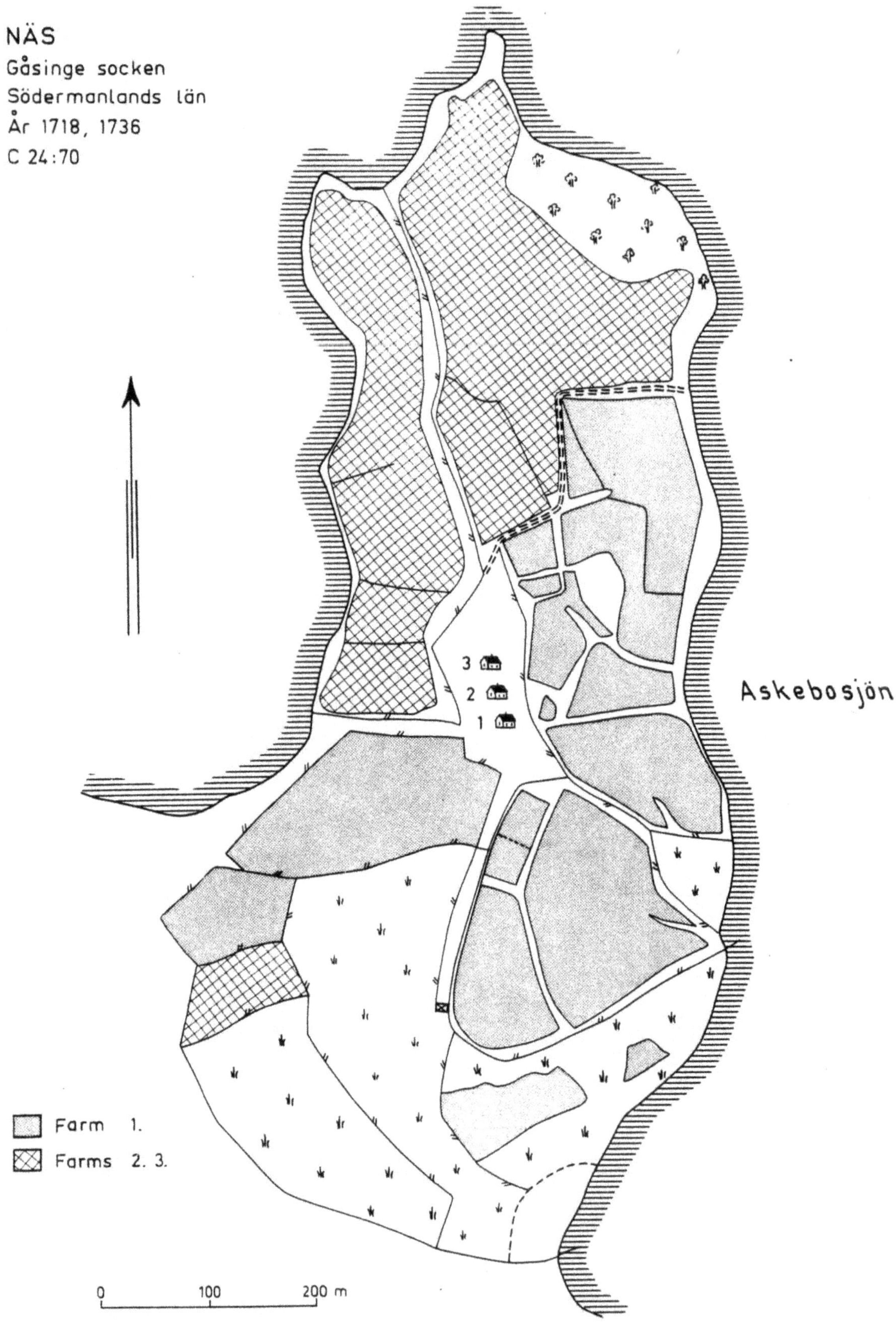

Fig. 5: Näs hamlet. An example of land division and settlement in the fissure valley terrain of eastern Sweden.

it is necessary for existing property ownership to be straightened out and the land to be redistributed in such a way that relatively regular fields can be laid out. The settlement should not be affected in this respect but, if it lies in the way of reorganization or new cultivation plans, this may be the case. This type of settlement should also be found in relatively "peripheral" areas - in other words, where villages lack sufficient room for expansion. An example of this type of landscape could be found in the south-eastern part of the province of Uppland and also in Södermanland (Fig. 5).

In both of these related situations the model works so that we imagine that the population increase, in spite of everything, has continued unchanged. If room for expansion is lacking, then the result is a moving away to eventual new settlements. This is illustrated by the fissure valley-terrain (Fig. 4) which lacks open areas. It ought to be noted that we do not in any way consider secondary settlements such as crofter's holdings or cottages.

In cases where the cultivated lands form a homogeneous surface, the development will appear in the forms which were illustrated by the flat land or river valley settlements in Fig. 4. Settlement becomes concentrated into villages, as we understand them today. A real splitting often goes further than in the peripheral areas. Let us examine one such case, a settlement unit consisting of three or more farms. There are two possibilities which are based upon the size of the village at the time of regulation. If this hamlet were the typical case for the Mälar Valley, say 3-4 farms, the development, in principle, would proceed the way it did for the 1-3 "farm hamlets" but the chances would now be much greater so that the original settlement arrangement in itself would be regarded as "inconvenient". The tendency to regulate the settlement itself would then increase and would be expressed in more or less concentrated village types, often with geometrically regular tofts. This type of settlement ought to be found in the central areas of the settled country, that is to say, in the province of Närke, the area around Rekarne, the northern Mälar coastline including the larger river valleys, the Uppsala Flat Lands and possibly several other especially favourable areas (Fig. 6).

With regard to the very large villages, a special problem arises at the time of regulation. We must take into account the fact that they have often had a relatively long period of development although this need not necessarily be the case. New techniques for example, have made quick cultivation possible. At any rate, these villages have acquired an intricate pattern of ownership accompanied by encroachments on the cultivated landscape. In this way, the regulation rules mentioned in the medieval laws of the provinces have been followed. The result ought to be that large villages also often have strictly regulated settlements. However, this is not always the case in very large villages with approximately 8-10 farms, where the cooperation required for a total reorganization of cultivation and settlement is more difficult to achieve. For this reason, these large villages frequently have special arrangements. (Helmfrid 1962, p.220-257). The fields are perhaps affected and the settlement often has several nuclei or is complex in other ways (Fig. 7). This line of reasoning leads to the idea that it ought to be possible to follow the line of development in the Mälar Valley morphogenetically and to identify different characteristics with regard to settlement arrangement and land use.

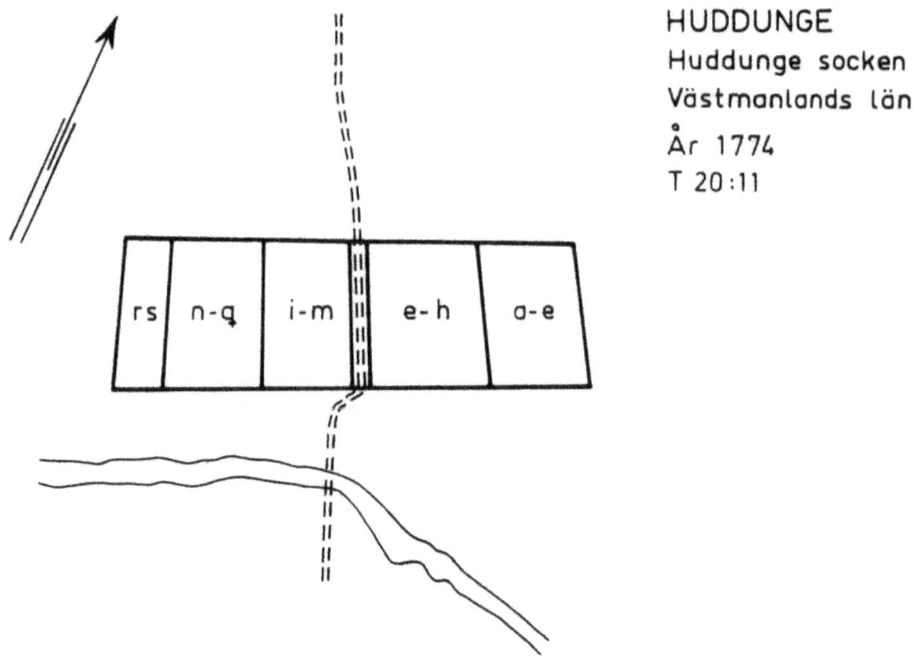

Fig. 6: The regulated tofts of Huddunge hamlet in the province of Uppland.

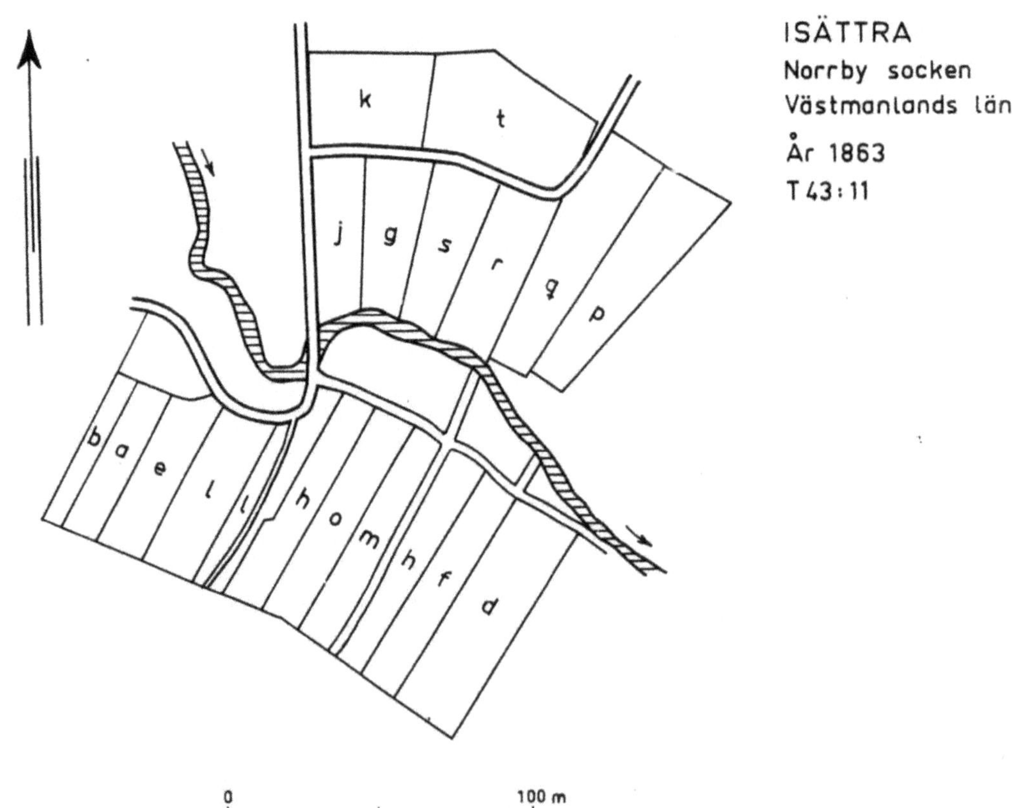

Fig. 7: Isättra - an example of a complex settlement unit.

The model is chronological, but not in absolute terms. Development can begin at different times in different areas, and rates of development can vary. The most important phases in the model can be depicted in the following chronological sequence:

a) A field system within regular fallow

In central Sweden this means two-course rotation. The idea of introducing two-course rotation was one of the main factors that definitively, in this part of Europe, changed the older, collective cultivation system into privately-owned strips connected to a new field system. It meant at the end of the process a total reorganisation of the village and a new distribution of land, in both a physical and a social sense.

b) Taxation of land

For a reorganisation of the distribution of land to take place, there must have been some kind of land-taxation ("jordrevning") in the preceding system.

c) Land division

The new distribution of land was obviously carried out with the help of new ideas of land division. The privately-owned and intermixed parcels that emerged out of the new technique were often in the shape of long and narrow strips. We do not know the reason for this formation yet but, in my opinion, the strip-fields merely represent a special technique which arose as individualistic features in a communal landscape.

d) Settlement regulation

As previously mentioned, even the settlement itself could be involved in the process of reorganisation - but generally at a relatively late stage. It was at this time that the so-called regulated villages emerged, above all in the central districts of Sweden. Building-plots were drawn up according to specific geometric patterns and measurement rules. Some hamlets were laid out with the help of medieval length and square measures, while more recent measures were used for those hamlets not regulated until the 17th and 18th centuries (Göransson 1978, Hannerberg 1977, Sheppard 1976).

The above explanation requires further supporting evidence, and later I shall present the results of my own field work on this matter. However, let us first examine some important characteristics of the Mälar region with the help of the earlier mentioned written sources.

4. Plains and periphery. Some characteristics of the agrarian landscape in central Sweden.

In order to illustrate some features of the actual settlement structure and rural economy, I would like to present some maps covering the area of investigation. These maps could also be used as a starting point for more detailed studies. Anyhow, I think it is important to be acquainted with the

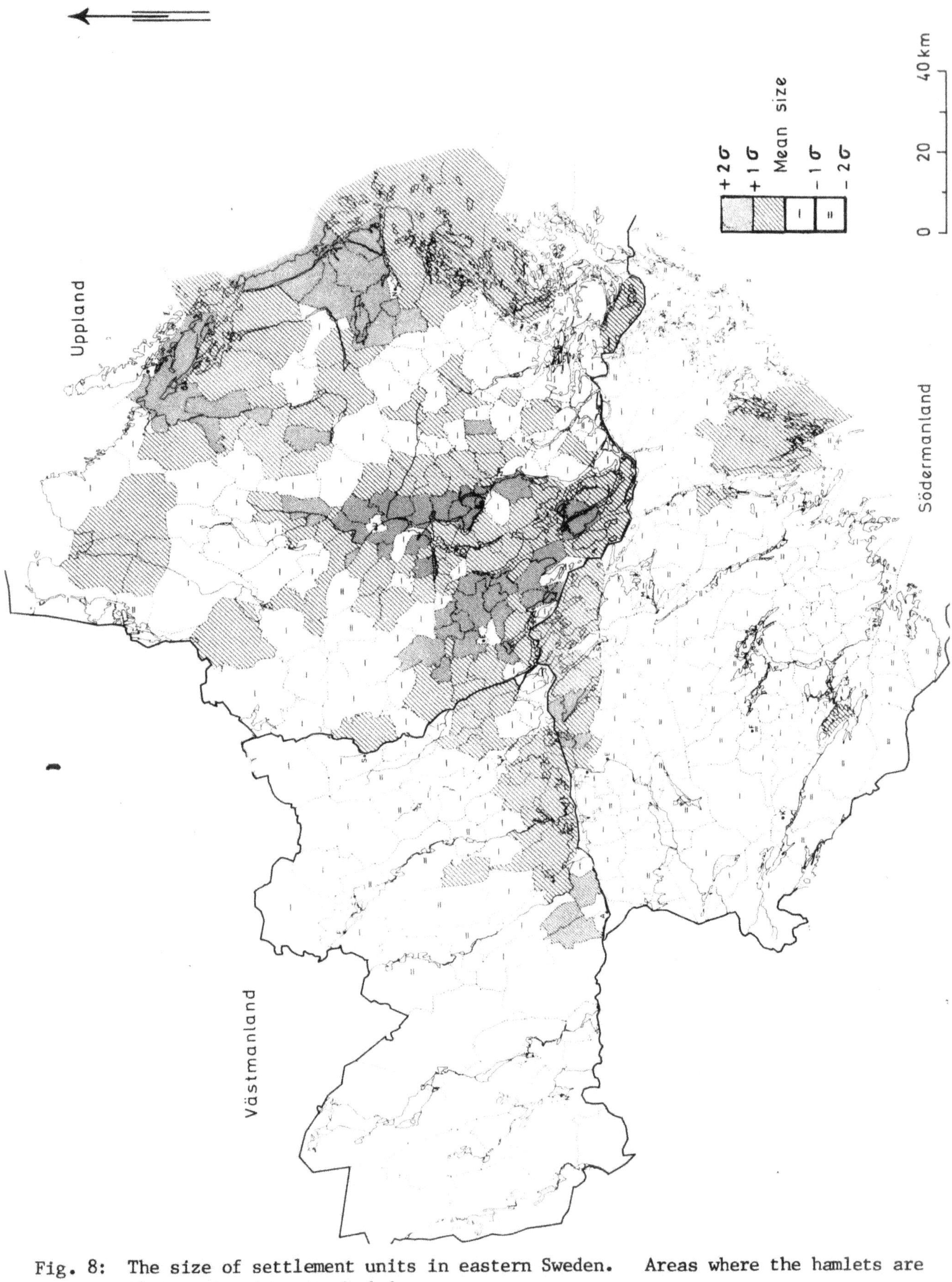

Fig. 8: The size of settlement units in eastern Sweden. Areas where the hamlets are above mean size are shaded.

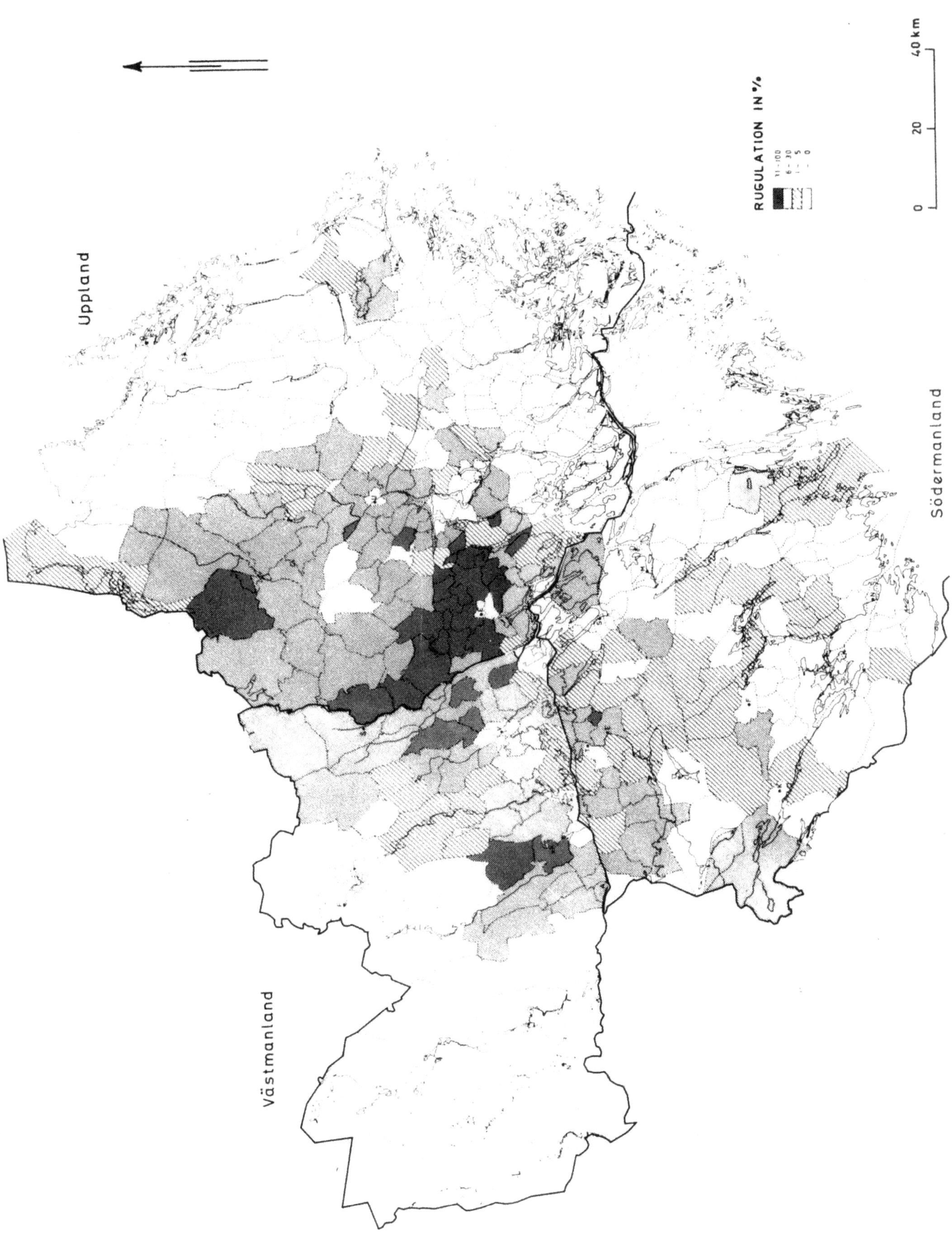

Fig. 9: The district of regulated hamlets in eastern central Sweden.

TABLE   The size of the "mantal" (farm) in different counties of Sweden 1560 AD.

County	Size in hectares
Stockholms	10.9
Skärgårdsdelen	2.5
Uppsala	11.4
Södermanlands	7.7
Ostergötlands	9.6
Kalmar l. fastl	3.8
Oland	5.1
Jönköpings	4.3
Kronobergs	3.8
Alvsborgs	3.5
Skaraborgs	5.6
Värmalands	7.5
Orebro	6.8
Västmanlands	12.3
Kopparbergs	
Gävleborgs	3.0
Västernorrlands	1.6
Västerbottens	1.2
Norrbottens	1.2

region as a whole before presenting any of the details about common trends.

a) The size of the settlement units in the Mälar area.

Fig. 8 shows the mean size of the settlement units (number of farms) for every parish in the three eastern provinces of the Mälar valley (Södermanland, Uppland and Västmanland). The shaded areas are dominated by hamlets greater than the mean size for the whole region. As source-material I have used a land register of the National Land Survey, which describes the situation at the beginning of the 20th century. The figures in the register have been compared with a sample of taxation lists from the middle of the fifteenth century 6). There is a strong statistical correspondence between the two series of figures, which means that the relation between big and small settlement units in this area is almost the same in the 16th and 20th centuries.

Furthermore, the map shows a fair correspondence between the physical prerequisities of the region and settlement size. The hamlets are relatively large in the central, plain areas to the north of lake Mälar, along the river valleys and around the town of Uppsala in central Uppland. There are also many large hamlets along the Baltic coast due to the combination of rural production and fishing. The cultivated area belonging to each individual farm in these coastal districts is rather small however. So, the maps show the settlement strucure at the end of the Middle Ages and some hundred years afterwards. On the basis of the model, we would expect the most developed forms of settlement and land-use to be in central districts of the area.

b) Settlement regulation

The map in Fig. 9 shows the percentage number of regulated tofts in every parish of the Mälar area. As can be seen, settlement regulation is most frequent in central districts although there are some exceptions. Hence, we find a spatial correspondence between an open landscape suitable for cultivation and large hamlets, many of which are regulated, as is predicted by the model. On the other hand, in the peripheral areas of the region we find many small unregulated hamlets (in eastern Uppland, northern Västmanland and a great part of Södermanland). A district of special interest in this respect lies in eastern Uppland, where there is a small area of regulated hamlets situated in an open, plain landscape which in its turn is due to the local occurrence of fertile morain-clay.

c) The mean size of the farms in different districts of the area.

It is possible to reconstruct the areal size of a farm ("mantal", a fiscal unit) as early as the 16th century. There are significant differences between the counties ("län") around Lake Mälar. If we examine the table V (p. 212) we can see that the biggest units are to be found in the counties of Västmanland and Uppsala - the two central districts (Arrhenius 1947). So in general, where we find good prerequisities for agriculture we also find relatively large fiscal units. It should be noted that such a unit could consist of several farms.

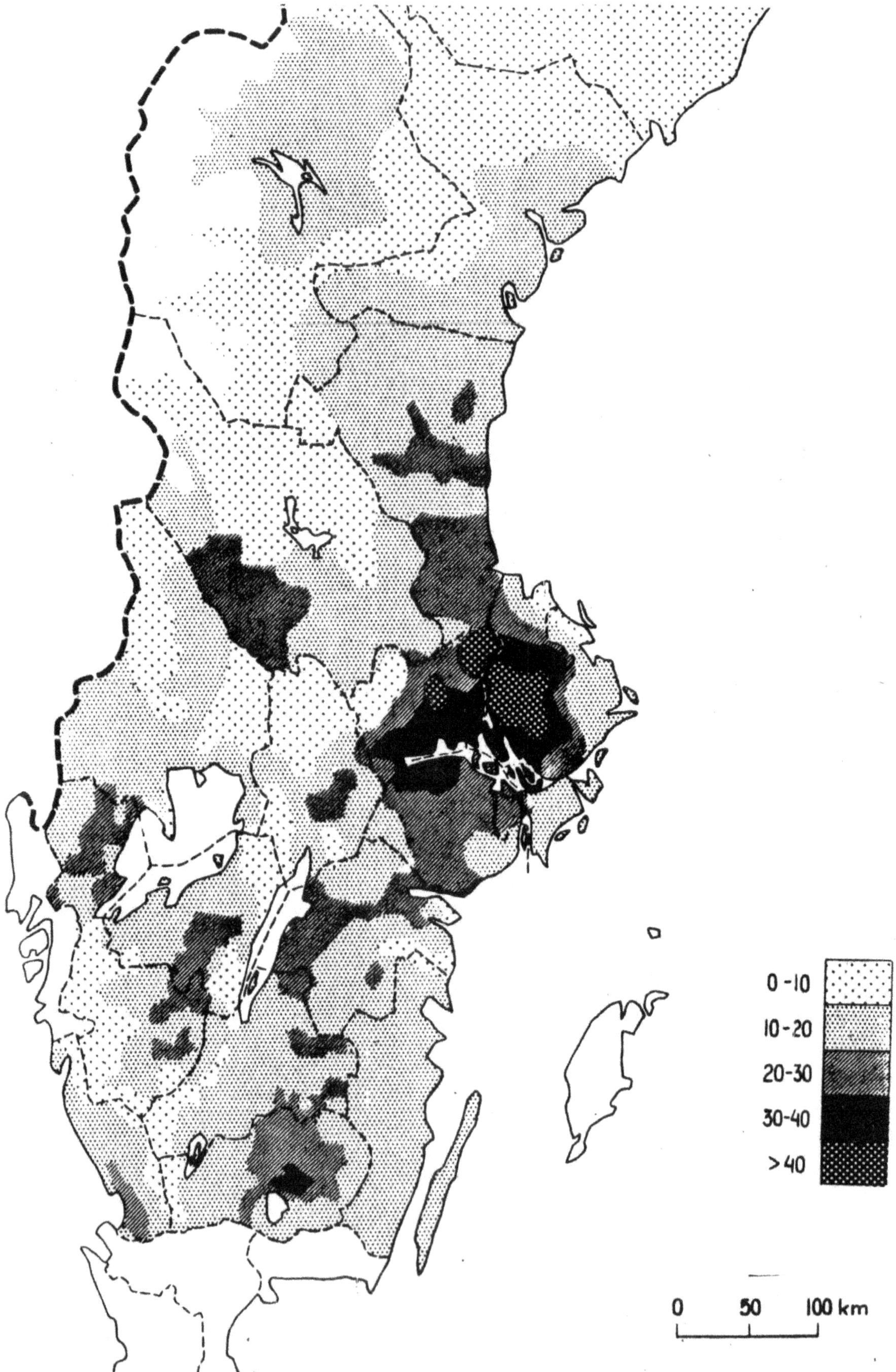

Fig. 10: The harvest (in barrels) in Sweden around 1550 AD.

d) Tithe per person registered in the middle of the 16th century.

Looking at Fig. 10 we can see that, according to the tithe register, the harvest per person for the central districts is of a considerable size and is much bigger than in the peripheral areas. The plains to the north of the lake and around Uppsala are especially significant (Friberg, N. - Friberg I, 1977).

5. What do traces of cultivation say about medieval society?

As well as documenting and dating different kinds of traces in the field, we can also use them to interpret medieval society if we can show that they represent a certain kind of social and economic organisation. I think that the most interesting strategy in this respect is to investigate the evolution of the strip-fields - a land division between separate land-owners belonging to the same rural unit (a village). In some outstanding examples we can find well preserved traces as well as being able to recognize them on maps from the 16th century. Many strips seem to have remained unchanged for hundreds of years. Thus they can be used as a document of early farming.

Another important element consists of the "original" fencing system of a certain unit. What did it look like? During the early Iron Age period we think that the fences around the cultivated area were of an irregular shape. There was probably no rotation system although such a system must have been introduced later in accordance with more regular principles. The village of today originated with, and was later organized around, a system consisting of common fields as well as privately owned strips - a somewhat peculiar form of land-use in terms of modern ideas. I think that the reason for this kind of cultivation was the transformation from a system of collective land-use during the early Iron Age to more individualistic forms later on. In other words, we still find cooperative forms of farming but, due to the redistribution of land inside new two-course rotation fields, we can also see that the society must have been changed as a result of new ideas and rules for farming and land-owning.

Another important change within rural society during the Middle Ages was the reorganisation of settlement and land-use that took place in the central districts. There we find the same kind of farming as in the rest of the region but even more regulated. In areas which have the best prerequisties for farming we also find regulations of the settlement. So, a change in rural society is not always due to steps taken by administrators. Two-course rotation and the strip-fields were accepted by every farmer of the area, but not settlement regulation. New ideas may have been introduced by big landowners, monasteries or even a central administration but they had to be accepted by the farmers before they could be put into practice. A need for reorganisation had to exist.

In order to find different kinds of features and traces of cultivation, I have used modern and historical maps, a register of antiquities made for antiquarian research and have also made an inventory of my own all over the Mälar basin. In the periphery one can still often find "undeveloped" forms of farming; a primary stage of evolution. There the hamlets and the fields are sometime old in origin (fossilized), but more often they belong to a landscape not colonized until the Middle Ages. In the central districts, on the other hand one can seldom find ancient features of farming because they

Fig. 11: Stone-wall near Vad in the province of Närke (Figure 1, area marked 1).

Fig. 12: Field and strips of the hamlet of Barknåre in northern Uppland (Figure 1, area marked III).

have been destroyed by cultivation. However, even here one can sometimes find a few village tofts and fences suitable for excavation.

To sum up we could say that we are looking for four main groups of cultivation traces:

a. Fences denoting two-course rotation. We must be able to identify it on an old map in order to be sure of the earlier use of the fence. In the terrain the traces often appear as stone wall.

b. Strips and parcels inside the field. The borderlines consist of ditches or of stone walls. There must be a specific identification on an old map.

c. Village tofts of different kinds, denoting a deserted village.

d. Small enclosures outside the field. They indicate further cultivation of the hamlet after a proper field system had already been introduced.

6. The field material

During a rather long period (1965-79), I have been excavating traces of cultivation in the Mälar region (Fig. 1). The function of those traces has often been identified with the help of old maps, especially from the 17th century. The age of the traces has mostly been determined with the help of radio carbon datings, as there are few archaeological artefacts. The next part of the paper reports some results from on-going fieldwork in which the following parts of the region have been of special interest.

a. Central Närke including the Orebro area

b. Eastern Uppland to the south of the town of Norrtälje

c. Northern Uppland, the parish of Hållnäs

d. Preliminary results from four minor localities: Skarp-Osby and Väsby in Uppland, Konugla in Västmanland and finally Hornby in Södermanland (Fig. 1).

In some places, charcoal has been found in walls and terraces, thus indicating the earlier use of fire for clearing new land. A common habit was to burn bushes and shrubs on the stone walls. The walls represent an unused part of the cleared land where the farmer put stones, branches, litter etc. Today, therefore, we can date those traces and sometimes we can even find small pieces of charcoal under the walls and fences 7). Hence, I think, that it is possible to get an idea of the age of those stone constructions using only radio carbon dating. The construction must either be of the same age or else more recent than the charcoal taken from a layer under the stones. Charcoal from the inside of the wall indicates a period when the wall was still in use. Finally, charcoal in the soil over the construction seems to be more recent than the wall itself. Of course you need several samples from different layers of the same construction before you can trust such a dating.

Fences surrounding fields in two-course rotation

In the following I shall report on some excavations of stone fences

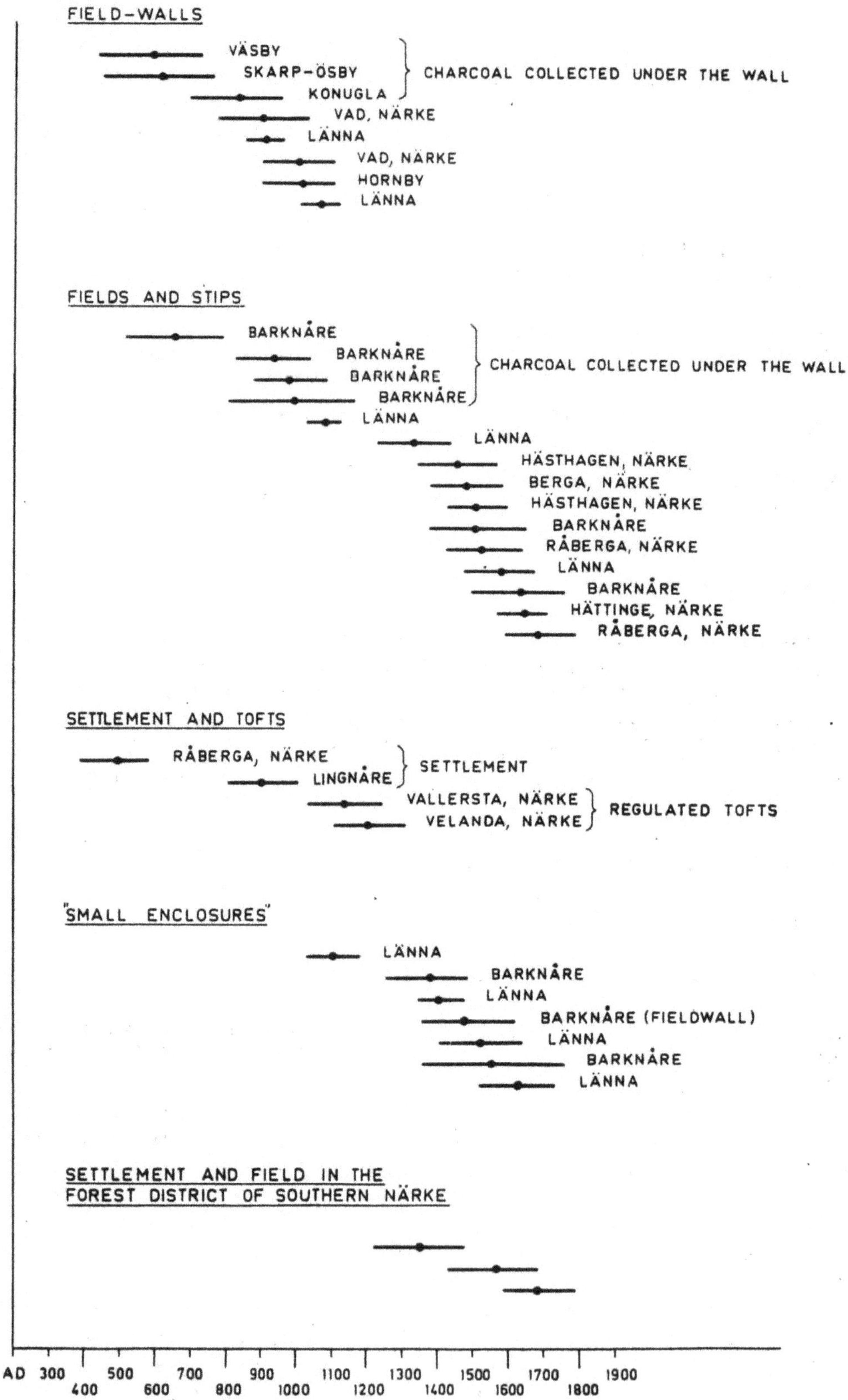

Fig. 13: Radio-carbon dating of field walls, strips, tofts and small enclosures in eastern Sweden.

that have evidently been used as field boundaries. It is easy to compare the situation in the field with an old map as most of the hamlets of the region have such a document. After that, it is relatively easy to determine the earlier use of the wall. For example: in the hamlet of Vad, situated in central Närke, one can still find the former limit of the two fields now, in an open pasture land. It has the shape of a stone wall (Fig. 11) and here are no problems with the identification of the traces. The wall can be seen on the map. It is built in the traditional manner, in combination with a wooden fence in this case, the stones have been put directly onto heaps of untouched charcoal. This gives us an opportunity to date the time of construction, and we have obtained two datings around 1000 AD (900 ± 130AD, 945 ±100 AD).

A fairly similar situation is to be found in Konugla hamlet near Västerås in the county of Västmanland. The earlier fences of the two field system are easily recognized in the terrain. Three radio carbon datings tells us that this construction may be somewhat younger than the example from Vad - around 4206 AD.

Further excavations of walls belonging to a two-field system have been carried out in Väsby and Skarp-Osby in the county of Uppland. In this case the charcoal has been taken from under the fences, so the field-wall must be more recent than tht radio carbon dating. In both cases we have obtained an age of about 600 AD.

In Hornby in the province of Södermanland there is a deserted settlement with the fields still partly in use. These fields were formerly surrounded by a stone fence, which has sunken in a swampy part of the area. Charcoal has been collected from the lowest part of it and also from a layer of soil covering the wall. According to the radio carbon datings the stone wall in this case must have been in use around 1000 AD but was evidently abandoned six hundred years later (1000 ± 90AD, inside the wall, and 1650 ± 105 AD).

In the Länna district of eastern Uppland we have obtained two more datings of walls surrounding deserted fields. Unfortunately, maps are missing in this case, but the datings are of the same age as those from the localities just mentioned (915 ± 65AD, 1070 ± 65AD). From the same district we have also found a cattle path dividing the cultivated area of one of the hamlets into two equal parts (two fields). Traces of an earlier field system are to be found inside the broad cattle path. According to metrological investigations this earlier field system is of medieval origin, which means that the two fields must have been laid out relatively late in this case - say around 1250.

Strip fields

In this case one has to collect charcoal from inside the walls in order to determine the period in which the walls were still in use. It seems that the original boundaries between the strips consisted of shallow ditches into which the farmers threw stones continuously while clearing their land. In this way, the ditch was quickly transformed into a long stone-heap - a wall. I have investigated such field walls in eastern and northern Uppland. (Fig. 12). Charcoal from the bottom layer is often early medieval, while the top layer often represents modern times.

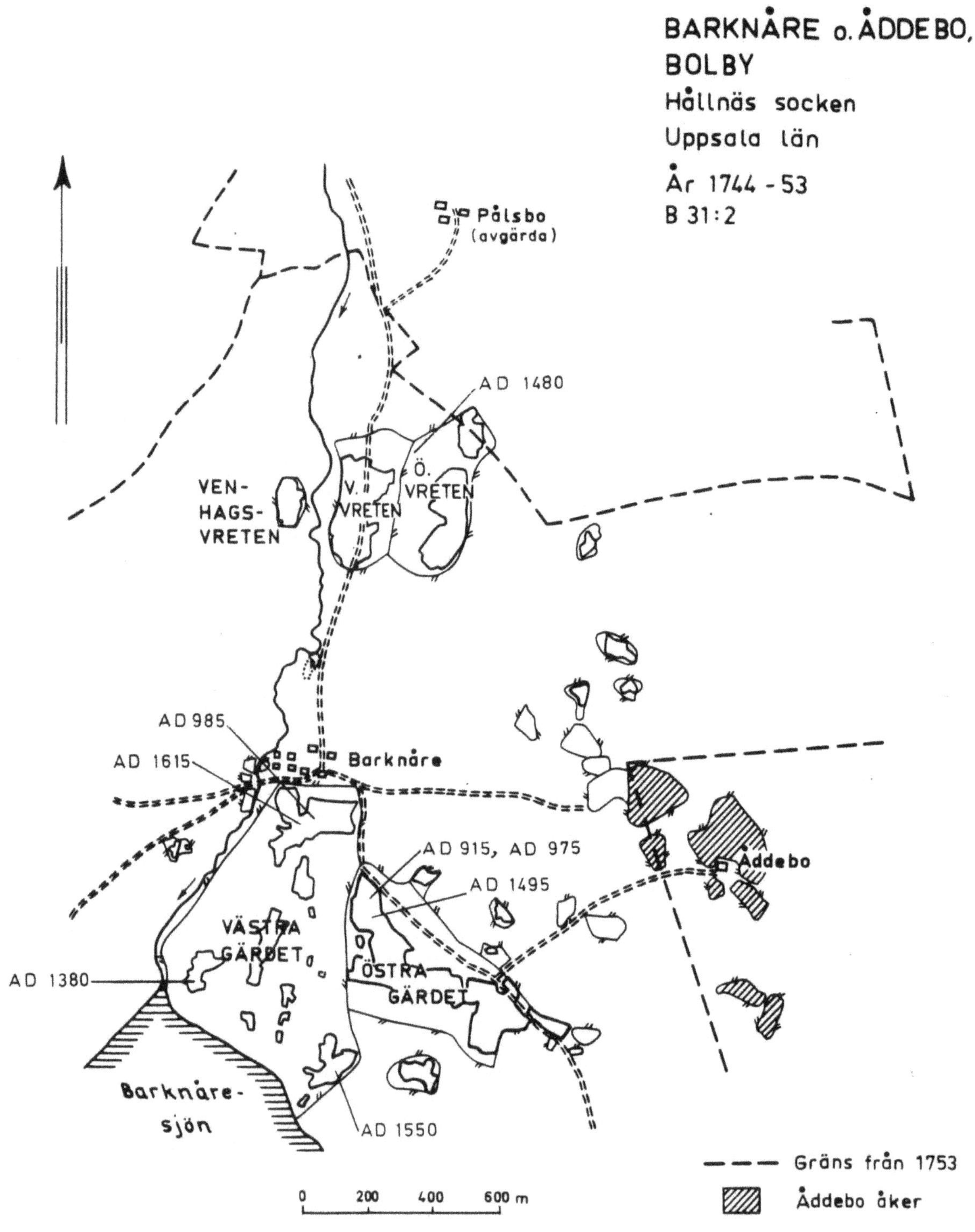

Fig. 14: Some radiocarborn datings of fields and strips in the hamlet of Barknåre (Figure 1, area III).

The earliest datings of that kind that I could find are about 1000 years old. In both districts, stone walls seem to have separated field strips as early as the 11th century. There are also many datings from the latter part of the Middle Ages and onwards (Fig. 13).

Some metrological tests have also been carried out concerning old regular strips in the field. In many cases we have found that an early medieval ell-measure (0.52 m) has been used to divide land. More frequently, however, the test confirms the use of a late medieval cubit of 0.55 cm. A good example of the latter can be seen in Hästhagen, quite near the town of Orebro, in Närke (Sporrong 1978). According to the metrological analysis, one of two separate fields belonging to a deserted village had been divided with the help of a measuring rod of 4.40 m (8 x 0.55 m). The strips have the shape of ridges and furrows and radio carbon datings from the deserted parcels confirm a medieval land division (1445 ± 115AD, 1505 ± 80 AD).

Tofts

The regulated village-tofts have generally been investigated only through map studies, in conjunction with metrological and statistical tests. So far, our results illustrate the precedence of the medieval cubit over the older ell-measure in toft-planning (Göransson 1978, Sporrong 1980). It means that the regulated tofts that we find on our old maps are no older than late medieval. Sometimes, however, it is possible to find an earlier stage of toft-planning that might even be prehistoric (Hannerberg 1977).

I have tried to do some excavation inside village tofts - deserted or sometimes still "living" - in order to get an absolute dating of regulated settlement. We know that the establishment of the actual hamlets had already taken place by the lat Iron Age, but reorganization into a regulated form must have come later. I can give only one example from a deserted, regulated village in central Sweden where the boundaries around each farm are still to be found. The fences are made of stone. In this case they were constructed around 1100 AD, according to a couple of radio carbon datings, but of course the planning *per se* could be older.

Small enclosures ("vretar") outside the field

The regulation of settlement and land-use in the Middle Ages interfered with the pattern of ongoing evolution in many ways. It was no longer possible to clear new land inside the fields and expansion therefore took place on common land outside the field system. In eastern Uppland some of these small enclosures are dated as early as 1100 AD but most of them seem to appear later - from 1300 AD and onwards. I have obtained many datings of that kind and, as an example, we can examine figure 14 showing Barknåre hamlet in northern Uppland about 1752. The field system drawn on the map still exists and I have tried to date the fields as well as the small enclosures outside them. The so-called "Ostervreten" is of special interest. It is the biggest of all enclosures outside the fields and it has been put into two-course rotation! The fence that divides Ostervreten into two equal parts is no older than 1480 AD according to one two carbon datings of charcoal which was collected from under the fence.

The medieval regulation of settlement and farmland caused a new pattern of settlement because the regulated hamlet was "locked in". Further expansion took place on common land in the shape of small enclosures or sometimes as small new settlement units around the central farming districts. In the forest area to the south of the plains of Näke, for instance, many such small settlement units seem to have been established at the end of the Middle Ages.

7. Some conclusions.

We have been discussing certain traces of the cultivation of a rural society preceding the agrarian revolution. The traces represent some main lines of agrarian evolution but they also correspond to certain events which occurred within the society itself. So far, the oldest datings we have discussed generally represent the "outlines" of the hamlet - for instance, parts of the fencing system (Figure 10). The land division into elongated strips seems to be somewhat more recent and so also does the settlement regulation. The small enclosures outside the field system are often late medieval or less.

As far as we understand, there was a change in the early Iron Age settlement pattern. The outcome of that change, medieval society, is fairly clear, but between those two temporal "poles" there seems to have been a long period of reorganization. There are no signs of a radically different rural social system in the meantime. So, I argue that there was a slow social and economic change from cooperative forms of living to a new family structure which introduced new ideas of land owning and farming. In broad terms, this transformation was finished around the year 1000 AD.

The first sign of a "new society" that I can identify with the help of field-material in the Mälar area belongs to the Viking age, when a new settlement structure and elements of a new spatial organisation emerge in the shape of hemlets and villages. The culmination of that process is to be found at the beginning of the Middle Ages. The settlement units were clearly separated from each other according to certain rules of land owning, land taxation and land division: the strip fields represent that stage. In terms of the field evidence, we can return to the model and describe the process as follows:

- the farmers wanted to introduce a rotation system (fields and fallow)

- that idea was accompanied by a need for the reorganization of land (land division)

- this in its turn implied taxation of the holdings before reorganisation

- afterwards, land use continued in cooperative forms but the division of land facilitated a transformation into strict private holdings.

We have been using our model in order to understand the logical sequences of evolution and have also tried to identify and map some important features of settlement structure of the whole region. The physical prerequisties play an important role as almost everywhere we find that the most developed forms of settlement occur in the central rural districts. The field traces give us rough dating of the main lines of evolution but, on the basis of other sources, I think that the process was even more differentiated. There are for instance important differences between central and peripherial areas of the Mälar basin and there were also differences in the economic and social structure within the area of investigation. What did for instance the increase in urbanisation and trade mean for the surrounding rural landscape? I hope to be able to return to and discuss that question later on.

NOTES

1) The social structure of the early Middle Ages in Scandinavia has been discussed for a long time by the historians. (For a summary - see Lindkvist 1979). The Medieval period in Sweden last for four hundred years, 1050 - 1500 AD.

2) According to a traditional archaeological view the society of the early iron age differs a great deal from that of later periods. A transformation took place around 500 AD. However, this opinion is under discussion (Sjöholm 1978).

3) With reference to "Medeltidsstaden" - an ongoing research project about medieval towns and their hinterland in the Mälar-valley. The Central Board of Antiquities - (Riksantikvarieämbetet), Box 5405, 114 84 Stockholm.

4) The argumentation upon conditions in a preindustrial society. The relation between technological level and population pressure has been thoroughly discussed in the literature of economic history. (Gould 1972).

5) We are here coming in touch with a scientific discussion of long tradition in Western Europe.
Some recent works can be referred to - Baker, A. - Butlin, R. (eds) 1973, Dodgshon 1980.

6) I have used excerpts made by "Det Medeltida Sverige" (The Medieval Sweden) - a research project at the Central Board of National Antiquities, Stockholm.

7) The method has been developed by Lindquist and it is reported in "Lindquist 1968 and 1975".

References

Arrhenius, O. 1974. Sveriges åkerareal vid mitten av 1500-talet. Kgl Lantbruksakademiens tidskrift 86.

Baker, A. - Butlin, R. (eds) 1973. Studies of Field Systems in the British Isles. (Cambridge).

Dodgshon, R. 1980. The origin of British Field Systems, an interpretation. (London).

Friberg, N. - Friberg, I. 1977. Alvkarlebymarknaderna vid 1500-talets mitt. Kulturgeografiska Institutionen. (Stockholm).

Fritz, B. 1972. Hus, land och län. Förvaltningen i Sverige 1250 - 1434. Stockholm. _Studies in History_ 16.

Göransson, S. 1978. _Viking Age Traces in Swedish Systems of Territorial Organisation_. (Uppsala).

Hafström. G. 1964. Die altschwedishe Hundertschaft. _Vorträge und Forschungen_ VIII. (Stuttgart).

Hannerberg, D. 1976. Models of Medieval and Pre-medieval terriotorial organisation, with select biblography. _Journal of Historical Geography_ 1976:1.

Hannerberg, D. 1977. _Kumlabygden, Forntid-Nutid-Framtid_. IV By, gård och samhälle. (Kumla).

Helmfrid, S. 1962. Ostergötland Västanstång/ Studien über die ältere Agrarlandschaft und ihre Genese. _Geografiska Annaler_ 1962: 1-2.

Lindquist, S.-O. 1968. _Det förhistoriska kulturlandskapet i östra Ostergötland_. (Stockholm).

Lindquist, T. 1979. _Landborna i Norden under äldre medeltid_. (Uppsala).

Sheppard, J. 1976. Medieval village planning in Northern England: Some evidence from Yorkshire. _Journal of Historical Geography_ 1976:1.

Sjöholm, E. 1978. Rättshistorisk metod och teoribildning. _Scandia_ 44. 1978:2.

Sporrong, U. 1976. _Mälardalen mellan historia och förhistoria_. Kulturgeografiska institutionen. (Stockholm).

Sporrong, U. 1978. Ryggade åkrar. (Ridge and furrow) _RIG_.

Sporrong, U. 1980. _Mälarbygden under tidig medeltid_. Medeltidsstaden. Rapport 18. (Stockholm).

Welinder, S. 1975. _Prehistoric Agricuture in Eastern Middle Sweden_. (Lund).

www.ingramcontent.com/pod-product-compliance
Lightning Source LLC
LaVergne TN
LVHW071206210926
848482LV00015B/736
9780860542728